21世纪内容语言融合（CLI）系列英语教材

*An Introduction to European Culture*
*(Second Edition)*

# 欧洲文化入门

（第2版）

常俊跃 黄洁芳 赵永青 主编

北京大学出版社
PEKING UNIVERSITY PRESS

图书在版编目(CIP)数据

欧洲文化入门 / 常俊跃，黄洁芳，赵永青主编. —2版. —北京：北京大学出版社，2020.9
21世纪内容语言融合(CLI)系列英语教材
ISBN 978-7-301-31591-0

Ⅰ.①欧… Ⅱ.①常… ②黄… ③赵… Ⅲ.①英语—高等学校—教材 ②文化—概况—欧洲 Ⅳ.①H319.39：G

中国版本图书馆CIP数据核字(2020)第174749号

| | |
|---|---|
| 书　　名 | 欧洲文化入门（第2版）<br>OUZHOU WENHUA RUMEN (DI-ER BAN) |
| 著作责任者 | 常俊跃　黄洁芳　赵永青　主编 |
| 责任编辑 | 刘文静　吴宇森 |
| 标准书号 | ISBN 978-7-301-31591-0 |
| 出版发行 | 北京大学出版社 |
| 地　　址 | 北京市海淀区成府路205号　100871 |
| 网　　址 | http://www.pup.cn　新浪微博:@北京大学出版社 |
| 电子邮箱 | 编辑部 pupwaiwen@pup.cn　总编室 zpup@pup.cn |
| 电　　话 | 邮购部 010-62752015　发行部 010-62750672　编辑部 010-62759634 |
| 印 刷 者 | 河北滦县鑫华书刊印刷厂 |
| 经 销 者 | 新华书店 |
| | 787毫米×1092毫米　16开本　14.25印张　281千字<br>2011年9月第1版<br>2020年9月第2版　2024年7月第5次印刷 |
| 定　　价 | 58.00元 |

未经许可，不得以任何方式复制或抄袭本书之部分或全部内容。
版权所有，侵权必究
举报电话：010-62752024　电子邮箱：fd@pup.cn
图书如有印装质量问题，请与出版部联系，电话：010-62756370

国家社会科学基金项目"英语专业基础阶段内容依托式课程改革研究"的研究成果

**本书主编** 常俊跃 黄洁芳 赵永青

**对本项目教材编校有贡献的其他教师**
李雪梅 宋杰 李莉莉 夏洋 赵秀艳 吕春媚 霍跃红
高璐璐 姚璐 李文萍 傅琼 刘晓蕖 范丽雅

# 第2版前言

　　长期以来,"以语言技能训练为导向"(SOI)的教学理念主导了我国高校外语专业教育,即通过开设语音、语法、基础英语、高级英语、听力、口语、阅读、写作、翻译等课程开展语言教学,帮助学生提高语言技能。该理念对强化学生的语言技能具有一定的积极作用,但也导致了学生知识面偏窄、思辨能力偏弱、综合素质偏低等问题。

　　为了探寻我国外语专业教育的新道路,大连外国语大学英语专业教研团队在北美内容依托教学理念(CBI)的启发下,于2006年开展了校级和省级"内容本位教学"改革项目,还于2007年和2012年开展了2次国家社会科学基金项目推进课程体系改革,对CBI在我国的应用进行了系统探索,为推出内容语言融合教育理念(Content and Language Integration, CLI)奠定了实践基础。教研团队批判性地吸收了国外CBI、内容语言融合学习(CLIL)、以英语为媒介的教学(EMI)、沉浸式教学(Immersion)等理念关注内容的优点,以我国外语教学背景下12年内容依托课程改革实践为依托,提出了具有中国特色的内容语言融合教育理念,即将目标语用于教授、学习内容和语言这两个重点,达到多种教育目的的教育理念。其特点如下:

**1. 教育目标**　　有别于诸多外语教学理念,CLI不局限于语言,而是包含知识、能力和素质培养三个方面的目标。知识目标包含专业知识、相关专业知识、跨学科知识;能力目标包含语言能力、认知能力、交际能力、思辨能力等;素质目标包含人生观、价值观、世界观、人文修养、国际视野、中国情怀、责任感、团队意识等。

**2. 教学特点**　　有别于单纯训练语言的教学,CLI主要特点体现在:语言训练依托内容,内容教学依靠语言;语言内容融合教学,二者不再人为割裂。

**3. 师生角色**　　有别于传统教学和学生中心理念对师生角色的期待,CLI是在充分发挥教师主导作用的同时发挥学生的主体作用。教师可以扮演讲授者、评估者、建议者、资源提供者、组织者、帮助者、咨询者,同时也不排斥教师的权威角色、控制者等角色。学生角色也更加多元,包括学习者、参与者、发起者、创新者、研究者、问题解决者,乃至追随者。

**4. 教学材料**　　有别于我国传统的外语教科书,它具有多类型、多样化的特点,包括课本、音频资料、视频资料、网站资料、教学课件、学生作品等。整个教材内容具有连续性和系统性;每个单元的内容都围绕主题展开。

**5. 教学侧重**　　教学过程中,教师根据教学阶段或教学内容的特点确定教学重点,或侧重语言知识教学,或侧重语言技能教学,或侧重专业知识教学,或在语言教学和内容教学中达成某种平衡。

**6. 教学活动**　　教学活动不拘泥于某一种教法所规定的某几种技巧,倡导充分吸收各种教法促进语言学习、内容学习、素质培养的技巧,运用多种教学手段,通过问题驱动、输出驱动等方法调动学生主动学习;运用启发式、任务式、讨论式、结对子、小组活动、课堂展示、项目依托教学等行之有效的方法、活动与学科内容教学有机结合,提高学生的语言技能,激发学生的学习兴趣,培养学生的自主性和创造性,提升学生的思辨能力和综合素质。

**7. 教学测评** 其测评吸收测试研究和评价研究的成果,包括形成性评价和终结性评价。形成性评价可以有小测验、课堂发表、角色扮演、小组活动、双人活动、项目、撰写论文、撰写研究报告、创意写作、创意改写、反馈性写作、制作张贴作品等;终结性评价可以包括传统的选择题等各种题型和方法。

**8. 互动性质** 它有别于传统教学中信息从教师向学生的单向传送,其课堂互动是在师生互动基础上的生生互动、生师互动乃至师生与其他人员的互动。

**9. 情感处理** 它重视对学生的人文关怀,主张教师关注学生的情感反应,教学中要求有效处理影响学生学习的各种情感因素。

**10. 母语作用** 它尊重外语环境下师生的母语优势并加以利用。不绝对禁止母语的使用。母语的使用取决于教学的需要,母语用于有效支持教育目标的达成。

**11. 应对失误** 它认可失误是学生获得语言或知识内容的过程中不可避免的现象,对学生失误采取包容的态度。针对具体情况应对学生的失误,或不去干预,允许学生自我纠正,或有针对性地适时给予纠正。

**12. 理论支撑** 它的语言学理论支撑包括:语言是以文本或话语为基础的;语言的运用凭借各种技能的融合;语言具有目的性。它的学习理论支撑包括:当人们把语言当成获取信息的工具而不是目的时学习语言更成功,作为语言学习的基础使得一些内容比另外一些内容更有用;当教学关注学生的需求时学生的学习效果会更好;教学应该以学生以前的学习经历为基础。

在CLI教育理念指导下,依托2个国家社会科学基金项目,我们将《高等学校英语专业英语教学大纲》规定的语言技能课程(包括英语语音、英语语法、英语听力、英语口语、英语阅读、英语写作、基础英语、高级英语、英语视听说、英汉笔译、英汉口译等)和专业知识课程(包括英语国家概况、英国文学、美国文学、语言学概论、学术论文写作)进行系统改革,逐步构建了全新的英语专业课程体系,包括八个系列的核心课程:

**1. 综合英语课**:美国文学经典作品、英国文学经典作品、世界文学经典作品、西方思想经典。依托美国、英国及其他国家的英语文学经典作品和西方思想经典的内容,提高学生综合运用英语的能力,丰富对英语文学及西方思想的认知,提高综合能力和综合素养。

**2. 英语视听说课**:美国社会文化经典电影、英国社会文化经典电影、环球资讯、专题资讯。依托美英社会文化经典电影、环球资讯、专题资讯内容,提高学生的英语听说能力,同时增加学生对相关国家社会文化的了解。

**3. 英语口语课**:功能英语交际、情景英语交际、英语演讲、英语辩论。依托人际交往的知识内容,提高学生的英语口语交际能力,增进对人际沟通的了解。

**4. 英语写作课**:段落写作、篇章写作、创意写作、学术英语写作。依托笔头交际的知识内容,提高学生的英语笔头表达能力。

**5. 英汉互译课**:英汉笔译、汉英笔译、交替传译、同声传译、专题口译。依托相关学科领域的知识内容,提高学生的英汉笔译、交传、同传、专题口译技能,增加学生对相关领域的了解。

**6. 社会文化课**:美国社会与文化、美国自然人文地理、美国历史文化、英国社会与文化、英国自然人文地理、英国历史文化、澳新加社会与文化、欧洲文化、中国文化、古希腊罗马神话、《圣经》与文化、跨文化交际。依托相关国家或区域的社会、文化、史地等知识,扩展学生的社会文化知识,增加学生专业知识的系统性,拓宽学生的国际视野,同时提高学生的英语能力。

**7. 英语文学课**:英语短篇小说、英语长篇小说、英语散文、英语戏剧、英语诗歌。依托各种体

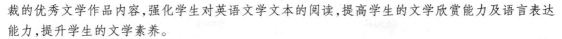

裁的优秀文学作品内容，强化学生对英语文学文本的阅读，提高学生的文学欣赏能力及语言表达能力，提升学生的文学素养。

**8. 语言学课程：** 英语语言学、英语词汇学、语言与社会、语言与文化、语言与语用。依托英语语言学知识内容，帮助学生深入了解英语语言，增加对语言与社会、文化、语用关系的认识，同时提升学生的专业表达能力。

此外，每门课程均通过开展多种教学活动，服务于学生的综合能力和综合素质培养目标。

研究表明，CLI指导下的课程改革在学生的语音、词汇、语法、听力、口语、写作、交际、思辨、情感、专业知识等诸多方面产生了积极的教学效果，对学生的文学作品分析能力、创新能力、思辨能力及逻辑思维能力发展也大有裨益。

CLI教育理念一经推出，在国际、全国、区域研讨会及我国高校广泛交流，产生了广泛的积极影响。

**1. CLI教育理念影响了教师的教育理念。** 随着教学研究成果的不断出现，越来越多的英语教师开始关注CLI教育理念及其指导下的改革，数以百计的教师积极参与CLI教育教学研讨与交流，国际关系学院、华中农业大学等数十所高校领导积极与团队交流理念及课程建设，两百多所高校引介了改革的理念、课程建设理念及开发的课程，而且还结合本校实际开展了课程改革，取得了积极成果。

**2. CLI教育教学研究成果影响数万师生。** 在CLI教育理念指导下开发了系列课程和教材在北京大学出版社、上海外语教育出版社等出版社出版，推出的校级、省级和国家级教学研究成果开始发挥辐射作用，通过《外语教学与研究》《中国外语》等期刊发表的研究论文向同行汇报了改革遇到的问题及取得的进展，数以万计的师生使用了开发的教材，在提高语言技能的同时扩展专业知识，提高综合素质。改革成果在我国的英语专业教育中发挥着积极的作用。

该理念不仅得到一线教师的广泛支持，也得到了戴炜栋、王守仁、文秋芳等知名专家的高度肯定。蔡基刚教授认为其具有"导向性"作用。孙有中教授认为，该理念指导的教学改革"走在了全国的前列"。教育部高等学校外语专业教学指导委员会前主任委员戴炜栋曾表示，开发的课程值得推广。此外，该理念被作为教学要求写入《普通高等学校本科外国语言文学类专业教学指南（上）：英语类专业教学指南》，用于指导全国的外语专业教育，对我国的外语教育及教育教学改革必将产生深远的影响。

《欧洲文化入门（第2版）》是CLI教育理念指导下英语专业知识课程体系中"欧洲文化"课程所使用的教材。教材针对的学生群体是具有中学英语基础的大学生，适用于英语专业一、二年级学生，也适用于具有中学英语基础的非专业学生和英语爱好者。总体看来，本教材具有以下主要特色：

**1. 打破了传统的教学理念。** 本教材改变了"为学语言而学语言"的传统教材建设理念，在具有时代特色且被证明行之有效的CLI教育理念指导下，改变了片面关注语言知识和语言技能、忽视内容学习的做法。它依托学生密切关注的西方文明和文化内容，结合社会文化内容组织学生进行语言交际活动，在语言交流中学习有意义的知识内容，既训练语言技能，也丰富相关知识，起到的是一箭双雕的作用。

**2. 涉及了丰富的教学内容。** 《欧洲文化入门（第2版）》共设计十五个单元。内容从欧洲文明发展的源头——两河文明和古埃及文明——开始，以历史发展的时间先后为序，一直延伸到当代欧洲社会的主要文艺动向，基本涵盖了西方文明发展的主要历程。

**3. 引进了真实的教学材料。** 英语教材是英语学习者英语语言输入和相关知识输入的重要渠道。本教材大量使用真实、地道的语言材料，为学生提供了高质量的语言输入。此外，为了使课文内容更加充实生动，易于学生理解接受，编者在课文中穿插了大量的插图、表格、照片等真实的视觉材料，表现手段活泼，形式多种多样，效果生动直观。

**4. 设计了新颖的教材板块。** 本教材每一单元的主体内容均包括 Before You Read, Start to Read, After You Read 和 Read More 四大板块，不仅在结构上确立了学生的主体地位，而且系统的安排也方便教师借助教材有条不紊地开展教学活动。它改变了教师单纯灌输、学生被动接受的教学方式，促使学生积极思考、提问、探索、发现、批判，培养自主获得知识、发现问题和解决问题的能力。

**5. 提供了有趣的训练活动。** 为了培养学生的语言技能和综合素质，本教材在关注英语语言知识训练和相关知识内容传授的基础上精心设计了生动多样的综合训练活动，例如头脑风暴、话题辩论、角色表演、主题陈述、故事编述等。多样化的活动打破了传统教材单调的训练程式，帮助教师设置真实的语言运用情境，组织富于挑战性的、具有意义的语言实践活动，培养学生语言综合运用能力。

**6. 推荐了经典的学习材料。** 教材的另一特色在于它对教学内容的延伸和拓展。在每个章节的最后部分，编者向学生推荐经典的书目、影视作品、名诗欣赏以及英文歌曲等学习资料，这不仅有益于学生开阔视野，也使教材具有了弹性和开放性，方便不同院校不同水平学生的使用。

本教材是我国英语专业综合课程改革的一项探索，凝聚了全体编写人员的艰苦努力。然而由于水平有限，本教材还存在疏漏和不足，希望老师和同学们能为我们提出宝贵的意见和建议。您的指导和建议将是我们提高的动力。

编者
2019 年 11 月 27 日
于大连外国语大学

# Contents

**Unit 1  The First Civilizations** ·········································································· **1**
  Text A  The Cradle of Civilization ·······································································  2
  Text B  Pyramids in Egypt ···················································································  9
  Text C  Ötzi's Last Meal ····················································································· 11

**Unit 2  Ancient Greece (I)** ················································································· **14**
  Text A  The Classical Greece ············································································ 15
  Text B  A Tale of Two Cities: Sparta vs. Athens ············································· 22
  Text C  Alexander the Great: The King of Kings ············································· 24

**Unit 3  Ancient Greece (II)** ················································································ **26**
  Text A  The Hellenistic Greece ·········································································· 28
  Text B  The Ancient Olympic Games ······························································· 34
  Text C  The Parthenon ······················································································· 36

**Unit 4  Ancient Rome (I)** ···················································································· **40**
  Text A  Rome: From Republic to Empire ·························································· 41
  Text B  Conversion of the Roman Republic to the Roman Empire ················ 49
  Text C  The Burning of Rome ············································································ 51

**Unit 5  Ancient Rome (II)** ··················································································· **55**
  Text A  Roman Art and Architecture ································································· 57
  Text B  Roman Baths ························································································· 64
  Text C  The Roman Forum ················································································ 66

**Unit 6  The Middle Ages** ···················································································· **70**
  Text A  Between Ancient and Modern ······························································ 72
  Text B  The Crusades ························································································ 80
  Text C  The Black Death ···················································································· 83

**Unit 7  The Making of Renaissance** ································································· **86**
  Text A  The Dawn of a New Age ······································································ 87
  Text B  Humanism of the Renaissance ···························································· 96
  Text C  Johannes Gutenberg ············································································· 98

## Unit 8  High Renaissance .................................................. 102
Text A  Renaissance Art and Artists .................................... 103
Text B  Mystery behind the *Mona Lisa* ............................. 111
Text C  William Shakespeare ............................................. 112

## Unit 9  The Reformation ..................................................... 116
Text A  The European Reformation .................................... 117
Text B  The Roman Catholic Church in 1500 ...................... 125
Text C  Driven to Defiance ................................................. 127

## Unit 10  The Baroque Age ..................................................... 130
Text A  The Age of Revolution ........................................... 131
Text B  Newton, the Apple, and Gravity .............................. 139
Text C  Baroque Style ........................................................ 140

## Unit 11  The Age of Enlightenment ....................................... 144
Text A  The Enlightenment ................................................. 146
Text B  Wolfgang Amadeus Mozart .................................... 153
Text C  Women in the Enlightenment ................................. 155

## Unit 12  The French Revolution ............................................ 159
Text A  The French Revolution ........................................... 160
Text B  The Storming of the Bastille .................................. 168
Text C  The Reign of Terror ............................................... 170

## Unit 13  Romanticism ........................................................... 174
Text A  Romanticism .......................................................... 175
Text B  The Sorrows of Young Werther .............................. 182
Text C  The Romantic Painting ........................................... 184

## Unit 14  Realism .................................................................. 188
Text A  Science and Culture in an Age of Realism ............... 189
Text B  *A Tale of Two Cities* ............................................ 196
Text C  Charles Darwin ...................................................... 198

## Unit 15  Modernism and Other Contemporary Trends .......... 202
Text A  Modernism Defined ................................................ 204
Text B  Modernism after World War II (I) .......................... 211
Text C  Modernism after World War II (II) ......................... 214

## Bibliography ........................................................................ 217

# Unit 1
## The First Civilizations

> The history of civilization, if intelligently conceived, may be an instrument of civilization.
> —Charles Beard, US historian

### Unit Goals

- To have a general understanding of the early civilizations in the world
- To appreciate the cultural achievements of the Mesopotamians and ancient Egyptians
- To learn the useful words and expressions that describe the early civilizations
- To improve language skills by learning this unit

### Before You Read

1. What do you know about ancient civilizations of the world?

   The ancient civilizations I know are:
   (1) _____
   (2) _____
   (3) _____
   (4) _____

2. Do you know the following architectural constructions? What civilization does each of them symbolize?

3. Form groups of three or four students. Try to find, on the Internet or in the library, more information about the constructions in the pictures above. Choose one as your topic and prepare a five-minute classroom presentation.

## Start to Read

### Text A  The Cradle of Civilization

The word civilization comes from Latin *civis*, meaning a citizen or resident of a city. This term is similar to and often interchangeable with culture, but the former refers mostly to cultures that have complex economic, governmental, and social systems. That is, a civilization is technologically more advanced than the cultures of its time, whereas a culture, as a body of learned behaviors common to a given human society, acts rather like a template, shaping behavior and consciousness within a human society from generation to generation.

The development of writing is a prerequisite for civilization. Therefore, the first civilizations were those highly organized societies in which the only efficient way of communication between individuals and groups across larger space and time was writing. In this sense, the four earliest civilizations were Mesopotamian, Egyptian, Indian and Chinese.

By western civilization we mean the civilization that has consummated in the most industrially advanced regions in the world today, mostly in Europe and North America. Nevertheless, it is not a geographically defined concept. Western civilization belongs to no particular place, and the origin of western civilization was oriental rather than occidental. The civilization that later spread to and left its legacy for the West appeared first outside the "West", in Mesopotamia at the Tigris and Euphrates river basins in present-day Iraq and Iran, a region that westerners today call the Middle East. At every stage of its growth, western civilization drew heavily on heritages of oriental civilizations in Egypt, Asia Minor, the Middle East, Indus and China.

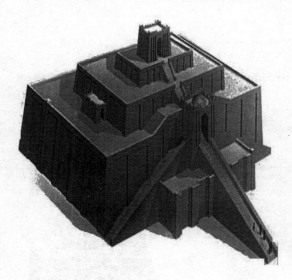

### Civilization in Mesopotamia

Mesopotamia is a region in the Middle East, lying between the rivers Euphrates and Tigris in what is Iraq today. The name "Mesopotamia" comes from Greek, which means "between rivers". Important ancient civilizations in the region were the Sumerian, the Babylonian and Assyrian.

It was the two rivers that became the basis of the wealth of the region. Through relatively easy irrigation, agriculture could yield heavy crops. There were fish in the rivers, the area had diversified agriculture and wildfowl was available out near the coast.

Hence, there was an easy surplus of food products—a prerequisite for urbanization, so cities developed. The cities were centers of trade, as well as the production of handicrafts, state administration and military defense. Mesopotamia also had other important raw materials available although stone and wood were rare, and they had to be imported. The most important local raw material was clay, which was used to build houses and create tablets to write on.

Mesopotamian people made great cultural achievements. Much mathematical and astronomical science owes its beginnings to the Mesopotamians. They developed the sexagesimal system, which was used for all types of calculations and is still used for the clock all around the world.

Architecture and art are often impressive, but cannot be compared to what is found in Egypt. However, one achievement is among the greatest found in antiquity: The Ziggurat, a temple structure of impressive size and high aesthetical values.

It was in Mesopotamia that cuneiform writing was developed, and with this, much literature of high value was produced. *Enuma Elish* and *Gilgamesh* are examples of great religious literature, while the *Code of Hammurabi* is one of the greatest early examples of juridical literature. Still, much of the available literature remains untranslated.

## Ancient Egyptian Culture

Ancient Egypt is a civilization that thrived along the Nile River in northeastern Africa for more than 3,000 years, from about 3100 BC to 30 BC. It was the longest-lived civilization of the ancient world.

The Nile River, which formed the focus of ancient Egyptian civilization, originates in the highlands of East Africa and flows northward throughout the length of what are now Sudan and Egypt. Northwest of modern-day Cairo, it branches out to form a broad delta, through which it empties into the Mediterranean Sea. Because of seasonal rains farther south in Africa, the Nile overflowed its banks in Egypt every year. When the floodwaters receded, a rich black soil covered the floodplain. This natural phenomenon and its effects on the environment enabled the ancient Egyptians to develop a successful economy based on agriculture.

Other natural factors combined to give rise to a great civilization in the Nile region. In the relatively cloudless sky in Egypt, the Sun almost always shone, consistently providing heat and light. The Nile served as a water highway for the people, a constant source of life-giving water, and the sustainer of all plants and animals. In addition, natural barriers provided good protection from other peoples. The desert to the west, the seas to the north and east, and the Nile's rapids to the south prevented frequent hostile attacks.

In this setting, a sophisticated and creative society came into being. That society was the only one in the area to endure for thousands of years. It was in this land that two of the Seven Wonders of the World were found: the pyramids at Giza and the lighthouse at Alexandria.

The ancient Egyptians processed thin flat sheets from the papyrus, a plant that grew along the

Nile, and on these paperlike sheets they wrote their texts. Their earliest script, now known as hieroglyphs, began as a type of picture writing in which the symbols took the form of recognizable images. They originated many basic concepts in arithmetic and geometry, as well as the study of medicine and dentistry. They devised a calendar based on their observations of the Sun and the stars.

Although the ancient Egyptians worshiped many gods, Egypt is also often recognized as the origin of the first recorded monotheist (worshiper of one god). Egypt also developed one of the first religions to have a concept of the afterlife. No culture before or since paid as much attention to preparations as the Egyptians for what was to come after death. Both royalty and private individuals built, decorated, and furnished tombs, which the ancient Egyptians understood to represent their eternal existence.

Politically, Egypt was a major power in the ancient world. Its kings governed the land through an elaborate bureaucratic administration. At certain periods, ancient Egypt's influence extended even farther south and west in Africa as well as east into Asia.

Great pyramids, hieroglyphs, elaborately decorated underground burial chambers, sprawling temple complexes, and statues combining human and animal forms are only a few of the many remnants that survive from ancient Egypt. These relics of an extinct world raised numerous questions during the centuries after the civilization died out and still fascinate people today.

## Proper Nouns

1. the Tigris-Euphrates 底格里斯河—幼发拉底河流域
2. Mesopotamia 美索不达米亚
3. Ziggurat 美索不达米亚的金字塔形塔庙
4. *Enuma Elish* 美索不达米亚史诗《埃努玛—埃利什》
5. *Gilgamesh* 古巴比伦史诗《吉尔伽美什》
6. *Code of Hammurabi* 《汉穆拉比法典》
7. the Nile River 尼罗河
8. the pyramids at Giza 吉萨金字塔
9. lighthouse at Alexandria 亚历山大灯塔

## After You Read

**Knowledge Focus**

**1. Fill in the blanks according to what you have learned in the text above.**

(1) _____ is a region in the Middle East lying between the Euphrates and Tigris.

(2) The most important ancient civilizations in the Mesopotamian region were _____, _____, _____, and _____.
(3) The Mesopotamian people developed the _____ system, which is still used for the clock all around the world.
(4) The most famous architectural construction in the Mesopotamian time was called _____.
(5) The writing system invented by the Mesopotamian people was called _____.
(6) The *Code of Hammurabi* is one of the greatest early examples of _____ literature.
(7) It was in ancient Egypt that two of the Seven Wonders of the World were found: _____ and _____.
(8) The writing system adopted by the Egyptians is called _____.
(9) Egyptians devised a calendar based on their observations of _____ and _____.
(10) Egypt developed one of the first religions to have a concept of _____.

## 2. Discuss the following questions with your partner.
(1) What are the four earliest civilizations in the world?
(2) What does the term "Mesopotamia" refer to?
(3) Which two rivers are related to the Mesopotamian culture?
(4) Why did civilization develop in the Mesopotamian region?
(5) What cultural achievements were made by the Mesopotamian people?
(6) Why is Egypt often called "the gift of the Nile"?
(7) What contributed to the emergence of a great civilization in the Nile region?
(8) What cultural legacy has been left by the people in ancient Egypt?

## Language Focus
### 1. Fill in the blanks with the words or expressions you have learned in the text.

| prerequisite | diversified | cradle | give rise to | devise |
| --- | --- | --- | --- | --- |
| remnant | consistently | recede | eternal | sophisticated |

(1) The company is engaged in the _____ search for a product that will lead the market.
(2) In many Third World regions, land reform remains a _____ for development.
(3) China _____ holds that economic development should be coordinated with environmental protection.
(4) What is learned in the _____ is carried to the tomb.
(5) Managerial economics is becoming a _____ art.
(6) International support has _____ a new optimism in the company.
(7) He is good at _____ language games that you can play with students in the class.
(8) Like marriage dance, funeral dance is also varied and _____.
(9) His hair is beginning to _____ from his forehead.

(10) It matters little where we pass the _____ of our days.

2. Fill in the blanks with the proper form of the word in the brackets.
   (1) The school has received _____ (vary) grants from the education department.
   (2) The city's first _____ (inhabit) arrived in the 16th century.
   (3) _____ (urban) is the process by which more and more people leave the countryside to live in cities.
   (4) Scientists concluded that ancient people probably built the ledge as an _____ (astronomy) observation platform.
   (5) He constructed his house with an eye to _____ (architecture) beauty.
   (6) The town relies on the _____ (season) tourist industry for jobs.
   (7) The reform program was greeted with _____ (hostile) by conservatives.
   (8) A dentist is a person who is trained and licensed to practice _____ (dentist).
   (9) The _____ (extinct) of the dinosaurs occurred millions of years ago.
   (10) The Eiffel Tower in Paris is an instantly _____ (recognize) landmark.

3. Fill in the blanks with the proper prepositions or adverbs that collocate with the neighboring words.
   (1) The kings of ancient Egypt governed the land _____ an elaborate bureaucratic administration.
   (2) Let me cite an incident that happened last semester _____ an example.
   (3) Having failed my French exams, I decided to concentrate _____ science subjects.
   (4) It is mutual respect that their relationship was based _____.
   (5) A surplus of exports _____ imports will boost employment.
   (6) He owes his life _____ the staff at the hospital.
   (7) These lights are used _____ illuminating the playing area.
   (8) She was torn _____ loyalty to her father and love for her husband.

4. Error Correction: Each of the following sentences has at least one grammatical error. Identify the errors and correct them.
   (1) Ancient Egypt is the civilization that thrived along Nile River in northeastern Africa for more than 3000 years from about 3300 BC to 30 BC.
   (2) The river branches out to form into a broad delta, which it empties into Mediterranean Sea.
   (3) By western civilization we mean civilization that has consummated in the most industrially advanced regions in the world today, mostly in the Europe and the North America.
   (4) At every stage of its growth, western civilization drew heavy on heritages of oriental civilizations in Egypt, Asia Minor, the Middle East, Indus and China.
   (5) Mesopotamia is a region in the Middle East lied between the rivers Euphrates and Tigris in that is Iraq today.
   (6) It was the Tigris and the Euphrates which became the basis upon which the wealth of the region

was based.

(7) Much mathematical and astronomical science owe its beginnings to the Mesopotamians.

(8) Architecture and art are often impressive, but cannot be compared to that is found in Egypt.

(9) Much of the available literature in the Mesopotamian culture remains to be untranslated.

(10) The Nile River was the long-lived civilization of the ancient world.

(11) Many natural factors combining to give rise to a great civilization in the Nile region.

(12) In the relatively cloudless sky in Egypt, the Sun almost always shone, consistently provide heat and light.

(13) It was in this land where two of the Seven Wonders of the World was found: the pyramids at Giza and the lighthouse at Alexandria.

(14) The ancient Egyptians processed thin flat sheets that they wrote their texts.

(15) No culture before or since paid as many attentions to preparations as the Egyptians for what was to come after death.

## Comprehensive Work

### 1. Sharing Ideas: *Code of Hammurabi*

The following statements are taken from the *Code of Hammurabi*. Read carefully and discuss the following questions with your partner.

25. If a fire breaks out in a house, and someone who comes to put it out casts his eye upon the property of the owner of the house and takes the property of the master of the house, he shall be thrown into that self-same fire.

**Question:**
Is the punishment fair? Why or why not?

---

196. If a man has destroyed the eye of another man, his eye shall be destroyed.
198. If he has destroyed the eye of a freed man or broken the bone of a freed man, he shall pay one mina of silver.
199. If he has destroyed the eye of a man's slave or broken the bone of a man's slave, he shall pay one-half of its value.

**Question:**
What do these rules say about the social structure of the Mesopotamian society?

---

### 2. Seven Wonders of the Ancient World

The *Seven Wonders of the Ancient World* is the first known list of the most remarkable man-made creations of classical antiquity, and was based on guide-books popular among Ancient Greek sight-seers and only includes works located around the Mediterranean rim. Search the Internet for related information about the seven wonders, and complete the following tasks.

**a. Match the following wonders with their respective pictures and the places where they can be found.**

| How does it look? | What is the name? | Where is it now? |
|---|---|---|
| | Statue of Zeus at Olympia | Cairo, Egypt |
| | Temple of Artemis | Izmir, Turkey |
| | Hanging Gardens of Babylon | Olympia, Greece |
| | Great Pyramid of Giza | Iraq |
| | Lighthouse of Alexandria | Pharos, Egypt |
| | Mausoleum at Halicarnassus | Rhodes, Greece |
| | Colossus of Rhodes | Bodrum, Turkey |

b. Questions for Discussion:

(1) What do you think are the qualities of an object that is considered a "wonder of the world"?

(2) Which of the seven wonders would you like to visit? Why?

## 3. Writing

Suppose you work in a travel agency. Write to a local newspaper, advertising for the travel to one of the Seven Wonders of the Ancient World. Describe its location and its history, and explain why it is a good idea to travel there.

### Text B  Pyramids in Egypt

During Egypt's Old Kingdom, the pharaohs established a stable central government in the fertile Nile Valley. Perhaps the greatest testaments to their power were the pyramids and other tombs built to shelter them in the afterlife.

**Kings of the Dead**

Ancient Egyptians believed that when the pharaoh died, he became *Osiris*, king of the dead. The new pharaoh became *Horus*, god of the heavens and protector of the Sun god. This cycle was symbolized by the rising and setting of the Sun.

Some part of a dead pharaoh's spirit, called his *ka*, was believed to remain with his body. And it was thought that if the corpse did not have proper care, the former pharaoh would not be able to carry out his new duties as king of the dead. If this happened, the cycle would be broken and disaster would befall Egypt.

To prevent such a catastrophe, each dead pharaoh was mummified, which preserved his body. Everything the king would need in his afterlife was provided in his grave—vessels made of clay, stone, and gold, furniture, food, even doll-like representations of servants, known as *ushabti*. His body would continue to receive food offerings long after his death.

**Tombs Fit for Kings**

To shelter and safeguard the part of a pharaoh's soul that remained with his corpse, Egyptians built massive tombs—but not always pyramids.

Before the pyramids, tombs were carved into bedrock and topped by flat-roofed structures called *mastabas*. Mounds of dirt, in turn, sometimes topped the structures.

The pyramid shape of later tombs could have come from these mounds. More likely, Egyptian pyramids were modeled on a sacred, pointed stone called the *benben*. The *benben* symbolized the rays of the Sun; ancient texts claimed that pharaohs reached the heavens via sunbeams.

**Who Built the Pyramids?**

Contrary to some popular depictions, the pyramid builders were not slaves or foreigners. Excavated skeletons show that they were Egyptians who lived in villages developed and overseen by the pharaoh's supervisors.

The builders' villages boasted bakers, butchers, brewers, granaries, houses, cemeteries, and probably even some sorts of health-care facilities—there is evidence of laborers surviving crushed or amputated limbs. Bakeries excavated near the Great Pyramids could have produced thousands of loaves of bread every week.

Some of the builders were permanent employees of the pharaoh. Others were conscripted for a limited time from local villages. Some may have been women: Although no depictions of women builders have been found, some female skeletons show wear that suggests they labored with heavy stone for a long period.

Graffiti indicates that at least some of these workers took pride in their work, calling their teams "Friends of Khufu", "Drunkards of Menkaure", and so on—names indicating allegiances to pharaohs.

An estimated 20,000 to 30,000 workers built the Pyramids at Giza over 80 years. Much of the work probably happened while the River Nile was flooded.

Huge limestone blocks could be floated from quarries right to the base of the Pyramids. The stones would likely then be polished by hand and pushed up ramps to their intended positions.

It took more than manual labor, though. Architects achieved an accurate pyramid shape by running ropes from the outer corners up to the planned summit, to make sure the stones were positioned correctly. And priests-astronomers helped choose the pyramids' sites and orientations so that they would be on the appropriate axis in relation to sacred constellations.

From stone pusher to priest, every worker would likely have recognized his or her role in continuing the life-and-death cycle of the pharaohs, and thereby in perpetuating the glory of Egypt.

***Questions for Reflection***

1. Explain the meaning of the following terms according to what you read in the text above.

    (1) Osiris   _____

    (2) Horus   _____

    (3) ka   _____

    (4) ushabti   _____

    (5) mastabas   _____

    (6) benben   _____

2. Why was every pharaoh of Ancient Egypt made into a mummy after they died?
3. What kind of people took part in the construction of Egyptian Pyramids?
4. How did the workers build the Pyramids? How did they feel about their work?

### Text C  Ötzi's Last Meal

The idea that we can visit an ancestor from three hundred generations past seems incredible. And yet a discovery in the Italian Alps in 1991 has brought us face to face with Ötzi (so-named for the valley where he was found), an ordinary man who faced a cruel death more than five thousand years ago. Ötzi's perfectly preserved body, clothing, tools, and weapons allow us to know how people lived and died in Western Europe before it was Europe—before indeed it was the West.

Ötzi was small by modern European standards: he stood at just 5 feet 4 inches. Around 40 years old, he was already suffering from arthritis, and his several tattoos were likely a kind of therapy. He probably lived in a village below the mountain whose inhabitants survived by hunting, simple agriculture, and goat herding.

One spring day around 3000 BC, Ötzi enjoyed what would be his last meal of meat, some vegetables, and flat bread made of einkorn wheat. He dressed warmly but simply in a leather breechcloth with a calfskin belt covered by a leather upper garment of goatskin sewn together with animal sinews. Below, he wore leather leggings and sturdy shoes made of bearskin soles and deer hide tops, lined with soft grasslike socks. On his head was a warm bearskin cap.

Ötzi carried an ax with a blade of almost pure copper and a flint knife in a fiber scabbard. He secured his leather backpack to a pack-frame made of a long hazel rod bent into a U-shape and reinforced with two narrow wooden slats. Among other things it held birch bark containers, one filled with materials to start a fire, which he could ignite with a flint he carried in his pouch. He also equipped himself with a multipurpose mat made from long stalks of Alpine grass and a simple first-aid kit consisting of inner bark from the birch tree—a substance with antibiotic and styptic properties.

For so small a man, Ötzi carried an imposing weapon: a yew-wood bow almost six feet long and a quiver of arrows. He must have been working on the weapon shortly before he died; the bow and most of the arrows were unfinished.

For ten years after the discovery of Ötzi's body, scholars and scientists studied his remains and speculated on why and how he died. Was he caught by a sudden storm or did he perhaps injure himself and die of exposure? And what was he doing so high in the mountains—six hours from the valley where he had his last meal, without adequate food or water? Finally, another X-ray of his frozen corpse revealed a clue: the shadow of a stone point lodged in his back.

Apparently, Ötzi left the lower villages that fateful spring day frightened and in a great hurry. Alone at an altitude of over 10,000 feet, desperately trying to finish his bow and arrows, he was fleeing for his life, but his luck ran out, Ötzi was shot in the back with an arrow. It pierced his shoulder between his shoulder blade and ribs, paralyzing his arm and causing extensive bleeding. Exhausted, he lay down in a shallow cleft in the snowy rocks. In a matter of hours, he was dead, and the snows of centuries quietly buried him.

What do Ötzi's life and death tell us about the story of western civilization? Although during his lifetime radically new urban societies and cultures were appearing just east of the Mediterranean, Ötzi still belonged to the Stone Age. None of his clothing was woven, although such basic technology was common in western Asia. The only metal was his ax head of soft copper, not the much harder bronze favored in the eastern Mediterranean. And yet, something vital connected Ötzi's world and that distant cradle of civilization: his last meal. Einkorn wheat is not native to western Europe but originated in the region of the Tigris and Euphrates. From there, both the grain itself and the technology of its cultivation spread slowly, ultimately reaching Ötzi's Alpine village. Other components of civilization would be: weaving, metalworking, urbanization, writing, and ways to kill men and women like Ötzi with great efficiency.

**Questions for Reflection**
1. Who is Ötzi? What did he look like?
2. What did Ötzi have for his last meal on a spring day around 3000 BC? How was he dressed? What did he carry with him?
3. How did Ötzi die? What was he doing so high in the mountains?
4. What do Ötzi's life and death tell us about the story of western civilization?

**Websites to Visit**
http://www.d.umn.edu/cla/faculty/troufs/anth1602/pccivil.html (accessed Apr. 28, 2020)
This website provides links to information about major ancient civilizations in the world.

http://www.ancientcivilizations.co.uk/home_set.html (accessed Apr. 28, 2020)
This website provides detailed information on various ancient cultures.

*Movie to Watch*

### The Prince of Egypt (1998)

*The Prince of Egypt* is a 1998 American animated film, the first traditionally animated film produced and released by DreamWorks. The story follows the life of Moses from his birth, through his childhood as a prince of Egypt, and finally to his ultimate destiny to lead the Hebrew slaves out of Egypt, which is based on the Biblical story of Exodus.

The film presents an extraordinary tale of two brothers named Moses and Ramses, one born of royal blood, and one an orphan with a secret past. Growing up the best of friends, they share a strong bond of free-spirited youth and good-natured rivalry. But the truth will ultimately set them at odds, as one becomes the ruler of the most powerful empire on Earth, and the other the chosen leader of his people! Their final confrontation will forever change their lives and the world.

# Unit 2
## Ancient Greece (I)

> I am not an Athenian or a Greek, but a citizen of the world.
> —Socrates
>
> Wise men speak because they have something to say; fools because they have to say something.
> —Plato

### Unit Goals

- To learn the general history of the Classical period of ancient Greece
- To be acquainted with the cultural achievements made in the Classical period of Greece
- To learn the useful words and expressions that describe Classical Greece
- To improve language skills by learning this unit

### Before You Read

1. **Test Your Knowledge: What do you know about Greece?**
   (1) Location: _____
   (2) Capital city: _____
   (3) Neighboring countries: _____
   (4) Famous Greek people: _____
   (5) Places of interest: _____
   (6) More about Greece: _____

2. **A Legendary Horse**
   **Look at the picture and answer the following questions.**
   (1) What is the name of the "horse" in the picture?
   _____
   (2) In which war did it appear?
   _____

(3) What was it used for?

(4) Do you know anything else about the horse or the war?

3. **Form groups of three or four students. Try to find, on the Internet or in the library, more information about Ancient Greece. Choose a topic that interests you most and prepare a five-minute classroom presentation.**

## Start to Read

### Text A  The Classical Greece

Ancient Greece was known as the "Cradle of Western Civilization". From this mountainous peninsula and scattered group of islands came the first democracy, epic stories, and advancements in math, science, medicine, and philosophy.

The ancient Classical and Hellenistic eras of Greece are undoubtedly the most splendid in the history of Greece, having left behind a host of ideas, concepts, and art to provide the foundation of what we call "western civilization".

**The Classical Greece**

In the context of the art, architecture, and culture of Ancient Greece, the classical period corresponds to most of the 5th and 4th centuries BC, from the fall of the last Athenian tyrant in 510 BC to the death of Alexander the Great in 323 BC.

Between 580 and 323 BC, Athens and Sparta dominated the Hellenic world with their cultural and military achievements. These two cities rose to power through alliances, reforms, and a series of victories against the invading Persian armies. They eventually resolved their rivalry in a long, and particularly nasty war that concluded with the demise of Athens first, Sparta second, and the emergence of Macedonia as the dominant power of Greece. Other city-states like Miletus, Thebes, Corinth, and Syracuse among many others played a major role in the cultural achievements of this period we came to call Classical Greece.

The Classical Period produced remarkable cultural and scientific achievements. The city of Athens introduced to the world a direct Democracy, the likes of which had never been seen hitherto, or subsequently, with western governments like Great Britain, France, and the USA emulating it a thousand years later. The rational approach to exploring and explaining the world as reflected in Classical Art, Philosophy, and Literature became the well-grounded springboard that

western culture used to leap forward, beginning with the subsequent Hellenistic Age. The thinkers of the Classical Greek era have since dominated thought for thousands of years, and have remained relevant to our day. The teachings of Socrates, Plato and Aristotle among others, either directly, in opposition, or mutation, have been used as reference points of countless western thinkers in the last two thousand years. Hippocrates became the "Father of modern medicine", and the Hippocratic Oath is still used today. The dramas of Sophocles, Aeschylus, Euripides, and the comedies of Aristophanes are considered among the masterpieces of western culture.

The art of Classical Greece began the trend towards a more naturalistic depiction of the world, thus reflecting a shift in philosophy from the abstract and supernatural to more immediate earthly concerns. Artists stopped merely "suggesting" the human form and began "describing" it with accuracy. Man became the focus, and "measure of all things" in daily life through Democratic politics, and in cultural representations.

Even after its defeat at the Peloponnesian war, Athens remained a guiding light for the rest of Greece for a long time, but this light that shone so bright, began to fade slowly. Sparta won the Peloponnesian war and emerged as the dominant power in Greece, but her political prowess failed to match her military reputation. While Sparta fought against other city-states all over Greece, Athens reconstructed her empire after rebuilding her walls, her navy and army. Sparta's power and military might were eventually diminished, especially after two crushing defeats in 371 BC and 363 BC. This power vacuum was quickly filled, however, by the Macedonians who under the leadership of Philip II emerged as the only major military authority of Greece after their victory against the Athenians in 338 BC.

Through diplomacy and might, Philip II, who became the king in 359 BC, managed to consolidate the areas around northern Greece under his power, and until his assassination in 336 BC had added central and southern Greece to his hegemony. But his sight was fixed beyond the borders of Greece. His ambition was to lead a military expedition of united Greece against the Persian Empire to avenge the Persian incursions of Greece. This ambition was fulfilled by his son Alexander the Great who became king after his father's assassination.

With a copy of *The Iliad* and a dagger in his hand, Alexander continued the centuries-old conflict between East and West by leading a united Greek army into Asia. His success on the battlefield and the amount of land he conquered became legendary and earned him the epithet "the Great". Besides brilliant military tactics, Alexander possessed leadership skills and charisma that made his army unbeatable in numerous battles against more numerous opponents, pushing the Greeks all the way to Egypt, India and Bactria (today Afghanistan).

The conquests of Alexander the Great changed the course of Ancient history. The center of gravity of the Greek world moved from the self-containment of city-states to a more vast territory that spanned the entire coast of the Eastern Mediterranean and reached far into Asia. Alexander's conquests placed diverse cultures under common hegemony and Greek influence around the

Mediterranean and southern Asia, paving the way for the distinct Hellenistic culture that followed his death.

## Proper Nouns

1. the Hellenistic Age 希腊化时代(公元前4世纪至公元前1世纪的希腊文明全面繁荣的时代)
2. Alexander the Great 亚历山大大帝
3. Athens 雅典
4. Sparta 斯巴达
5. Macedonia 马其顿
6. Miletus 米利都(古希腊城市之一)
7. Thebes 底比斯(古希腊城市之一)
8. Corinth 科林斯(古希腊城市之一)
9. Syracuse 锡拉库扎(古希腊城市之一)
10. Socrates 苏格拉底(古希腊哲学家)
11. Plato 柏拉图(古希腊哲学家)
12. Aristotle 亚里士多德(古希腊哲学家)
13. Hippocrates 希波克拉底 (古希腊医学家)
14. Sophocles 索福克勒斯(古希腊剧作家)
15. Aeschylus 埃斯库罗斯(古希腊剧作家)
16. Euripides 欧里庇得斯(古希腊剧作家)
17. Aristophanes 阿里斯托芬(古希腊剧作家)
18. The Peloponnesian war 伯罗奔尼撒战争(公元前5世纪雅典和斯巴达之间进行的战争)
19. Philip II of Macedonia 马其顿国王腓力二世(亚历山大的父亲)

## After You Read

### Knowledge Focus

**1. Fill in the blanks according to what you have learned from the text.**

(1) The classical period of Greece corresponds to most of the 5th and 4th centuries BC, from _____ in 510 BC to _____ in 323 BC.

(2) The most famous city-states in ancient Greece were _____ and _____.

(3) The city of Athens first introduced to the world the concept of _____, which is still worshipped by many modern countries in the West.

(4) People in the Classical Greece adopted a _____ approach to exploring and explaining the world as reflected in Classical Art, Philosophy, and Literature.

(5) The great philosophers in the Classical Greece were _____, _____, and _____.
(6) _____ was called "the father of modern medicine".
(7) The _____ of Sophocles, Aeschylus, Euripides, and the _____ of Aristophanes are still considered among the masterpieces of western culture.
(8) The art of Classical Greece began the trend towards a more _____ depiction of the world, and focused on _____.
(9) Under the leadership of _____, the Macedonians invaded Greece, and Philip II became the King in _____.
(10) Alexander's success on the battlefield was so legendary that he was given the epithet _____.

2. **Decide whether the following statements are true or false.**
   (1) ( ) Athens and Sparta were two friendly city-states in Ancient Greece.
   (2) ( ) The idea of democracy was first introduced by the city of Athens, and has influenced western governments for thousands of years.
   (3) ( ) The Hippocratic Oath is still used today by millions of law school graduates.
   (4) ( ) Aristophanes is famous for his tragedies.
   (5) ( ) Artists in Ancient Greece paid more attention to human form and began to describe it with accuracy.
   (6) ( ) Athens defeated Sparta in the Peloponnesian war.
   (7) ( ) By year 336 BC, Philip II had conquered northern Greece, the central part of Greece, and the southern Greece as well.
   (8) ( ) It was Alexander's ambition to lead a military expedition against the Persian Empire.
   (9) ( ) After numerous battles against numerous opponents, Alexander expanded his empire to Egypt, India and today's Afghanistan.
   (10) ( ) As a result of Alexander's conquest, Greek culture was spread to much of the Mediterranean region and southern Asia, paving the way for the development of the Hellenistic culture.

3. **Discuss the following questions with your partner.**
   (1) Why was ancient Greece known as the "cradle of western civilization"?
   (2) What period does the Classical Greece refer to?
   (3) What cultural and scientific achievements were made in the Classical period?
   (4) What did the art of Classical Greece focus on?
   (5) Who became the king of ancient Greece in 359 BC? What was his ambition?
   (6) Please draw a character sketch of Alexander the Great.

## Language Focus

**1. Fill in the blanks with the following words or expressions you have learned in the text.**

| a host of | resolve | demise | like (n.) | consolidate |
| emulate | charisma | correspond to | springboard | epithet |

(1) She hoped that marriage would _____ their relationship.
(2) The firm's director is confident that the new project will act as a _____ for/to further contracts.
(3) He was a very great actor—we will not see his _____ again.
(4) The couple _____ their differences and made an effort to get along.
(5) Our era produces _____ heroes and heroines.
(6) In "Alfred the Great", "the Great" is an _____.
(7) The arms of a man _____ the wings of a bird.
(8) How did a man of so little personal _____ get to be prime minister?
(9) The _____ of the company was sudden and unexpected.
(10) It is customary for boys to _____ their fathers.

**2. Fill in the blanks with the proper form of the word in the brackets.**

(1) The painting is _____ (undoubted) genuine.
(2) This, the president promised us, was a war against _____ (tyrant).
(3) _____ (rival) among business firms grew more intense.
(4) The _____ (emerge) of small Japanese cars in the 1970s challenged the US and European manufacturers.
(5) Meeting you here in Rome is a _____ (remark) coincidence.
(6) Do you think Australia is a more _____ (democracy) country than Britain?
(7) It can be very hard to think _____ (rational) when you are feeling so vulnerable and alone.
(8) We discourage waste of time on items _____ (relevant) to the object of study.
(9) We can predict changes with a surprising degree of _____ (accurate).
(10) A plot to _____ (assassination) the President was uncovered by government agents.

**3. Fill in the blanks with the proper prepositions or adverbs that collocate with the neighboring words.**

(1) Karl Marx left _____ him a great revolutionary theory for us.
(2) Economic independence would develop _____ the context of the liberation of all oppressed people.
(3) Liverpool chalked up another home victory _____ Arsenal.
(4) The meeting will conclude _____ the National Anthem.
(5) The most important lesson we have learned, _____ a great many others, is that we must be

clear about those questions.

(6) The work fills (in) a gap which has _____ existed in our archaeological literature.

(7) She shifted her weight uneasily _____ one foot _____ the other.

(8) Asia may well emerge _____ the world's largest producer, as well as the world's largest consumer market.

(9) To ease the tension, the manager added a few more names of laborers _____ the list.

(10) Such opinions pave the way _____ social change.

4. **Error Correction**: Each of the following sentences has at least one grammatical error. Identify the errors and correct them.

(1) The ancient Classical and Hellenistic eras of Greece are undoubtedly the most splendid in the history of Greece, left behind a host of ideas, concepts, and art.

(2) Ancient Greece was known the "Cradle of Western Civilization".

(3) Athens and Sparta rose to power by alliances, reforms, and a series of victories with the invaded Persian armies.

(4) Many city-states as Athens, Sparta, Miletus, and Corinth among many others played a major role in the cultural achievements of this period what we came to call Classical Greece.

(5) The city of Athens introduced to the world a direct Democracy, the likes of what had never been seen hitherto.

(6) The rational approach to explore and explain the world that reflected in Classical Art, Philosophy, and Literature became the well-grounded springboard that western culture used to leap forward.

(7) The teachings of Socrates, Plato and Aristotle like others have been used as reference points of countless western thinkers in the last two thousand years.

(8) Sparta won the Peloponnesian war and the dominant power was emerged in Greece, but her political prowess failed to fit her military reputation.

(9) His ambition was leading a military expedition of united Greece against the Persian Empire to avenge the Persian incursions of Greece.

(10) Alexander is one of the most puzzled great figures in history.

(11) By diplomacy and might, Philip II became the king in 359 BC, managed to consolidate the areas around northern Greece.

(12) Alexander's conquests placed diverse cultures under common hegemony and Greek influence around Mediterranean and southern Asia, pave the way for the distinct Hellenistic culture that followed his death.

### Comprehensive Work
### 1. Qualities of Great Leaders

The number of leaders in world history who have been called "the Great" is very small. What unique qualities in Alexander's personality and heritage contributed to his "greatness" and popularity? Do we have a similar or different definition of "greatness" for today's leaders?

What contributed to Alexander's greatness? {  _____
_____
_____
_____

What contributed to the "greatness" of today's leaders? {  _____
_____
_____
_____

## 2. Who rules?

In ancient Greece, there are different ways of ruling the cities.

| | |
|---|---|
| Sparta | Power held in family line —Monarchy and Aristocracy |
| Corinth | One person rules —Tyranny |
| Later Corinth | A small group rule —Oligarchy |
| Athens | People share power —Democracy |

Form groups of three or four. Discuss the following questions, and get ready to present your ideas to the whole class.

(1) Which of the four types of government would you prefer? Why?

_____

(2) And which would you prefer to be ruled by? Why?

**3. Writing**

What do you think are the qualities of a great leader? Please write a composition of about 200 words on this topic. Give one or two examples to illustrate your idea.

### Text B  A Tale of Two Cities: Sparta vs. Athens

In Ancient Greece there were two different major forms of government, Oligarchy and Democracy. The two city-states that best represented each form of government were Sparta (oligarchy) and Athens (democracy). The democratic government in Athens, though decently equal, fair and fairly advanced for its time, did not meet the needs of the Greeks. During a time of many military battles, Athens decided to worry more about comfort and culture. It is the oligarchy in Sparta that put a war-like attitude as its first priority and best met the needs of Ancient Greece.

The Athenian democratic government, which may have given the citizens in Greece more freedom, was not the best form of government at the time. The democracy in Athens cannot really be called a true democracy since there were several flaws in the government and the way it worked. Only ten percent of the total population of Athens actually had voting rights and all of these citizens were upper-class men who were over thirty years old.

Women, no matter what class or age, were given no freedom at all. They were first owned by their fathers and then were passed from them to their husbands who then gave them nothing more than the responsibilities of managing the household and educating the children. During a meeting of the Assembly, a policy could be adopted and formed into law. But once the meeting of the assembly ended, the enforcement of that law was left in the hands of people who may not agree with that specific law. Also, a rule of the Assembly said that if a certain speaker became too powerful, he could be expelled from the country if given a majority vote by the Assembly. This rule could easily be abused and really infringed on the freedom of speech that most democracies have. The Assembly was made up of five hundred men who were chosen from a list of those who

were eligible to serve on the council. Since most of the population was of a lower economic class, the time taken away from their normal work by serving on the Assembly lowered their earning potential, causing their already poor situation to worsen. Life may have been sophisticated and graceful in Athens but the Athenians were often mocked by opposing countries and other city-states for having no bravery, patriotism or courage. This was shown by the repeated attacks on Athens. If the Athenians had a more war-like reputation, they probably could have avoided many of those conflicts that eventually led to the loss of the power Athens held in Ancient Greece.

In the city-state of Sparta, the government was controlled by an oligarchy in which the power was held by a group of five men called ephors. It may not seem very fair in that the citizens had little say in the decisions made by the government but, at the time, this was the better government. The Spartans needed to give up comfort and culture for a more disciplined military approach to control the rebelling Messenians which eventually turned them into a deadly war machine. Over the years, the Spartan's ruthless and brutal reputation in war grew so large that other nations and city-states were so frightened that they would not attack Sparta even though the Spartan army was no larger than eight thousand men. The Spartan men in the army would start their military training at the age of seven and were trained to be tough and very self-sufficient. Every man in the army would fight with a great deal of passion for his country. Life in Sparta may have been rough but the rest of the Greeks envied the Spartans for their simplicity, straightforwardness, and fanatical dedication. There was a law in Sparta that banned all foreign trade and foreign traveling. This kept out all foreign ideas and allowed them to have the element of surprise when it came to attacks. This law did not affect their economy, which was already self-sufficient. Unlike the rest of Greek women, Spartan women had the freedom of equal rights except for voting rights. Since men were in the military, the women had full authority over their households and were not forced into a life of only childbearing and housekeeping like the Athenian woman.

The best example of why the Spartan government was better than the Athenian government happened in 404 BC when the Spartan army was able to conquer the mighty power known as Athens. The Spartan government was clearly better for that time period because they could handle the rigors of the military craze which was growing amongst its enemies.

For that specific time period, the oligarchy government in Sparta was better for the Ancient Greeks than the democratic government in Athens. The government in Athens worried more about the citizens of its city-state than its own well-being. The Spartan oligarchy may not have given its citizens a lot of freedom but it was successful in gaining attention and respect from the other Greeks and their rival nations.

## Questions for Reflection

1. What were the two major forms of government in ancient Greece? Which two city-states had best represented the two forms of government respectively?
2. Please define oligarchy and democracy. How do you understand the two terms?
3. Why did the author say that "the democracy in Athens was not a true democracy"?

4. What was the government like in Sparta? Why did the author say that the Spartan government was a better government at that time?
5. Do you agree with the author on his opinion? Why or why not?

### Text C  Alexander the Great: The King of Kings

On July 20th, 356 BC, the world changed forever.

King Philip II of Macedon and his wife, Olympias of Epirus, were given a child that would change the course of history. Alexander, they called him, was born in Pella, Macedonia on July 20th in the middle of summer. At a very young age, Alexander began his extensive education routine under some famous scholars at that time. At the age of 13, Philip requested philosopher Aristotle to tutor his son in literature and rhetoric. Alexander quickly took his subject, and began to expand his knowledge into botany, zoology, medicine, general science, geography, and philosophy. He is said to have loved the Greek theatre and reading immensely, as he became nearly attached to his copy of Homer's *The Iliad* that Aristotle had written down for him. The young prince would take this book everywhere he went, and slept with it under his pillow.

As he grew into a young man, Alexander began challenging physical activities such as hunting, riding, swordplay, archery, and running. At the age of 12, he was given a horse, Bucephalus, as a present, but the horse could not seem to be tamed. Young Alexander, however, was easily able to tame the black stallion and quickly bond with the animal to create a lasting friendship that would cease only in death.

In 338 BC, King Philip II of Macedonia had defeated the Greeks and established his control over the Greek peninsula. When Alexander became king after Philip's death, he led the Macedonians and Greeks on a spectacular conquest of the Persian Empire and opened the door to the spread of Greek culture throughout the ancient Near East. In just twelve years, Alexander the Great conquered vast territories. Dominating lands from west of the Nile to east of the Indus, he brought the Persian Empire, Egypt, and much of the Middle East under his control and laid the foundation for the Hellenistic world.

Alexander is one of the most puzzling great figures in history. Historians relying on the same sources give vastly different pictures of him. Some portray him as an idealistic visionary and others as a ruthless Machiavellian. No doubt he was a great military leader—a master of strategy and tactics, fighting in every kind of terrain and facing every kind of opponent. Alexander was a brave and even reckless fighter who was quite willing to lead his men into battle and risk his own life. His example inspired his troops to follow him into unknown lands and difficult situations. We know that he sought to imitate Achilles, the warrior-hero of Homer's *The Iliad*, who was an ideal still important in Greek culture. He also claimed to be descended from Heracles, the Greek hero who came to be worshiped as a god. Alexander also aspired to divine honors; as the pharaoh of Egypt, he became a living god according to Egyptian tradition and at one point even sent instructions to the Greek cities to "vote him a god".

Regardless of his ideals, motives, or views about himself, one fact stands out: Alexander truly created a new age, the Hellenistic era. As a result of his conquests, Greek language, art, architecture, and literature spread throughout the Near East. The urban centers of the Hellenistic Age, many founded by Alexander and his successors, became springboards for the diffusion of Greek culture. Alexander had established a number of cities and military colonies named Alexandria to guard strategic points and supervise wide areas. Most of the settlers were Greek mercenaries. It has been estimated that in the course of his campaigns, Alexander summoned 60,000 to 65,000 additional mercenaries from Greece, at least 36,000 of whom took up residence in the garrisons and new cities. While the Greeks spread their culture in the East, they were also inevitably influenced by Eastern ways. Thus Alexander's legacy became one of the hallmarks of the Hellenistic world: the clash and fusion of different cultures.

## Questions for Reflection

1. What kind of education did Alexander receive when he was young? How did his education influence his later life?
2. Find a map of the Greek kingdom of that time and describe the empire that Alexander had established.
3. Why did the author say that Alexander is one of the most puzzling great figures in history?
4. What new age was created by Alexander? What are the characteristics of this new age?

## Website to Visit

http://ancienthistory.about.com/cs/greecehellas1/a/classicalgreece.htm (accessed Apr. 28, 2020)
This website provides a brief introduction to the Classical Age in Greece as well as various links to what you may be interested in about Ancient Greece.

## Movie to Watch

### Troy (2004)

It is the year 1250 BC during the late Bronze Age. Two emerging nations begin to clash after Paris, the Trojan prince, convinces Helen, Queen of Sparta, to leave her husband Menelaus, and sail with him back to Troy. After Menelaus finds out that his wife was taken by the Trojans, he asks his brother Agamemnon to help him get her back. Agamemnon sees this as an opportunity for power, so they set off with 1,000 ships holding 50,000 Greeks to Troy. With the help of Achilles, the Greeks are able to fight the never-before-defeated Trojans. But they come to a stop by Hector, Prince of Troy. The whole movie shows their battle struggles and the foreshadowing of fate in this remake by Wolfgang Petersen of Homer's *The Iliad*.

# Unit 3
## Ancient Greece (II)

> A knowledge of Greek thought and life...is essential to high culture. A man may know everything else, but without this knowledge, he remains ignorant of the best intellectual and moral achievements of his own race.
> —Charles Eliot Norton

### Unit Goals

- To have a general understanding of the legacy of the Hellenistic Greece
- To be familiar with the intellectual and cultural trends in the Hellenistic Greece
- To learn the useful words and expressions that describe the Hellenistic Greece
- To improve language skills by learning this unit

### Before You Read

**1. Greek Mythology**

There are many powerful Gods and Goddesses in Greek mythology. What do you know about them? Fill in the blanks with what you know.

(1) _____ is the king of the gods and he controls the heavens.

(2) _____ is the wife of Zeus and is the queen of the gods. She is the most beautiful goddess.

(3) Ares is a son of _____ and god of _____. He is young and handsome.

(4) Athena is the goddess of _____ and _____. Her symbol is an _____.

2. Artists in the Hellenistic Greece created many great works of art, some of which are still admired by people today. The following three statues were famous ones made in the Hellenistic Greece. Do you know their names?

(1) _____   (2) _____   (3) _____

3. Form groups of three or four students. Try to find, on the Internet or in the library, more information about Ancient Greece. Choose a topic that interests you most and prepare a five-minute classroom presentation.

## Start to Read

### Text A  The Hellenistic Greece

The Hellenistic Age marks the transformation of Greek society from the localized and introverted city-states to an open, cosmopolitan, and exuberant culture that permeated the entire eastern Mediterranean, and Southeast Asia. While the Hellenistic world incorporated a number of different people, Greek thinking, mores, and way of life dominated the public affairs of the time. All aspects of culture took a Greek hue, with the Greek language being established as the official language of the Hellenistic world. The art and literature of the era were transformed accordingly. Instead of the previous preoccupation with the Ideal, the Hellenistic art focused on the Real. Depictions of man in both art and literature revolved around exuberant, and often amusing themes that for the most part explored the daily life and the emotional world of humans, gods, and heroes alike.

The autonomy of individual cities of the Classical era gave way to the will of the large kingdoms that were led by one ruler. As Alexander left no apparent heir, his generals controlled the empire. They fought common enemies and they fought against each other as they attempted to establish their power, and eventually, three major kingdoms emerged through the strife that followed the death of Alexander in 323 BC and persisted for the most part over the next three hundred years.

Many famous thinkers and artists of the Hellenistic era created works that remained influential for centuries. Schools of thought like the Stoics, the Skeptics, and the Epicureans continued the substantial philosophical tradition of Greece, while art, literature, and poetry reached new heights of innovation and development. The sculptures and canons of Polykleitos remained influential and were copied throughout the Hellenistic and Roman Eras, and even centuries later during the Italian Renaissance. Great works of art were created during the Hellenistic Era. In Architecture, the classical styles were further refined and augmented with new ideas like the Corinthian order which was first used on the exterior of the Temple of Olympian Zeus in Athens. Public buildings and monuments were constructed on a larger scale in more ambitious configuration and complexity. The Mausoleum of Pergamum merged architectural space and sculpture by the placement of heroic sculptures in the close proximity of a grand staircase.

The Hellenistic Greece became a time of substantial maturity of the sciences. In geometry, Euclid's *Elements* became the standard all the way up to the 20th century, and the work of Archimedes on mathematics along with his practical inventions became influential and legendary. Eratosthenes calculated the circumference of the Earth within 1,500 miles by simultaneously measuring the shadow of two vertical sticks placed one in Alexandria and one in Syene. The fact that the Earth was a sphere was common knowledge in the Hellenistic world.

The Hellenistic Age was by no means free of conflict, even after the major kingdoms were established. Challenges to the Hellenistic kingdoms appeared from internal conflict and new external enemies. The size of the empire made securing it next to impossible, and life outside the orderly large cities was filled with danger from bandits and pirates. Internal strife and revolutions caused the borders of the kingdoms to be shifted several times as the rulers of the major and minor kingdoms engaged in continuous conflict. At the same time, serious threats to the Hellenistic world came from external threats.

At the time of the Hellenistic Era, Rome had risen to a formidable power and by 200 BC occupied not only Italy, but also the entire coastal Adriatic Sea and Illyria. In the end, a large part of the Hellenistic kingdoms disintegrated by constant incursions by tribes of the fringes, many parts were simply given to Rome through the will of deceased rulers, and others won brief independence by revolution. In 31 BC, Octavian (later Augustus) defeated the rulers of Egypt Anthony and Cleopatra in the naval battle of Actium, and completed the demise of the Hellenistic Era.

The battle of Actium is considered the pivotal moment that defines the end of Ancient Greece. After the battle of Actium, the entire Hellenic world became subject to Rome. Greece in the next two thousand years was to undergo a series of conquests that made its people subjects of numerous powers and did not gain its self-determination until the 19th century AD.

## Proper Nouns

1. the Stoics 斯多葛学派
2. the Skeptics 怀疑论学派
3. the Epicureans 伊壁鸠鲁派(享乐主义学派)
4. Polykleitos 波利克里托斯(古希腊雕塑家)
5. Corinthian order 科林斯柱式。古希腊建筑的石柱主要有三种式样：多立斯柱式(Doric)、爱奥尼亚柱式(Ionic)和科林斯柱式(Corinthian)。
6. Temple of Olympian Zeus 奥林匹亚宙斯神庙
7. Mausoleum of Pergamum 帕加马陵墓(现位于土耳其伊斯坦布尔)
8. Euclid 欧几里得，古希腊数学家，以其所著的《几何原本》(Elements)闻名于世。
9. Archimedes 阿基米德(古希腊物理学家、数学家)
10. Eratosthenes 埃拉托斯特尼(古希腊数学家)
11. Alexandria 亚历山大港(古埃及城市之一)
12. Syene 赛伊尼(古埃及城市之一，现名为阿斯旺)
13. The Adriatic Sea 亚得里亚海
14. Illyria 伊利里亚(古代沿巴尔干半岛环绕亚德里亚海岸地区)
15. Octavian 屋大维(即后来的奥古斯都大帝)
16. Anthony and Cleopatra (古罗马将军)安东尼和(埃及女王)克莉奥帕特拉
17. Battle of Actium 亚克兴战役

## After You Read

**Knowledge Focus**

1. Fill in the blanks with what you have learned from the text.

   (1) The Hellenistic Age marks the transformation of Greek society from the _____ and _____ city-states to an _____, _____, and _____ culture.

   (2) The Hellenistic art focused on the _____.

   (3) After the death of Alexander, _____ controlled the empire.

   (4) Many schools of thought continued the philosophical tradition of Greece. They are _____, _____ and _____.

   (5) The _____ and _____ of Polykleitos remained influential throughout the Hellenistic Age.

   (6) In architecture, _____ order was first used on the exterior of the Temple of Olympian Zeus in Athens.

   (7) In geometry, _____'s *Elements* became the standard textbook all the way up to the 20th century.

   (8) The most famous mathematician in the Hellenistic period was _____, who was also noted for many of his practical inventions.

   (9) Eratosthenes calculated _____ of the Earth.

   (10) In _____, Octavian defeated the rulers of Egypt _____ and _____ in the naval battle of Actium, and completed the demise of the Hellenistic Era.

2. Decide whether the following statements are true or false.

   (1) ( ) The Hellenistic Age was characterized by an open, cosmopolitan and exuberant culture.

   (2) ( ) The official language of the Hellenistic world was the Latin language.

   (3) ( ) The Hellenistic art focused on the Ideal, and explored the daily life and the emotional world of humans, gods, and heroes alike.

   (4) ( ) A stable and prosperous period of time followed Alexander's death in 323 BC.

   (5) ( ) The sculptures of Polykleitos remained influential even during the Italian Renaissance.

   (6) ( ) Archimedes' *Elements* became the standard of geometry all the way up to the 20th century.

   (7) ( ) The fact that the Earth was a sphere was common knowledge in the Hellenistic world.

   (8) ( ) The peace in the Hellenistic Age was frequently disturbed by internal conflicts and external enemies.

   (9) ( ) The end of the Hellenistic Era was marked by the defeat of Anthony and Cleopatra in the battle of Actium.

   (10) ( ) Greece did not regain its self-determination until the fall of Rome.

3. Discuss the following questions with your partner.
   (1) What transformation was made during the Hellenistic Age of Ancient Greece?
   (2) What cultural achievements were made in the Hellenistic Age?
   (3) Why was the Hellenistic Greece a time of substantial maturity of the sciences?
   (4) What event marked the demise of the Hellenistic Era?

**Language Focus**

1. Fill in the blanks with the following words or expressions you have learned in the text.

| formidable | autonomy | give way to | permeate | substantial |
| proximity | next to impossible | pivotal | be subject to | incursion |

   (1) The findings show a _____ difference between the opinions of men and women.
   (2) It is _____ to catch a taxi at night during the year-end party season.
   (3) The universities are anxious to preserve their _____ from the central government.
   (4) Water will easily _____ a cotton dress.
   (5) Foreign trade occupies a _____ position in Mexico's economy.
   (6) _____ to a good shopping center was very important.
   (7) The arms trade should _____ rigorous controls.
   (8) He displayed remarkable energy and became the most _____ personality among the defendants.
   (9) Our employer will not _____ our demands for higher wages.
   (10) They repelled a sudden _____ of enemy troops.

2. Fill in the blanks with the proper form of the word in the brackets.
   (1) President Nixon's visit led to a _____ (transform) of American attitudes toward China.
   (2) The painter's _____ (depict) of the horror of war won her a worldwide reputation.
   (3) My computer makes a _____ (continue) low buzzing noise.
   (4) This is a matter that comes within the jurisdiction of the _____ (autonomy) region.
   (5) Great _____ (persist) is necessary for success.
   (6) He consoled himself by _____ (philosophy) reflections.
   (7) The story is written in richly _____ (poem) language.
   (8) Which team is likely to be more _____ (innovation) and creative?
   (9) Another attraction here is a _____ (legend) monster: the Loch Ness Monster.
   (10) As he reached _____ (mature), Bandit became more difficult to live with.

3. Fill in the blanks with the proper prepositions or adverbs that collocate with the neighboring words.
   (1) I suggest that we establish Mr. Jeffrey _____ our representative.

# 欧洲文化入门(第2版)
## An Introduction to European Culture (Second Edition)

(2) It is a difficult job and they should be paid _____.

(3) Their troubles revolve _____ money management.

(4) In response _____ tremendous demand, they began to manufacture radio _____ a large scale in 1922.

(5) The students ran all the way up _____ the station only _____ find that the train had left 10 minutes before.

(6) Along _____ the increase of age, then people do not like the illusion.

(7) Our government officials seem free _____ corruption.

(8) _____ hard work and determination the team has achieved remarkable success.

4. **Error Correction**: Each of the following sentences has at least one grammatical error. Identify the errors and correct them.

   (1) All aspects of culture took a Greek hue, with the Greek language was established as the official language of the Hellenistic world.

   (2) After the death of Alexander, the generals fought common enemies and they fought against each other where they attempted to establish their power.

   (3) Eventually, three major kingdoms emerged through the strife followed the death of Alexander in 323 BC and persisting for the most part over the next three hundred years.

   (4) Public buildings and monuments constructed on a larger scale in more ambitious configuration and complexity.

   (5) The Hellenistic Greece became a time of substantial maturity of the science.

   (6) Eratosthenes calculated the circumference of the Earth within 1,500 miles by simultaneous measuring the shadow of two vertical sticks placed one in Alexandria and one in Syene.

   (7) The size of the empire made securing it next to impossible, and life outside the orderly large cities filled with danger from bandits and pirates.

   (8) Internal strife and revolutions caused the borders of the kingdoms to shift several times as the rulers of the major and minor kingdoms engaged in continuous conflict.

   (9) In the end, a large part of the Hellenistic kingdoms integrated by constant incursions by tribes of the fringes, many parts were simply given to Rome through the will of deceased rulers.

   (10) Greece in the next two thousand years was undergoing a series of conquests that made its people subjects to numerous powers and did not gain its self-determination until the 19th Century AD.

   (11) While Hellenistic world incorporated a number of different people, Greek thinking, mores, and way of life dominated the public affairs of time.

## Comprehensive Work
### 1. Write a Story: Alexander the Great

Alexander the Great is one of the most prominent figures in history. There are many interesting stories about his legendary life. In this activity, we will try to describe a story that had happened between Alexander and Diogenes, a great thinker in ancient Greece.

Unit 3  Ancient Greece (II)

a. Look at this picture and answer the questions that follow.

(1) Who are the two people in the picture? Which one is Alexander the Great?
_____

(2) How will you describe their appearance?
   Alexander:
   _____

   Diogenes:
   _____

(3) What are they doing? What do you think they are talking about?
_____

(4) Do you know the story revealed by the picture? Tell what you know to your classmates.
_____

b. Please write a composition about the encounter between Alexander and Diogenes. Use as much detailed information as possible to describe their encounter. Don't forget to choose an appropriate title for your composition.

## 2. Debate

One significant byproduct of Alexander's reign was the establishment of Greek as a universal language throughout the empire. Historians say that a single, universally spoken language helped to simplify commerce, education, and daily communication in the vast empire Alexander created.

In the 20th century, people often disagree over whether a single national language is still a beneficial concept in modern countries. What do you think of the idea of having a universal language in today's world?

1. I am in favor of having a universal language today for the following reasons:

   (a) _____

   (b) _____

   (c) _____

2. I am against the idea of having a universal language today for the following reasons:

   (a) _____

   (b) _____

   (c) _____

3. Debate in the class on the advantages and disadvantages of having a universal language today.

### Read More

### Text B  The Ancient Olympic Games

The first written accounts of the Olympic Games date from 776 BC, although it is sure that these Games were not the first ones to be held. The Games, like all Greek Games, were an intrinsic part of a religious festival held in honor of Zeus (supreme among the gods) in Olympia, a worshipping place for the Greek gods near the town of Elis. Here the Greeks erected statues and built temples dedicated to Zeus. The greatest shrine was an ivory and gold statue of Zeus created by the Greek sculptor Phidias. The statue was considered to be one of the Seven Wonders of the World.

The Olympic Games were held in four-year intervals, and later the Greek method of counting the years even referred to these Games, using the term Olympiad for the period between two Games. The Games took place during the first full moon after the summer solstice.

When it was time for the games, the rulers of Elis sent out messengers all over Greece and to the Greek colonies around the Black Sea and the Mediterranean. They declared a truce throughout the Greek world for a month. No matter who you had a war with, you had to stop the war and let their athletes and performers go through your city-state safely to get to the Olympic Games.

According to Hippias of Elis, who compiled a list of Olympic victors c.400 BC, at first the only Olympic event was the stadion race, a race over about 190 meters, measured after the feet of Hercules. The word stadium is derived from this foot race. This was the only event until 724 BC when a two-stadium race was added.

Over the years, other events were added: boxing, wrestling, pankration (combination of boxing and wrestling), horse and chariot racing, several other running events, as well as a pentathlon, consisting of wrestling, running, long jump, javelin throw and discus throw (the latter three were not separate events). The addition of these events meant the festival grew from 1 day to 5 days, 3 of which were used for competition. The other 2 days were dedicated to religious rituals.

Only freeborn male Greek citizens not accused of murder or sacrilege were eligible to participate. Training began as early as one year before the games in the athlete's home city. A month before the games, the athletes were obligated to move to Elis or Olympia for their final training. It was here that the athletes were taught the rules of fair play and honorable competition.

Athletes usually competed nude. They originally wore shorts but, according to one ancient writer, Pausanias, a competitor deliberately lost his shorts so that he could run more freely during the race in 720 BC, and clothing was then abolished.

Spectators also abided by strict rules. Only free men not convicted of any sacrilege could attend. Women were not allowed to watch the games, but that had nothing to do with the nudity of the male athletes. Rather, it was because Olympia was dedicated to Zeus and was, therefore, a sacred area for men. Punishment for breaking the rules was an automatic death sentence by being thrown off Mt. Typeo.

The first day of the games began with sacrifices to the gods, for the games were meant as religious tributes. At the great altar of Zeus, the athletes vowed that they were eligible to participate in the games and that they would obey the Olympic rules while competing. Judges, trainers, and even the athlete's parents all had to make a similar vow.

On the final fifth day, there was a banquet for all of the participants, consisting of 100 oxen that had been sacrificed to Zeus on the first day. It started with a procession to the Temple of Zeus, referred to by the Greeks as the Altis, where each winner received his wreath of live branches from olives. Then crowds showered them with flowers.

The victors of the Olympic games were hailed as heroes. Statues were built in their honor around the magnificent Temple of Zeus and the stadium of Olympia. Parades with chariots, songs, and poems written in their honor were given in their hometowns. Other special privileges awarded to the athletes were choice seats at all public spectacles; statues carved in their image were placed in prominent locations in the city, and they were also exempt from paying taxes. Cash rewards were common. In some Greek cities, part of a wall was torn and victorious athlete was led in through the opening. This ritual signified that any city with strong citizens had no need to defend itself with a wall from its enemies.

In 146 BC, the Romans gained control of Greece and, therefore, of the Olympic games. In 85 BC, the Roman general Sulla plundered the sanctuary to finance his campaign against Mithridates. Sulla also moved the 175th Olympiad (80 BC) to Rome.

The ancient Olympic Games were abandoned in AD 394 by the Roman emperor Theodosius I, who considered the Games to be a savage celebration.

Centuries of earthquakes and floods buried Olympia and the Temple of Zeus until 1870 when German excavations unearthed the beauty and magnificent statues of the classical Greek Games. These archeological findings in the sacred ground of Olympia fascinated French historian and educator Baron Pierre de Coubertin so much that he was inspired to conceive the idea of reviving the modern Olympic Games. On June 23, 1894, speaking at the Sorbonne in Paris to a gathering of international sports leaders from nine nations proposed that the ancient Games be revived on an international scale. The idea was enthusiastically received and the Modern Olympics, as we know them, were born.

**Questions for Reflection**
**Decide whether the following statements are true or false.**
1. (　) The Games, like all Greek Games, were an intrinsic part of a religious festival held in honor of Zeus.
2. (　) The Greeks used the term Olympiad to refer to the year when the Games were held.
3. (　) When it was time for the Games, no matter who you had a war with, you had to stop the war and let their athletes go through your city-state safely to get to the Olympic Games.
4. (　) At first, the only Olympic event was the stadion race, a race over about 190 meters, measured after the feet of Achilles.
5. (　) In the beginning years, the Olympic festival lasted for 5 days, 3 of which were used for competition. The other 2 days were dedicated to religious rituals.
6. (　) Athletes in Ancient Olympics usually competed nude.
7. (　) In Ancient Greece, women were not allowed to watch the games, because male athletes competed nude in the games.
8. (　) The victors of the Olympic games were entitled to choice seats at all public spectacles.
9. (　) The ancient Olympic Games were abandoned by a Roman emperor because he considered the Games to be uncivilized.
10. (　) Baron Pierre de Coubertin was the first person in history to propose the idea of reviving the modern Olympic Games.

### Text C　The Parthenon

The Parthenon stands today as the epitome of Greek architectural design, still perched on its spot on the Athenian Acropolis, though in quite a state of disrepair. It still holds up relatively well, considering the abuse it has endured since it was built well over 2,000 years ago. It remains a symbol of the strength and power of Ancient Greece, and its design has been emulated the world over in modern structures.

The Parthenon was a shrine to Athena, the patron goddess of the city-state of Athens. It was the central point of worship to her, where all festivals in her honor culminated, including the Panathenaic Procession. However, the Parthenon was not only a grand temple for a patron goddess; it stood as a reminder and a reflection of the military power and political prowess of Athens, and its leader, Pericles. It was literally a monument to celebrate Athens' military victory over Sparta in one phase of the Peloponnesian War.

Earlier in the 5th century BC, the Athenians began construction on a temple to Athena on the Acropolis. This original Parthenon was not to be completed. When the Persians sacked Athens in 480 BC, the work that had been completed was destroyed, save for the foundation blocks. And when Pericles swore on the Oath of Plataia that no temples that had been destroyed by the "barbarians" were to be rebuilt (as a memorial and reminder of the senseless destruction of the city), it seemed that there would never be a Parthenon.

After several years had passed, and Pericles opened up the Delian Treasury for himself and his city-state, new plans were developed for another, even grander Parthenon, on the same site as the original. No expense was to be spared in its design and execution. Pericles turned to the top architects and artists of the day, including architects Iktinos and Kallicrates, and sculptor Pheidias. The temple was, after all, the embodiment of Athens' and Pericles' superiority over the rest of the world. Construction on the grand sanctuary began in 447 BC.

The Parthenon is widely considered the high point of Doric architecture, though it famously has several Ionic elements incorporated in its design, including a continuous sculptural frieze and four Ionic columns that support the roof of the opisthodomos. It was a peripheral temple, characteristic of the Doric style, with simple Doric columns surrounding the outer porches. It was also adorned with triglyphs and metopes on the entablature, as well as high relief sculptures on its pediment. The metopes were sculpted in high relief as well. The entire temple was constructed with Pentelic marble, which was readily available to the workers.

The Parthenon is considered to be a "perfect" temple. To look at it from its front, it looks perfectly straight. But, the genius of its temple lies in the optical refinements that were used in order to fool the eye into seeing something totally straight. From the foundation upwards, the horizontal lines of the columns and walls were made with a slight inward curvature. This gave an upward lift to the appearance, making the temple appear taller and giving it more strength. The individual columns were given this treatment as well. They were tapered vertically, growing slightly narrower as they went up.

Inside all Greek temples, there would have been a cult statue. The Parthenon was no exception, and the cult statue of Athena must have been truly an awesome spectacle. It is said to have been carved out of pure ivory, and embellished with gold. She would have stood 12 meters (or about 39 feet) tall, and would have been adorned with a heavy peplos that would have been changed during the Panathenaia. Unfortunately, nothing remains of this supposed sculptural wonder, as the statue was taken away to Constantinople during the late Roman Empire, and it was lost forever.

Construction on the Parthenon was completed in 432 BC. It was documented by ancient scholars and historians, who described its splendor and magnitude. It was truly a monument befitting Athena, and her city of Athens. It stood in all of its glory for nearly 1,000 years, through the Classical Period, the Hellenistic Period, and it even survived Roman times, when Athens was reduced to a mere province of the Empire. After the cult statue had been taken to Constantinople, the Parthenon was converted to a Christian church, which likely helped it to survive even longer. Then, in 1456, the Ottomans took Athens, and the Parthenon became a mosque.

But, the Parthenon received a great literal blow, when in 1687, under attack from the Venetians, the Ottomans used the Acropolis as a fortification, and stocked the Parthenon with gun powder. The Venetians fired from a nearby hill, and hit the temple, devastating its internal structure, collapsing its roof, and causing great damage to its sculptural decoration. And thus was the end of the Parthenon's long and majestic history. Today, it is a protected historical and archaeological site, having been undergoing restorative renovation in the last several years. Though it is only a shell of its formal self, one can still appreciate the skill and beauty of this once great and important structure.

### Questions for Reflection

1. Where is the Parthenon located? What does it symbolize?
2. What is the Parthenon originally built for?
3. What architectural features could be found in the Parthenon?
4. What is the inside of the Parthenon like?

### Websites to Visit

http://www.fordham.edu/halsall/hellenistic/index.html (accessed Apr. 28, 2020)
This is a comprehensive website providing information on various aspects of the Hellenistic culture.

http://www.perseus.tufts.edu/Olympics/ (accessed Apr. 28, 2020)
This website provides further information about Ancient Olympic Games as well as the link between Ancient Olympics and Modern Olympics.

http://academic.reed.edu/humanities/110Tech/Parthenon.html (accessed Apr. 28, 2020)
This website provides further information about the Parthenon, including its historical setting, architectural features, and other authors' descriptions of it.

*Movie to Watch*

### *Alexander* (2004)

Conquering 90% of the known world by the age of 25, Alexander the Great led his armies through 22,000 miles of sieges and conquests in just eight years. Coming out of tiny Macedonia, Alexander led his armies against the mighty Persian Empire, drove west to Egypt, and finally made his way east to India. This film will concentrate on those eight years of battles, as well as his relationship with his boyhood friend and battle mate, Hephaestion. Alexander died young, of illness, at 33. Alexander's conquests paved the way for the spread of Greek culture (facilitating the spread of Christianity centuries later), and removed many of the obstacles that might have prevented the expansion of the Roman Empire. In other words, the world we know today might never have been if not for Alexander's bloody, yet unifying, conquest.

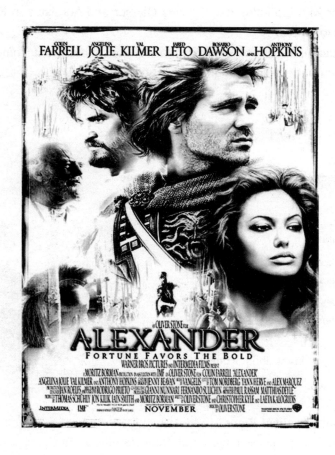

# Unit 4
## Ancient Rome (I)

> I came, I saw, I conquered.
> 
> —Julius Caesar

### Unit Goals

- To have a general understanding of the rise and development of the Roman Republic
- To be familiar with the influence of Julius Caesar and Augustus in Rome's transition from republic to empire
- To learn the useful words and expressions that describe ancient Rome
- To improve language skills by learning this unit

### Before You Read

1. Test Your Knowledge: What do you know about Rome?

   (1) Location

   _____

   (2) Current Population

   _____

   (2) Rome is famous for

   _____

   (3) Tourist attractions in Rome

   _____

   (4) Something else you know about Rome

   _____

2. Brainstorming: Sayings about Rome

   As an indication of its importance in the world, Rome features in numerous sayings. Do you know any English sayings about Rome?

   (1) _____

(2) _____

(3) _____

3. Search in the dictionary for the meaning of the following idioms/sayings. What do they tell about the history of Rome?

(1) See Rome and die.
_____

(2) I found Rome a city of bricks and left it a city of marble.
_____

(3) Fiddling while Rome burns.
_____

4. Form groups of three or four students. Try to find, on the Internet or in the library, more information about Ancient Rome. Choose a topic that interests you most and prepare a five-minute classroom presentation.

## Start to Read

### Text A  Rome: From Republic to Empire

The earliest empires had been in the East. Egypt, Mesopotamia, China, India, and Greece were all home to at least one powerful civilization. About 387 BC, a city on the Italian peninsula began acquiring land and building an empire. That city was Rome. For more than one thousand years, Rome controlled the western world.

Rome is an ideal place for a city. It is located along the banks of the Tiber River. The river made it easy to travel to and from the sea. The Tiber is very shallow near Rome. A shallow portion of a river is called a ford. The ford made it easier for people to cross the river. Seven hills surround Rome. The hills make it harder for invaders to approach the city and served as lookout areas for the Romans. Rome is also close to excellent farmland and an abundance of wood and stone. Civilizations have grown and prospered in Rome for thousands of years, which is why Rome is nicknamed "the Eternal City".

Rome had begun as a small city on the Italian peninsula. In 509 BC, Rome's citizens expelled their ruler. By 264 BC, they had committed the whole of Italy. The Roman expansion was briefly halted in 216 BC by General Hannibal of Carthage. Hannibal with his

army of elephants invaded Italy and threatened to destroy Rome. But Roman troops finally defeated Hannibal. In 146 BC, they burned Carthage and this gave them control of the western Mediterranean. The conquest of Greece and Macedonia had secured the eastern Mediterranean. The lands around the sea were the cores of Rome's empire, though later generals would extend its boundaries north and east.

Rome began as a republic. There were two classes of citizens: the aristocratic patricians and the majority of citizens, the plebeians. Both groups had some civic rights, but only the patricians could be elected to office. Rome's government was divided into executive and legislative branches. Two Consuls headed the executive branch. The Senate dominated the legislature. Its 300 patrician members, who were elected for life, advised the Consuls and debated foreign policy and legislation. In 494 BC, a revolt by the plebeians increased their political power and established the principle that all free citizens were protected by the laws.

Rome's military success was based on its well-organized and highly disciplined army. At first, when most Romans were small farmers, all male citizens served as soldiers. But military conquests changed that. Thousands of conquered people were brought as slaves to Rome and replaced the paid workers. At the same time, many small farmers lost their lands to great landowners who also used slave labor. Rome's swelling population of the poor and unemployed now provided army recruits.

These new soldiers were loyal to the generals who paid them, not to the state. Powerful generals used their soldiers to gain political control. The most important was Julius Caesar. After conquering Gaul and Britain, Caesar's army invaded Italy. In 45 BC, he began to rule as dictator for life, but some senators viewed him as a tyrant and murdered him in 44 BC. Caesar's nephew, Octavian, defeated his rivals and made himself Rome's first emperor as Augustus Caesar in 27 BC.

Emperor Augustus and the "good emperors" reformed the administration of the empire. They appointed capable governors to rule the provinces; fine new roads allowed them to communicate with Rome. Public buildings were constructed and aqueducts were built to carry water to the cities. Roman law applied to rich and poor alike and was used across the empire.

The provinces sent luxury items from the East and raw materials to Rome. Italian craftsman made pottery, cloth, glass, and jewelry for the provinces. The profits of trade and agriculture allowed wealthy Romans to lead comfortable and cultured lives. Most citizens were poor but they were consoled by free grain and public spectacles such as chariot races and gladiator fights.

The period of peace and prosperity between 27 BC and 180 AD is known as the Pax Romana—the peace brought by Rome. Literature, art, and science flourished. Latin poets like Virgil and Horace and historians like Livy celebrated Rome's greatness. Doctors and astronomers developed theories based on the observations made earlier by the Greeks and Egyptians.

But by 200, the Roman Empire was threatened from inside and out. Christianity was spreading, especially among poor city folk. Christians refused to fight in the army or honor Roman gods (including the emperor who was viewed as a god). They were widely persecuted and even though their numbers were small, their influence was considerable. By 392, Christianity was so widespread that it became the official religion of the empire.

After 192, emperors were appointed by the army. Most of them ruled only briefly. Army factions fought each other constantly. This internal fighting disrupted trade and industry and destroyed harvests and farms.

To make matters worse, Germanic groups whom the Romans called barbarians began to threaten the empire. Rome's army was too divided, and its borders were too long to be defensible. Emperor Diocletian recognized that it was impossible for one man to rule such a vast area and appointed separate rulers for the eastern and western provinces (the empire was formally divided into two halves in 395). In 330, Emperor Constantine moved the capital to the Greek city of Byzantium, which was easier to defend than Rome. The city of Rome was finally conquered in 476, but the eastern half of the empire survived for another 1,000 years.

## Proper Nouns

1. The Tiber River 台伯河(意大利第三大河流)
2. General Hannibal 汉尼拔将军(前247—前183),任迦太基统帅
3. Carthage 迦太基(非洲北部的古代城邦)
4. Consul 执政官
5. Julius Caesar 尤利乌斯·恺撒
6. Augustus Caesar 奥古斯都·恺撒
7. Pax Romana 罗马和平时期
8. Virgil 维吉尔(古罗马诗人)
9. Horace 贺拉斯(古罗马诗人)
10. Livy 李维(古罗马历史学家)
11. Emperor Diocletian 戴克里先大帝(罗马皇帝)
12. Emperor Constantine 康斯坦丁大帝
13. Byzantium 拜占庭

An Introduction to European Culture (Second Edition)

**After You Read**

*Knowledge Focus*

**1. Match the item in Column A with its corresponding description in Column B.**

| Column A | Column B |
|---|---|
| (1) General Hannibal | (a) the lower social classes in ancient Rome |
| (2) patricians | (b) the conqueror of Gaul and Britain |
| (3) plebeians | (c) the emperor who moved the capital to Byzantium |
| (4) Consuls | (d) military leader of Carthage |
| (5) the Senate | (e) a historian in ancient Rome |
| (6) Julius Caesar | (f) members of the aristocracy in ancient Rome |
| (7) Augustus Caesar | (g) the first emperor of Rome |
| (8) Virgil | (h) the head of the executive branch in Rome |
| (9) Livy | (i) a Latin poet |
| (10) Emperor Constantine | (j) the political body that dominated the legislature |

**2. Fill in the blanks according to what you have learned in the text above.**

(1) Rome is located along the banks of the _____ river.

(2) Civilizations have grown and prospered in Rome for thousands of years, which is why Rome is nicknamed _____.

(3) Rome begun as a _____ on the Italian peninsula. In 509 BC, Rome's citizens expelled their ruler and Rome became a _____ from then on.

(4) The two classes of citizens in the Roman Republic were _____ and _____.

(5) Rome's military success was largely based on its _____ and _____ army.

(6) In 45 BC, _____ began to rule Rome as a dictator for life.

(7) A period of peace and prosperity between 27 BC and 180 AD is known as _____.

(8) Roman citizens entertained themselves with public performances such as _____ and _____.

(9) By 392, _____ was so widespread that it became the official religion of the empire.

(10) In the year of _____, the Roman Empire was formally divided into _____ and _____.

**3. Discuss the following questions with your partner.**

(1) What regions were included in the Roman Empire?

(2) How could the patricians have a great deal of political power in the Roman Republic?

(3) How did the Plebeians receive equal protection under the law of Rome?

(4) Why was the Roman army able to achieve military success?

(5) In what way did Augustus reform the Roman Empire?
(6) Why was Pax Romana considered as the peak time in Roman history?
(7) How did the spread of Christianity disrupt the Roman Empire?
(8) Why did Diocletian split the Roman Empire into eastern and western provinces?

## Language Focus

**1. Fill in the blanks with the following words or expressions you have learned in the text.**

| abundance | expel | dominate | disciplined | revolt |
| recruit | view...as | barbarian | persecute | defensible |

(1) In television, the three networks clearly _____ the American television audience.
(2) John was enrolled in the army last week, so he is a very raw _____.
(3) A city built on an island is easily _____.
(4) At the feast there was a (an) _____ of food and drink.
(5) It was the dream of Isabella's life to _____ them forever.
(6) She _____ a strong candidate for the job.
(7) In ancient times, the Great Wall fortified China against _____ invasions.
(8) France plays with more flair and inventiveness, whereas England is a more _____ side.
(9) They _____ those who do not conform to their ideas.
(10) Troops were called in to put down the _____.

**2. Fill in the blanks with the proper form of the word in the brackets.**

(1) For over nine hundred years, the sea has defended Britain from _____ (invade).
(2) Our country has a large population, vast territory and _____ (abundance) resources.
(3) The basic aim of this institution is the _____ (conquer) of disease.
(4) The proposed national identity card system would help to tighten _____ (secure) against fraud.
(5) Byron was born of an _____ (aristocracy) family of doubtful reputation.
(6) The government has promised to introduce _____ (legislative) to limit fuel emissions from cars.
(7) A drastic _____ (reform) of the present housing system has been carried out.
(8) On the whole, the appearance of the house was _____ (luxury) and romantic.
(9) The dissidents went abroad to escape political _____ (persecute).
(10) —That's a new dress, isn't it?
   —Yes, you are _____ (observe)!

3. Fill in the blanks with the proper prepositions or adverbs that collocate with the neighboring words.

(1) The dramatic weekend first brought home _____ me the nature of Watergate.
(2) These philosophical views serve _____ a guide in life.
(3) If we all get behind Mr. Smith, we can easily elect him _____ that office.
(4) A good education should equip you _____ life.
(5) Evidence based _____ the reports of others rather than the personal knowledge of a witness is generally not admissible _____ testimony.
(6) The laws apply _____ everyone irrespective of race, creed or color.
(7) It is a show that appeals to young and old _____ .
(8) We cannot survive _____ long without food and drink.

4. Error Correction: Each of the following sentences has at least one grammatical error. Identify the errors and correct them.

(1) Civilizations have grown and prospered in Rome for thousands of years, that is why Rome is nicknamed "the Eternal City".
(2) The Roman expansion briefly halted in 216 by General Hannibal of Carthage.
(3) The 300 patrician members were elected for life, advised the Consuls and debated foreign policy and legislation.
(4) Rome's military success based on its well-organized and highly disciplined army.
(5) They appointed capable governors to rule the province, fine new roads allowed them to communicate with Rome.
(6) Roman law applied to rich and poor alike and used across the empire.
(7) The profits of trade and agriculture allowed wealthy Romans to lead comfortable and culture lives.
(8) Most citizens were poor but they were consoled by free grain and public spectacles as chariot races and gladiator fights.
(9) Christianity were spreading, especially among poor city folk.
(10) Germanic groups the Romans called barbarians began to threaten empire.
(11) Rome's army was too divided, and its borders so long to be defensible.
(12) The city of Rome was finally conquered in 476, but the eastern half of the empire survived for other 1,000 years.

**Comprehensive Work**

**1. Role Play: Interview with a Gladiator**

Imagine that you are Rome's most popular new gladiator. A top Roman magazine, *Gladiators Today*, has sent a journalist to interview about your life. Tell him about yourself.

Student A plays the role of a journalist.

Student B plays the role of a gladiator.

The journalist may use the questions as below:
(1) Firstly, introduce yourself.
___

(2) How did you become a gladiator? (slave, criminal, chance of winning freedom)
___

(3) What injuries have you suffered?
___

(4) Have you ever fought against animals? Which ones? (elephants, tigers, rhinos, lions, cheetah)
___

(5) What is it like underneath the arena? (corridors, hot, trapdoors, animals, gladiators)
___

(6) Can you tell us about the most spectacular show you've been involved in? (battle recreation, sea battle, animal fight)
___

(7) Now tell us a bit more about yourself, and about life as a gladiator.
___

(8) Other questions.
___

## 2. Research Report: Roman Emperors

The Roman Empire used to be one of the most powerful empires in the world. After Julius Caesar, many emperors of Rome made various contributions to the development of the empire. In this activity, we are going to search the Internet in order to find more information about Roman Emperors.

Here is a list of major Roman emperors:

| Augustus | Rome's first emperor. He also added many territories to the empire. |
|---|---|
| Claudius | He conquered Britain. |
| Nero | He was insane. He murdered his mother and his wife and threw thousands of Christians to the lions. |
| Trajan | He was a great conqueror. Under his rule, the empire reached its greatest extent. |
| Diocletian | He split the empire into two pieces—a western and an eastern empire. |

# An Introduction to European Culture (Second Edition)

| Constantine | He was the first Christian emperor. He united the empire again and chose his capital to be the small town Byzantium, which he renamed Constantinople. |
|---|---|
| Romulus Augustus | He was the last emperor of Rome, nicknamed Augustulus which means "little Augustus". |

Form groups of three or four. Choose one emperor from the above list and try to find enough information on the Internet to complete the following report. When you finish your report, share your findings with the whole class.

**Roman Emperor Report**

Name _____ Date _____
Emperor's Name _____
Years in Power _____
Date of Birth _____ Place of Birth _____
How did he become Emperor?
_____
Date of Death _____ Place of Death _____
How did he die?
_____

Accomplishments
(1) _____
(2) _____
(3) _____
(4) _____
Failures
(1) _____
(2) _____
(3) _____
Reputation
_____
Interesting anecdotes about him
_____

## 3. Writing

What kind of person is Julius Caesar? Why do you think so? Please write a composition commenting on Caesar's life and his achievements.

## Read More

### Text B  Conversion of the Roman Republic to the Roman Empire

In 509 BC, Rome became a republic, a government in which power is controlled by the common people. It was under this Republic that Rome grew and expanded by conquest into the most powerful nation in the world at the time. As Roman territory increased, however, politicians and generals became more and more powerful and hungry for power. A series of events during the 2nd and 1st centuries BC led to the demise of the Roman Republic. Under the reigns of Julius Caesar and Augustus Caesar, the Roman Empire was formed. The Empire was ruled by an emperor, who had complete control over his people. Power was no longer in the hands of the people, but Rome continued to prosper and expand for several centuries.

Under the Republic, senators were elected by the people to run the government. The vote of wealthy landowners counted for more than others and many elections were fixed by bribes. However, the common people still maintained a significant power in government affairs.

When Rome's Republic was formed, Rome was a mere small city-state, easily managed. However, as time went on, politicians found it harder to maintain the growing country. Extremely wealthy landowners, known as patricians, began to have more and more political power. After the Second Punic War, marking the destruction of Rome's enemy Carthage, the Roman economy and trade grew at a fast pace. Rich landowners and merchants were able to buy up most of the country land. Under Roman law, only landowners could serve in the military, but with the rich owning the land, the number of available soldiers dwindled. This caused instability in the Roman military.

Tiberius Gracchus, an enthusiastic politician, was elected tribune, an important political office, in 133 BC. He proposed several laws to reshape Rome into the honest, pure republic that it had once been. His propositions included giving an equal share of land to all citizens, limiting the amount of land one person could have, and allowing every free Roman citizen to vote (at the time, only residents of Rome could vote). Tiberius' ideas were very controversial, so he was murdered by a riot. His brother Gaius as tribune in 123 BC, also attempted to pass these laws, but he too was murdered.

More problems arose with the reforms of General Marius. In 104 BC, he established a new law which stated that people did not have to own land to be a soldier. This worked to strengthen the military. However, in return for their service, soldiers wanted to be granted land. Only under the general's influence over the Senate could soldiers be granted that land. The result was that soldiers tended to trust the general more and be more loyal to him than to the Senate. The generals started to gain significant political power in Rome.

In 88 BC, Sulla was elected Consul. He gained much power within the Senate, and was the first one to challenge Marius' position, for until then Marius had been the most powerful man in Rome. A civil war erupted. Marius marched his army on Rome forcing Sulla to flee. Marius soon died, but his supporters continued the fight. Sulla came back with an army of his own and marched on Rome, declaring himself dictator in 82 BC. He died in 78 BC, but his reign encouraged others to grab absolute power over Rome.

After Sulla's dictatorship was over, Rome temporarily went back to being controlled by the Senate. Meanwhile, Pompey, the most distinguished general of the time, was gaining public favor from his many military victories. At the same time, Crassus, the wealthiest man in Rome, also gained much popularity from the common people, for defeating a large slave uprising. Each held the ambition of someday ruling Rome. Another prominent general who was gaining popularity was Julius Caesar. Pompey, Crassus, and Caesar made a secret alliance to work together to gain control over the Senate. This alliance became known as the First Triumvirate.

Caesar was elected Consul in 60 BC. He proposed laws that would gain the triumvirate even more power. When these laws were opposed, Crassus and Caesar resorted to violence and intimidation in order to get them passed. After a short time, the First Triumvirate began to crumble. Crassus was killed in battle in 53 BC. Caesar, after his term as Consul ended, was given a governorship of the area of southern France. Unheeding the word of the Senate, Caesar raised his own army and led a path of conquest throughout all of Gaul.

After 8 years Julius Caesar returned. The Senate was afraid that he might march on Rome with his loyal army. The Senate's fears proved correct. Pompey could not organize a counteroffensive in time to save Rome, so he was forced to flee. Caesar marched into the city and appointed himself dictator. While the Senate still existed, it was practically powerless against Caesar's commands.

Desperate politicians Brutus and Cassius plotted against Julius and eventually killed him, stabbing him in the back on March 15, 44 BC. The conspirators believed that the Senate would regain control of Rome. However, strong generals Mark Antony and Marcus Lepidus unofficially established their power by intimidation through their armies. In the ensuing years, the Second Triumvirate was formed. This consisted of Mark Antony, Lepidus, and Julius Caesar's nephew Octavian, who had demanded a position in the Senate after Julius' death. The three men swept the Senate with terror, killing Cicero, who was the greatest supporter of the Republic.

Brutus and Cassius retaliated by raising an army against the triumvirs. However, Antony met their army and, after fierce fighting, defeated it. Brutus and Cassius killed themselves after viewing their defeat.

Now, Antony and Octavian received no more opposition from the Senate and were supreme rulers. They were powerful enough that they did not need Lepidus anymore, so they betrayed him by knocking him out of their alliance. Antony took control over Eastern Rome, while Octavian controlled Western Rome. After a few years, in 36 BC, Octavian, needing an excuse to wage war on Antony, accused him of being disloyal to Rome by becoming involved with Cleopatra of Egypt. Octavian attacked Eastern Rome and defeated Antony. Octavian, who had changed his name to Augustus, was finally supreme ruler over Rome.

The Republic had died. While the Senate still existed, it had little say in government matters and could certainly not challenge the word of the emperor. Ten Caesars came after Augustus to rule over Rome. Despite the crippling of the Republic, Rome continued to prosper and expand for several centuries until its eventual decline.

## Comprehension Questions
**Choose the answer that best completes the sentence.**
1. The First Triumvirate consisted of _____.
   a. Julius Caesar, Mark Antony, Sulla
   b. Pompey, Crassus, Cleopatra
   c. Pompey, Crassus, Julius Caesar
   d. Octavian, Brutus, Marius
2. The Second Triumvirate consisted of _____.
   a. Octavian, Mark Antony, Lepidus
   b. Octavian, Julius Caesar, Tiberius Gracchus
   c. Sulla, Crassus, Pompey
   d. Gaius, Cicero, Bill Clinton
3. Octavian accused Mark Antony of being disloyal to Rome by _____.
   a. murdering Julius Caesar
   b. leading an army into Rome
   c. getting involved with Cleopatra
   d. falling off his horse too many times
4. Tiberius Gracchus's proposals included all EXCEPT _____.
   a. giving an equal share of land to all citizens
   b. limiting the amount of land one person could have
   c. allowing every free citizen to vote
   d. granting absolute power to a dictator

## Text C  The Burning of Rome

During the night of July 18, 64 AD, a fire broke out in the merchant area of the city of Rome. Fanned by summer winds, the flames quickly spread through the dry, wooden structures of the Imperial City. Soon the fire took on a life of its own consuming all in its path for six days and seven nights. When the conflagration finally ran its course, it left seventy percent of the city in smoldering ruins.

Rumors soon arose accusing the Emperor Nero of ordering the torching of the city and standing on the summit of the Palatine playing his lyre as flames devoured the world around him. These rumors have never been confirmed. In fact, Nero rushed to Rome from his palace in Antium (Anzio) and ran about the city all that first night without his guards directing efforts to quell the blaze. But the rumors persisted and the Emperor looked for a scapegoat. He found it in the Christians, at that time a rather obscure religious sect with a small following in the city. To appease the masses, Nero literally had his victims fed to the lions during giant spectacles held in the city's remaining amphitheater.

From the ashes of the fire rose a more spectacular Rome. A city made of marble and stone with wide streets, pedestrian arcades and ample supplies of water to quell any future blaze. The debris from the fire was used to fill the malaria-ridden marshes that had plagued the city for generations.

The historian Tacitus was born in the year 56 or 57 probably in Rome. He was in Rome during the great fire. During his lifetime, he wrote a number of histories chronicling the reigns of the early emperors. The following eye witness account comes from his final work The Annals written around the year 116.

Now started the most terrible and destructive fire which Rome had ever experienced. It began in the Circus, where it adjoins the Palatine and Caelian hills. Breaking out in shops selling inflammable goods, and fanned by the wind, the conflagration instantly grew and swept the whole length of the Circus. There were no walled mansions or temples, or any other obstructions, which could arrest it. First, the fire swept violently over the level spaces. Then it climbed the hills—but returned to ravage the lower ground again. It outstripped every counter-measure. The ancient city's narrow winding streets and irregular blocks encouraged its progress.

Terrified, shrieking women, helpless old and young, people intent on their own safety, people unselfishly supporting invalids or waiting for them, fugitives and lingerers alike—all heightened the confusion. When people looked back, menacing flames sprang up before them or outflanked them. When they escaped to a neighboring quarter, the fire followed—even districts believed remote proved to be involved. Finally, with no idea where or what to flee, they crowded on to the country roads or lay in the fields. Some who had lost everything—even their food for the day—could have escaped, but preferred to die. So did others, who had failed to rescue their loved ones. Nobody dared fight the flames. Attempts to do so were prevented by menacing gangs. Torches, too, were openly thrown in, by men crying that they acted under orders. Perhaps they had received orders. Or they may just have wanted to plunder unhampered.

Nero was at Antium. He returned to the city only when the fire was approaching the mansion he had built to link the Gardens of Maecenas to the Palatine. The flames could not be prevented from overwhelming the whole of the Palatine, including his palace. Nevertheless, for the relief of the homeless fugitive masses, he threw open the Field of Mars, including Agrippa's public buildings, and even his own Gardens. Nero also constructed emergency accommodation for the destitute multitude. Yet these measures, for all their popular character, earned no gratitude. For a rumor had spread that, while the city was burning, Nero had gone on his private stage and, comparing modern calamities with ancient, had sung of the destruction of Troy.

By the sixth day, enormous demolitions had confronted the raging flames with bare ground and open sky, and the fire was finally stamped out at the foot of the Esquiline Hill. But before panic had subsided, or hope revived, flames broke out again in the more open regions of the city. Here there were fewer casualties, but the destruction of temples and pleasure arcades was even worse. This new conflagration caused additional ill-feeling because it started on Tigellinus' estate in the Aemilian district. People believed that Nero was ambitious to found a new city to be called after himself.

Of Rome's fourteen districts only four remained intact. Three were leveled to the ground. The other seven were reduced to a few scorched and mangled ruins.

## Questions for Reflection

1. When did the fire break out in Rome? Was the city seriously damaged in the disaster?
2. Why did Emperor Nero order to kill Christians after the fire?
3. According to historian Tacitus, what measures did Emperor Nero take to deal with the disaster?

## Website to Visit

http://www.vroma.org/~bmcmanus/romanpages.html (accessed Apr. 28, 2020)
This website gives a comprehensive introduction to the society and the culture of ancient Rome.

## Movie to Watch

### *Gladiator* (2000)

Maximus is a powerful Roman general, loved by the people and the aging Emperor, Marcus Aurelius. Before his death, the Emperor chooses Maximus to be his heir over his own son, Commodus, and a power struggle leaves Maximus and his family condemned to death. The powerful general is unable to save his family, and his loss of will allows him to get captured and put into the Gladiator games until he dies. The only desire that fuels him now is the chance to rise to the top so that he will be able to look into the eyes of the man who will feel his revenge.

# Unit 5
## Ancient Rome (II)

> While stands the Coliseum, Rome shall stand; When falls the Coliseum, Rome shall fall; And when Rome falls—the World.
>
> —Lord Byron

### Unit Goals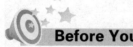

- To understand the achievements that Romans had made in terms of art
- To be able to appreciate the architectural wonders produced by ancient Romans
- To learn the useful words and expressions that describe ancient Rome
- To improve language skills by learning this unit

### Before You Read

**1. Greek Style vs. Roman Style**

Compare the two buildings in the following pictures. Can you tell which one is of Greek style? And which is of Roman style? What are the differences between the two styles?

## 2. Guess for Fun

Besides houses and temples, ancient Roman architects had built various forms of constructions. Look at the following pictures. Do you know what is the function of the construction in each picture?

## Start to Read

### Text A  Roman Art and Architecture

Roman art and architecture had a profound impact on the world we live in today by influencing modern city planning, architecture, and art. The early Roman structures were copies of Greek architectural forms, however, the Romans soon established their own identity by developing new building material and constructing unusual shapes and forms.

The Roman Empire's most impressive contribution is its architecture. They created numerous structures, blending utility with beauty. Quarried stone, used in conjunction with timber beams, terra-cotta tiles and plaques, as well as marble, was the essential Roman building material from Republican times on. They also developed a totally new type of material which they called caementum (cement) and concretus (concrete). Cement is a fine, gray powder that is mixed with water and materials such as sand, gravel, and crushed stone to make concrete. Concrete is fireproof, watertight, and comparatively cheap and easy to make. When first mixed, concrete can be molded into almost any shape. It quickly hardens into an extremely strong material that lasts a long time and requires little care. The cement that was used by the Romans had such great durability that some of their buildings, roads, and bridges still exist.

Concrete vaulting made possible the construction of the great amphitheaters and baths of the Roman world, as well as the dome of the Pantheon. They used huge vaulted halls, called basilica, for courtrooms and civic activities. Many of their most impressive buildings were constructed during the Imperial Period, from 27 BC to 476 AD. Roman theaters first appeared in the late Republic. They were semicircular in plan and consisted of a tall stage building abutting a semicircular orchestra and tiered seating area. The earliest known amphitheater (75 BC) is at Pompeii, and the grandest, Rome's Colosseum (70 – 80 AD), held approximately 50,000 spectators, roughly the capacity of today's large sports stadiums. The Pantheon is the only building of Imperial Rome to have withstood successfully the ravages of time and man. The porch reminds us of the Parthenon, but one can clearly see that the columns are Corinthian rather than Doric. The great vaulted dome is 142 feet in diameter, and the entire structure is lighted through one aperture, called an oculus, in the center of the dome. The Pantheon was erected between 118 AD and 128 AD, replacing a smaller temple built in 27 BC. In the early 7th century, it was consecrated as a church.

Another great achievement, attributed to the Romans, was the layout of cities and the construction of apartment buildings. The typical Roman city of the later Republic and empire had a rectangular plan and resembled a Roman military camp. It had two main streets; the main north-south thoroughfare was called the cardo and the east-west thoroughfare, the decumanus. A grid of smaller streets divided the town into blocks, and a wall with gates encircled the city. Recreational buildings, buildings for homes, and shops were dispersed throughout the area. The shops were usually one-room units opening onto the sidewalks. Large cities and small towns alike also had public baths. Under the

Republic, they were generally made up of a suite of dressing rooms and bathing chambers with hot-, warm-, and cold-water baths alongside an exercise area, the palaestra.

The city plan also included libraries, lecture halls, and vast vaulted public spaces elaborately decorated with statues, mosaics, paintings, and stuccos. In the second century AD, Rome had nearly a million inhabitants. The rich dwellings of the aristocracy and the emperors' palaces stood close to the communal apartment houses that were several stories high (about 60 feet). These apartment houses were hastily built and were supported only by beams as long and thin as flutes. Sometimes they fell down, and they were easy prey for the fires that periodically swept through the capital.

As Rome established herself as the center of civilization, it became clear that her destiny in the arts was to be realistic in sculpture, as she had been imperialistic in government. Throughout the Roman world, statues were regularly displayed in, on, and around public and private buildings. Statues were erected for deities, heroes, and mortals alike in a wide variety of contexts. Every temple had a cult Statue; marble and bronze images of the gods and heroes. In the Roman Imperial Period, portrait painting is best represented by a series of wooden panels recovered from sites throughout Roman Egypt. These works, traditionally called "Fayyum portraits", after the agricultural district in Egypt where they were first discovered, were painted in the encaustic technique, a method that uses pigment contained in a medium of hot wax. These panels are the only portraits that have survived in any number, and even though they are provincial works, they testify to a high level of accomplishment on the part of Roman painters. These images reflect the prevailing tastes of the times and provide a chronological overview of the development of portraiture during the Roman Imperial Period. Mural painting is, by contrast, well documented, especially in Pompeii and the other cities buried in 79 AD by the eruption of the volcano Mount Vesuvius. Wherever painted murals existed, colored floors were likely to be present. They were often simply painted in solid colors, but in many instances, they were made up of marble slabs of many hues or of thousands of tiny mosaic cubes.

Roman art and architecture have had a profound impact throughout the ages by influencing modern city planning, architecture, and art. From our city streets to our football stadiums, and even our tile floors, Roman art and architecture has provided important examples and has been emulated.

## Proper Nouns

1. the Pantheon 罗马万神殿

2. basilica (古罗马)长方形大会堂(教堂)
3. Colosseum 古罗马斗兽场
4. Doric 多利斯式立柱
5. Fayyum 法尤姆(埃及中部城市)
6. Pompeii 庞贝古城
7. Mount Vesuvius 维苏威火山

## After You Read

*Knowledge Focus*

**1. Fill in the blanks with what you have learned from the text.**

(1) The Roman structures developed their own identity by developing new _____ and constructing _____.

(2) The new building materials developed by the Romans were _____ and _____.

(3) _____ is fireproof, watertight and can be molded into any shape when mixed.

(4) _____ made possible the construction of great amphitheaters, baths and the dome of the Pantheon.

(5) The grandest amphitheater is Rome's _____.

(6) _____ is the only building of Imperial Rome to have withstood the ravages of time and man successfully.

(7) The typical Roman city had a _____ plan and resembled _____.

(8) Roman statues were erected for _____, _____ and _____.

(9) The _____ in Roman times were painted in the encaustic technique.

(10) _____ painting is well documented in Pompeii and other cities.

**2. Discuss the following questions with your partner.**

(1) How did Roman structures differ from Greek architectures?

(2) What building materials did the Romans use for their construction?

(3) How do you describe the Pantheon?

(4) What did a typical city look like in ancient Rome?

(5) What are the characteristics of Roman art?

(6) What art forms were prevailing in Roman times?

**An Introduction to European Culture (Second Edition)**

**Language Focus**

1. Fill in the blanks with the following words or expressions you have learned in the text.

| blend | in conjunction with | durability | withstand | testify |
|---|---|---|---|---|
| attribute to... | elaborately | prevailing | recreational | periodically |

(1) It was the most _____ decorated cake—all sugar flowers and bows.
(2) This method can be used _____ other methods.
(3) The _____ of the equipment should be tested.
(4) Their music _____ jazz and pop in a stylish contemporary sound.
(5) Marcello's work was at first _____ his brother Benedetto.
(6) The _____ market conditions are not favorable to small investors.
(7) These ruins _____ to the existence of the Roman occupation.
(8) The Provisional Urban Council provides and manages sports and _____ facilities.
(9) Their marriage did not _____ four years' separation during the war.
(10) My assessment is that nylon has an advantage over cotton in _____.

2. Fill in the blanks with the proper form of the word in the brackets.
  (1) That was an _____ (impression) performance from such a young tennis player.
  (2) The vitamins come in a form that is easily _____ (utility) by the body.
  (3) The _____ (essential) of his argument was that education should continue throughout life.
  (4) Nothing can rival cotton for _____ (durable).
  (5) _____ (erect) of the new hospital so near the main road is a mistake.
  (6) My secretary leaves us next week, so we are advertising for a _____ (replace).
  (7) Everybody says that my daughter bears a striking _____ (resemble) to me.
  (8) Above the blackboard, there was a _____ (portray) of Chairman Mao.
  (9) According to a survey, Weihai is regarded as one of the most _____ (inhabitant) cities in the world.
  (10) A few days later, Vesuvius was in violent _____ (erupt).

3. Fill in the blanks with the proper prepositions or adverbs that collocate with the neighboring words.
  (1) The integrated circuit has had a very significant impact _____ digital system development.
  (2) The novel should be read _____ conjunction with the author's biography.
  (3) Melted metal is poured _____ a mold to harden _____ shape.
  (4) Most people are familiar _____ the idea that all matter consist _____ atoms.
  (5) It took me about two hours and a half to dig a hole one meter _____ diameter and two meters _____ depth.
  (6) I finally come to understand how much I owe _____ my parents.

(7) Athletics should rank _____ soccer and cricket as a major sport.

(8) Homeless children were easy prey _____ drug dealers in the capital.

**4. Error Correction: Each of the following sentences has at least one grammatical error. Identify the errors and correct them.**

(1) Quarried stone, used in conjunction with timber beams, terra-cotta tiles and plaques, as well as marble, were the essential Roman building material from Republican times on.

(2) They also developed a total new type of material as they called caementum (cement) and concretus (concrete).

(3) Concrete is fireproof, watertight, and comparatively cheap and easy to be made.

(4) The cement that used by the Romans had such great durability that some of their buildings, roads, and bridges still exist.

(5) Concrete vaulting made it possible the construction of the great amphitheaters and baths of the Roman world.

(6) Roman theatres were semicircular in plan and were consisted of a tall stage building abutting a semicircular orchestra and tiered seating area.

(7) The earliest know amphitheater is at Pompeii, and the most grand, Rome's Colosseum, held approximately 50,000 spectators, roughly the capacity of today's large sports stadiums.

(8) The Pantheon is the only building of Imperial Rome to withstand successfully the ravages of times and men.

(9) Another great achievement, attributing to the Romans, was the layout of cities and the construction of apartment buildings.

(10) The city plan also included libraries, lecture halls, and vast vaulted public spaces elaborately decorating with statues, mosaics, paintings, and stuccos.

(11) Statues were erected for deities, heroes, and mortals like in a wide variety of contexts.

(12) Whatever painted murals existed, colored floors were like to be present.

## Comprehensive Work

### 1. Group Discussions

Roman architects were very talented. They left behind them a wealth of construction wonders which had a profound impact on the world we live in today. Read the following passage about Roman sewers. Then discuss the questions that follow.

**Roman Sewers**

The Romans built public and private toilets and these are found all over the empire. These toilets had well-designed drainage systems to carry away the sewage. In Rome itself, there were miles of sewers that carried the waste to the river Tiber where it flowed out to sea.

Water pipes, drains and toilets all go together. In Roman towns, there were drains laid along all of the streets and joined together with sewers to carry off the rainwater and sewage. Many public

toilets all had neat stone seats and even a hand basin, although the way they were laid out meant you were sat side by side with up to twenty other people! In Rome itself the sewers were massive (think of the "waste" that 1,000,000 people can produce) and flowed out through the Clocia Maxia into the river Tiber. A friend of Emperor Augustus once had himself rowed through the sewers in a boat. These sewers must have been smelly as even the Romans couldn't bring enough water to wash out the sewers properly. Roman drains were built to last and York still uses a section of Roman sewer, still doing its job after nearly 2,000 years when the Victorian sewer around it is crumbling.

### Source A

"Along your route, each open window may be a death-trap. So hope and pray, you poor man, that the local housewife drops nothing worse on your head than a bedpan full of slops."
(Juvenal, "Satires", Rome, 100 AD)

### Source B

"The results of the great number of reservoirs, works, fountains and water basins can be seen in the improved health of Rome. The city looks cleaner, and the causes of the unhealthy air which gave Rome a bad name amongst the people in the past are now removed. Compare such important engineering works with the idle pyramids and the useless though famous buildings of the Greeks."
(Frontinus, "The Aqueducts of Rome", Rome, 100 AD. Frontinus was the official in charge of aqueducts.)

### Questions for Discussion

(1) What three things made up the Roman sewer system?
(2) Where did the sewage from Rome eventually go?
(3) What features did the public toilets built by the Romans have?
(4) How do we know that the Roman sewers were very large?
(5) Are Sources A and B primary or secondary sources? Explain your answer.
(6) How do we know that the sewers lasted a long time?
(7) Why was Frontinus so proud of the Roman water system?
(8) In what way do Sources A and B disagree about the streets of Rome?

## 2. Research Report: The Colosseum

All nations of the world use famous statues or architectural constructions as symbols to identify themselves and express their ideals. Look at the following example.

Example:

| Symbol Name | The Statue of Liberty |
|---|---|
| Where? | In New York City's harbor, United States |
| Why was it built? | To welcome immigrants to America. Ships sailed past it on their way to Ellis Island. |
| Identity? | The statute identifies the US as being "a home for the homeless", "a land of opportunity". |
| What message is being told? | "We welcome immigrants from other lands." |

**(1) Complete the following form with the information you know about the Colosseum.**

| Symbol Name | Colosseum |
|---|---|
| Where? | |
| Why was it built? | |
| Identity? | |
| What message is being told? | |

## An Introduction to European Culture (Second Edition)

(2) Think about a Chinese symbol, and complete a similar form.

| Symbol Name |  |
|---|---|
| Where? |  |
| Why was it built? |  |
| Identity? |  |
| What message is being told? |  |

## 3. Writing

What statues or architectural constructions do you think can be regarded as a symbol of China? And why do you think so?

Please write a composition of about 200 words on the above topic. Give at least two reasons for your choice and illustrate with appropriate examples.

**Read More**

### Text B  Roman Baths

Roman baths were part of the day-to-day life in Ancient Rome. Bath in Somerset contains one of the best examples of a Roman bath complex in Europe. There are two good examples at Pompeii.

Roman houses had water supplied via lead pipes. However, these pipes were taxed according to their size, so many houses had just a basic supply and could not hope to rival a bath complex. Therefore, for personal hygiene, people went to the local baths. However, the local bath complex was also a gathering point and served a very useful community and social function. Here people could relax, keep clean and keep up with the latest news.

Taking a bath was not a simple chore. There was not one bath to use in a large complex such as the one at Bath. A visitor could use a cold bath (the frigidarium), a warm bath (the tepidarium) and a hot bath (the caldarium). A visitor would spend some of his time in each one before leaving. A large complex would also contain an exercise area (the palaestra), a swimming pool and a gymnasium. One of the public baths at Pompeii contains two tepidariums and caldaria along with a plunge pool and a large exercise area.

The building of a bath complex required excellent engineering skills. Baths required a way of heating up water. This was done by using a furnace and the hypocaust system carried the heat around the complex.

Water had to be constantly supplied. In Rome, this was done using 640 kilometers of aqueducts—a superb engineering feat. The baths themselves could be huge. A complex built by the emperor Diocletian was the size of a football pitch. Those who built them wanted to make a statement so that many baths contained mosaics and massive marble columns. The larger baths contained statues to the gods and professionals were on hand to help take the strain out of having a bath. Masseurs would massage visitors and then rub scented olive oil onto their skin.

It was very cheap to use a Roman bath. A visitor, after paying his entrance fee, would strip naked and hand his clothes to an attendant. He could then do some exercising to work up a sweat before moving into the tepidarium which would prepare him for the caldarium which was more or less like a modern sauna. The idea, as with a sauna, was for the sweat to get rid of the body's dirt. After this, a slave would rub olive oil onto the visitor's skin and then scrape it off with a strigil. The more luxurious establishments would have professional masseurs to do this. After this, the visitor would return to the tepidarium and then to frigidarium to cool down. Finally, he could use the main pool for a swim or to generally socialize. Bathing was very important to the ancient Romans as it served many functions.

> We quickly undressed, went into the hot baths and after working up a sweat, passed on to the cold bath. There we found Trimalchio again. His skin was glistening all over with perfumed oil. He was being rubbed down, not with ordinary linen, but with clothes of the purest and softest wool. He was then wrapped in a blazing scarlet robe, hoisted into a litter, and trundled off.
>
> —Petronius

However, not everyone was overjoyed by them:

> I live over a public bath-house. Just imagine every kind of annoying noise! The sturdy gentleman does his exercise with lead weights; when he is working hard (or pretending to) I can hear him grunt; when he breathes out, I can hear him panting in high-pitched tones. Or I might notice some lazy fellow, content with a cheap rub-down, and hear the blows of the hand slapping his shoulders. The sound varies, depending on whether the massager hits with a flat or hollow hand.
>
> To all of this, you can add the arrest of the occasional pickpocket; there's also the racket made by the man who loves to hear his own voice in the bath or the chap who dives in with a lot of noise and splashing.
>
> —Seneca

As the Romans advanced west in England, building the Fosse Way as they went, they crossed the River Avon. Near here they found a hot water spring. It brought over one million liters of hot water to the surface every day at a temperature of about 48 degrees centigrade. They built a reservoir to control the water flow, baths and a temple. A town, Bath, quickly grew around this complex. Many Romans viewed the springs as sacred and threw valuable items into the springs to please the gods. An altar was also built at Bath so that priests could sacrifice animals to the gods. The waters at Bath gained a reputation as being able to cure all ills. As a result, many traveled to Bath from all over the

Roman Empire to take to the waters there.

**Questions for Reflection**

1. Please describe how Ancient Romans take a bath.
2. What did a Roman bath complex look like?
3. What social functions did bathing serve in ancient Rome?
4. Why did Bath attract many travelers from all over the Roman Empire to take to the waters there?

## Text C  The Roman Forum

The Roman Forum (Forum Romanum) was the political and economic center of Rome during the Republic. It emerged as such in the 7th century BC and maintained this position well into the Imperial Period, when it was reduced to a monumental area. It was mostly abandoned at the end of the 4th century.

The Forum Romanum is located in a valley between the Capitoline Hill on the west, the Palatine Hill on the south, the Velia on the east and Quirinal Hill and the Esquiline Hill to the north. The Velia was leveled in Antiquity.

The importance of the Forum area is indicated by the presence of many of the central political, religious and judicial buildings in Rome. The Regia was the residence of the kings; the Curia, the meeting place of the Senate; and the Comitium and the Rostra, where public meetings were held. Major temples and sanctuaries in the Forum include the Temple of Castor and Pollux, the Temple of Saturn and the Temple of Vesta. Commercial and judicial activities took place in the basilicas, the two remaining are the Basilica Aemilia and the Basilica Julia. Due to the political importance of the area, there were also numerous honorary monuments.

Originally the area of the Forum was humid and covered in grass, as it was not suitable for construction. A necropolis has been found, dating from the 10th century BC, but otherwise the area does not seem to have been used much. This changed in the 7th century with the construction of the Cloaca Maxima. This sewer system was based on a natural stream, which was enclosed and covered to drain the area, a sign that the settlements on the Palatine Hill was spreading into the valley.

Gradually more public buildings were constructed around the square, thus forming a natural center for the rapidly growing town. According to legend, the second king of Rome, Numa Pompilius, instituted the cult of Vesta and built the Regia, Tullius Hostilius built the first Curia and enclosed the area of the Comitium, and Tarquinius Priscus ordered the Forum paved around 600 BC. While the role of the kings cannot be proven, the dates are largely confirmed by archaeological research. Other very old monuments in the Forum area are the Vulcanal and the Lapis Niger.

In republican times the construction on the Forum continued, with a series of basilicas, notably the Basilica Sempronia and the Basilica Aemilia. Also from this period are the Temple of Saturn, the Temple of Castor and Pollux and the Temple of Concord.

The current image of the Forum Romanum is a result of the changes made by Julius Caesar as pontifex maximus and dictator, which included the construction of the Basilica Julia where the Basilica Sempronia stood, the building of a new Curia and the renovation of the Rostra, the speaker's platform. Caesar did not see all his plans realized before his death, but most was finished by his successor Augustus, including the Temple of Divus Julius, dedicated to Caesar deified.

In imperial times the importance of the Forum as a political center diminished, but it remained a center of commerce and religious life. Construction and restoration continued, but now mostly in the form of honorary monuments, such as the Arch of Augustus, the Arch of Titus and the Arch of Septimius Severus. Other arches, such as the Arch of Tiberius, have disappeared completely. New religious buildings included the Temple of Antoninus and Faustina and the Temple of Vespasian and Titus. The Basilica of Maxentius from the 4th century is one of the last major additions to the Forum.

The Column of Phocas was the last monument to be erected in the Forum in 608 AD, but at this time the area was already half in ruin.

The Forum Romanum suffered damage and destruction repeatedly. When political strife in republican times deteriorated into violence, the Forum would regularly be the scene of fierce fights between rivaling factions, often followed by destructive fires. Fire was always a problem in ancient

Rome, and parts of the Forum burnt down several times, the worst fire being in 283 AD. Later the Forum suffered destruction and pillage at the hands of invaders. Most of the buildings on the Forum was destroyed completely in 410 AD when the Ostrogoths of Alaric sacked the town. Many religious sites were abandoned and fell in ruin after the ban of non-Christian cults in 394 AD.

After the fall of the empire in the west, the area was abandoned. A few buildings were converted into churches, including the Curia, the Temple of Antoninus and Faustina and the Temple of Divus Romulus; the rest was left to shepherds and their animals, to the extent that the popular name of the area became Campo Vaccino, the cattle field.

Many of the buildings served as quarries for other construction sites in the city during the Renaissance and later, and gradually dirt piled up to 5—7 meters above the street level of antiquity, covering all but the tallest ruins. This difference can be seen clearly on the church of San Lorenzo in Miranda (Temple of Antoninus and Faustina), where the door now sits halfway up the wall. It used to be level with the ground.

Archaeological excavations began in the 18th century, but the site has only been excavated systematically in the 20th century. Many of the later additions to buildings and monuments have now been removed and the original street level has been restored over large parts of the Forum.

**Questions for Reinforcement**
**Fill in the blanks according to what you have read in the passage.**
1. The Roman Forum is located in _____. It is the _____ and _____ center of Rome during the Republic.
2. The Roman Forum consisted of many separate constructions: the Regia was _____; _____ was the meeting place of the Senate, and the Comitium and the Rostra were where _____.
3. In imperial times, the importance of the Forum as a political center diminished, but it remained a center of _____. Constructions during this time were mostly in the form of _____.
4. The Forum suffered continuous damage and destruction caused by _____, _____, and _____.

**Website to Visit**
http://www.greatbuildings.com/buildings/Roman_Colosseum.html (accessed Apr. 28, 2020)
On this website, you can find all that you want to know about Roman Colosseum.

**Movie to Watch**

### Ancient Rome: The Rise and Fall of an Empire (2006)

*Ancient Rome: The Rise and Fall of an Empire* is a 2006 BBC docudrama series, with each episode looking at a different key turning point in the history of the Roman Empire. The six episodes are: "Nero", "Caesar", "Revolution", "Rebellion", "Constantine" and "Fall of Rome".

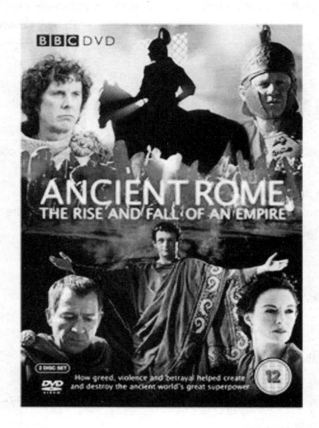

# Unit 6
## The Middle Ages

> If all the bones of all the victims of the Catholic Church could be gathered together, a monument higher than all the pyramids would rise.
> —Robert Green Ingersoll

### Unit Goals

- To be familiar with the major events and key cultural phenomena concerning the Middle Ages
- To understand the influence of the Church in the Middle Ages
- To learn the useful words and expressions that describe the Middle Ages
- To improve language skills by learning this unit

### Before You Read

**1. Story Telling**

What do you know about the Middle Ages? Describe the following pictures.

**Picture 1**

(1) Who are the people in the picture?
_____

(2) Where are they?
_____

(3) What are they doing?
_____

(4) What kind of life are they living?
_____

**Picture 2**

(1) Who is the man on the horse?

_____

(2) Who are the men in front of the church?

_____

(3) What are they doing?

_____

## 2. A Starter Quiz on the Middle Ages

Answer the following questions about the Middle Ages. Then search on the Internet for the correct answer to each question.

(1) The Middle Ages describes the period between the years _____.
    a. 500 and 1,000                  b. 1,000 and 1,050
    c. 1,000 and 1,500               d. 500 and 1,500

(2) The medieval period is also known as the _____.
    a. Age of Reason                 b. Dark Ages
    c. Germanic Era                  d. New Age

(3) What was a manor?
    a. A large estate or farm.          b. Land owned by serfs.
    c. A large body of water.          d. A road used for travel.

(4) Knights followed a code of conduct called _____.
    a. good manners                b. feudalism
    c. chivalry                        d. knighthood

(5) The Crusades were wars between the Christians and _____.
    a. the Greeks                  b. the Egyptians
    c. the Vikings                  d. the Muslims

(6) As much as half of the population of Europe was killed by _____.
    a. bad food                     b. poor medical care
    c. religious persecution          d. the Black Death

(7) The most powerful people in the Middle Ages were _____.
    a. the serfs                    b. the knights
    c. the pages                   d. the lords

(8) Medieval shields were used as protection and as _____.
    a. decoration                  b. mirrors to dress with
    c. identification of knights     d. sleds in snow

(9) What is a fief?
    a. Land granted to a knight by the king.    b. A poor worker on a manor.
    c. A type of landform.                       d. Home for orphans.

(10) Knights wore _____ for protection.
   a. armor  
   b. thick hats  
   c. long slacks  
   d. magic feathers

3. Form groups of three or four students. Try to find, on the Internet or in the library, more information about the Middle Ages. Choose a topic that interests you most and prepare a five-minute classroom presentation.

## Start to Read

### Text A  Between Ancient and Modern

In 476 AD, warriors attacked the city of Rome and ended more than 800 years of glory for the "eternal city". Historians mark the fall of Rome as the end of ancient history. The next one thousand years were called the Middle Ages. The Latin term for the Middle Ages is "medieval".

The beginning of the Middle Ages is often called the "Dark Ages" because the great civilizations of Greece and Rome had fallen. In the latter part of the fourth century, the Huns swept into Europe from central Asia, robbing and killing as they came along, and large numbers of the half civilized Germanic tribes such as the Visigoths, the Franks, the Angles and Saxons, and the Vandals fled their homelands in northern Europe and were pushed to cross the Danube River into the territory of the Roman Empire. In 476 AD, a Germanic general killed the last Roman emperor and took control of the government. While the Eastern Roman Empire continued, the power of ancient Rome was gone. In its place mushroomed a great many Germanic kingdoms, which in a few hundred years were to grow into the nations known as England, France, Spain, Italy, and Germany. Between the fifth and eleventh centuries, Western Europe was the scene of frequent wars and invasions. The political unity had given way to widespread destruction and confusion. Hunger and diseases killed many lives; towns and villages fell into ruin and great areas of land lay waste.

During the Medieval times, there was no central government to keep the order. The only organization that seemed to unite Europe was the Christian Church. It continued to gain widespread power and influence. In the late Middle Ages, almost everyone in Western Europe was a Christian and a member of the Christian Church. Christianity took the lead in politics, law, art, and learning for hundreds of years. It shaped people's lives. That is why the Middle Ages is also called the "Age of Faith".

Whatever names we may give to this span of time, this is a period in which classical, Hebrew and Gothic heritages merged. And it is this fusion and blending of different ideas and practices that paved the way for the development of what is the present-day European culture.

### Power of the Catholic Church

Christianity had spread throughout the Roman world and the Church had set up its own government by the time the Western Roman Empire fell. As time went by differences in practices as well as in beliefs arose between the church in the western Mediterranean areas and the Church in the eastern Mediterranean area. They even did not use the same language. After 1054, the Church was divided into the Roman Catholic Church and the Eastern Orthodox Church. In order to develop a civilization based on Christianity, the Catholic Church made Latin the official language and helped to preserve and pass on the heritage of the Roman Empire.

The Roman Catholic Church was the single, largest unifying structure in medieval Europe. It touched everyone's life, no matter what their rank or class or where they lived. The Church taught that all people had sinned and had to rely on God's favor to get to heaven. The only way to get this favor was by taking part in sacraments. Shortly after a child was born, he was baptized, and thus became a member of the Church. Later he was married by a priest. On Fridays, meat should not be touched and on Sundays everybody went to the church to worship God. One of the most important sacraments was Holy Communion, which was to remind people that Christ had died to redeem man.

People had to pay heavy taxes to their parish churches, part of which passed on to the Pope in Rome. In addition, nobles and kings often gave lands, crops or cattle to support the church. As a matter of fact, many high church officials were themselves big landowners and influential nobles. The Pope not only ruled Rome and parts of Italy as a king, but he was also the head of all Christian churches in Western Europe. Those who opposed the Pope lost their membership in the Church and their political right. The Church even set up a church court—the Inquisition to stamp out so-called heresy.

**Peasantry and Aristocracy**

Feudalism was the system of loyalties and protections during the Middle Ages. As the Roman Empire crumbled, emperors granted land to nobles in exchange for their loyalty. These lands eventually developed into manors. A manor is the land owned by a noble and everything on it. A typical manor consisted of a castle, small village, and farmland.

Two fundamental changes transformed rural society during the early Middle Ages. First, Roman slavery virtually disappeared. Second, the household emerged as the primary unit of social and economic organization. Across much of northwestern Europe, in particular in France in the eleventh century, the various gradations in status disappeared, and the peasantry formed a homogeneous social category loosely described as serfs. Although they were not slaves in a legal sense, their degraded status, their limited access to public courts of law, and their enormous dependency on their lords left them a situation similar to that of the slaves in the past. Each year, peasants paid their lords certain fixed portions of their meager harvests. In addition, they had to work a certain number of days on the demesne, or reserve of the lord, the produce of which went directly to him for his use or sale.

Most peasants led lives of constant insecurity. They were poorly housed, clothed, and fed; subject to the constant scrutiny of their lords; and defenseless against natural or human-made disasters. Their homes were typically small one- or two-room shacks constructed of mud and wood and shared with their most valuable domestic animals. These huts usually had no windows and, until the sixteenth century, no chimneys. Smoke from the open hearth escaped through a hole in the roof.

Peasants' houses were clustered in the villages on manors or large estates. In some parts of Europe, this was the result of their lord's desire to keep a close eye on his labor supply. In these villages, peasants were obligated to have disputes settled in the lords' court, to grind their grain in the lord's mill, and to bake their bread in the lord's oven—all primary sources of revenue for the lord. The same sort of monopoly applied to the Church. Villages had to contribute a tenth of their revenues to the Church and to make donations in order to receive the sacraments. In some villages, these payments may have actually gone to the Church, but usually they too went to the lord.

Beginning in the late tenth century, writers of legal documents began to use an old term in a novel manner to designate certain powerful free persons who belonged neither to the old aristocracy nor to the peasantry. The term was *miles*, which in classical Latin meant "soldier". As it was used in the Middle Ages, we would translate it as "knight". The knightly function gradually came to entail a certain status and lifestyle.

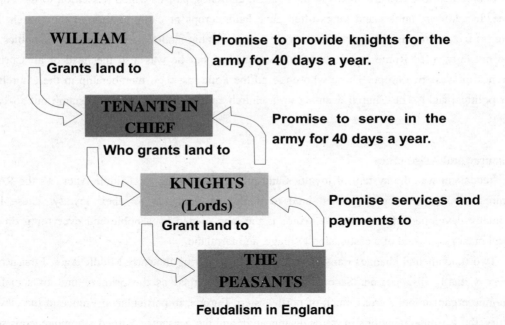

**Feudalism in England**

The center of the knightly lifestyle was northern France. From there the ideas of knighthood, or chivalry, spread out across Europe, influencing aristocrats as far east as Byzantium. The essence of this lifestyle was fighting. Through warfare this aristocracy had maintained or acquired its freedom, and through warfare it justified its privileges. The origins of this small elite were diverse. Many of its members were descended from the old aristocracy. They traced descent through the male line. Inheritance was usually limited to the eldest sons, and daughters were given a dowry but did not share in inheritance. Younger sons had to find service with some great lord or live in the household of their older brothers. Even the eldest sons who became heads of households could not dispose of family property without consulting their kinsmen.

Such noble families, proud of their independence and ancestry, maintained their position through complex kin networks, mutual defense pacts with other nobles, and control of castles, from which they could dominate the surrounding countryside. By the twelfth century, nobles lived safely behind the castle walls, often even independent of the local counts, dukes, and kings. This lesser nobility absorbed control of such traditionally public powers as justice, peace, and taxation.

The noble lifestyle required wealth, and wealth meant land. The nobility was essentially a society of heirs who had inherited not only land but also the serfs who worked their manors. Lesser nobles acquired additional property from great nobles and from ecclesiastical institutions in return for binding contracts of mutual assistance. Individual knights became vassals of lay or ecclesiastical magnates, swearing fealty or loyalty to the lord and promising to defend and aid him. In return, the lord swore to protect his vassal and granted him a means of support by which the vassal could maintain himself while serving his lord. Usually, this grant, termed a fief, was a parcel of productive land and the serfs and privileges attached to it, which the vassal and his heirs could hold as long as they provided the designated service to the lord.

## Proper Nouns

1. the Middle Ages 中世纪时期
2. the Huns 匈奴人
3. the Visigoths 西哥特人(日耳曼族的一支,于公元4世纪入侵罗马帝国并在法国和西班牙建立王国)
4. the Franks 法兰克人
5. the Angles and Saxons 盎格鲁人和撒克逊人
6. the Vandals 汪达尔人(4、5世纪时侵入罗马帝国的日耳曼民族)
7. the Danube River 多瑙河
8. Roman Catholic Church 罗马天主教
9. Eastern Orthodox Church 东正教
10. Holy Communion 基督教的圣餐礼

## After You Read

**Knowledge Focus**

1. True or False. Mark "T" if the statement is correct or "F" if incorrect.
   (1) (　) The Middle Ages is called the "Dark Ages" because many half-civilized Germanic tribes conquered the territory of the Roman Empire and brought an end to the glory of Greek and Roman civilization.

(2) (　) During the Medieval times, the Christian Church was the only organization that united Europe.
(3) (　) The official language of the Catholic Church was Greek.
(4) (　) Holy Communion was an important Christian sacrament in which people celebrate the birth of Jesus.
(5) (　) The head of all Christian churches in Western Europe in the Medieval times was the Pope.
(6) (　) A typical manor consisted of a noble, his many serfs and his land.
(7) (　) Peasant in Medieval times had to pay their lords heavy taxes.
(8) (　) Villages had to make donations to the church in order to receive the sacraments and these payments usually went to the church directly.
(9) (　) The essence of the knightly lifestyle was chivalry.
(10) (　) The noble heirs could inherit land from their predecessors but serfs were not inheritable.

## 2. Peasantry vs. Aristocracy

The medieval European society consisted of poor peasants and noble aristocrats. They lived quite different lives. Please find in the text as much evidence as possible to complete the following contrast between the life of a peasant and that of an aristocrat.

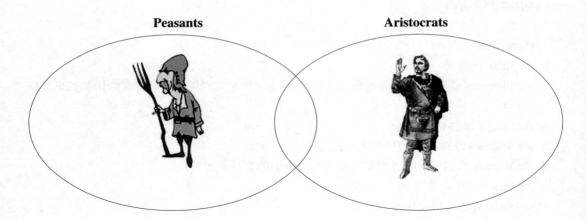

## 3. Discuss the following questions with your partner.

(1) What happened in Western Europe after the decline of the Roman Empire?
(2) Why is the Middle Ages also called the "Age of Faith"?
(3) How was the life of the medieval people influenced by the Catholic Church?
(4) What is a manor? Describe a typical manor.
(5) Did the serfs live a life similar to that of slaves in Roman times? Explain with examples.
(6) Who were knights? What privileges and obligations did they have?

# Unit 6  The Middle Ages

**Language Focus**

**1. Fill in the blanks with the following words or expressions you have learned in the text.**

| crumble | scrutiny | give way to | cluster (v.) | stamp out |
| mushroom(v.) | transform | keep a close eye | meager | entail |

(1) New blocks of flats and offices have _____ all over the city.
(2) Mrs. Jones did not _____ fears during the flood.
(3) This job would _____ your learning how to use a computer.
(4) The doctors are trying to _____ the disease.
(5) Even if the seas go dry and rocks _____, my will will remain firm.
(6) Whenever a camera was pointed at her, Marilyn would instantly _____ herself into a radiant star.
(7) Aside from his _____ savings, he has no resources to fall back on.
(8) The Government's record will come under close _____ in the weeks before the election.
(9) The men _____ together around the fire and sang songs.
(10) I'm going to _____ on my passport and other travel documents from now on.

**2. Fill in the blanks with the proper form of the word in the brackets.**

(1) A third party is formed by the _____ (fuse) of independent republicans and democrats.
(2) Don't allow personal _____ (loyal) to color your judgment.
(3) The situation is still _____ (secure), with many of the rebels roaming the streets.
(4) A city without a gun or water is _____ (defense) before an army.
(5) His real influence was asserted through his _____ (dominate) of the political bureau.
(6) The telecommunication service is a government _____ (monopolize).
(7) They used to _____ (donation) to the Red Cross every year.
(8) A particular gene is responsible for the _____ (inherit) of eye color.
(9) If you were the _____ (consult), what steps would you suggest to get the company to plan effectively?
(10) He traces his _____ (descend) back to an old Norman family.

**3. Fill in the blanks with the proper prepositions or adverbs that collocate with the neighboring words.**

(1) It's no easy task to take control _____ a class of young children.
(2) Ever since the economic reformation, many laid-off workers fall _____ poverty.
(3) As time goes _____, my memory seems to get worse.
(4) You can rely _____ your solicitor's professionalism in dealing _____ the house purchase.
(5) She caught my cold and passed it _____ to her husband.

(6) _____ a matter of fact, this was purely newspaper gossip and speculation.

(7) I gave Mary an apple _____ exchange for my favorite banana.

(8) As her private secretary, he has access _____ all her correspondence.

(9) Trains are subject _____ delays after the heavy snowfalls.

(10) His job is not only to dispose _____ problems but also to meet unexpected challenges.

4. **Error Correction**: Each of the following sentences has at least one grammatical error. Identify the errors and correct them.

(1) Historians mark the fall of Rome the end of ancient history.

(2) In the latter part of the fourth century, the Huns swept into Europe from central Asia, robbed and killed as they came along.

(3) In its place mushroomed a great many Germanic kingdoms, where in a few hundred years were to grow into the nations known as England, France, Spain, Italy, and Germany.

(4) Whichever names we may give to the Middle Ages, this is a period in which classical, Hebrew and Gothic heritages merged.

(5) It is this fusion and blending of different ideas and practices that paved the way for the development of that is the present-day European culture.

(6) The Church touched everyone's life, no matter their rank or class or what they lived.

(7) People had to pay heavy taxes to their parish churches, part of those passed on to the Pope in Rome.

(8) Those opposed the Pope lost their membership in the Church and their political right.

(9) The serfs had to work a certain number of days on the demesne, or reserve of the lord, the produce of them went directly to him for his use or sale.

(10) The nobility were essentially a society of heirs whom had inherited not only land but also the serfs whom worked their manors.

(11) In return, the lord swore to protect his vassal and granted him a means of support which the vassal could maintain himself while serving his lord.


*Comprehensive Work*

**1. Becoming a Knight**

Nobles could become knights in the Medieval days. But no one was born a knight—knighthood had to be earned. The training was both long and hard.

In the following activity, you will find that a noble boy had to go through three stages if he wanted to become a knight. Meanwhile, you will also find some descriptions concerning the things he had to learn or do in each stage.

Discuss with your partner what obligations a knight had to fulfill in each period of his training, and then put the descriptions into their corresponding columns.

## Becoming a Knight

| The Duties of A Page (Ages 7 – 15) | The Duties of A Squire (Ages 16 – manhood) | Final Steps in Becoming a Knight (Manhood) |
|---|---|---|
| | | |

a. learns manners
b. waits on tables
c. polishes the knight's armor
d. keeps vigil
e. plays chess
f. composes songs
g. rides horse
h. prays and fasts all night
i. dresses in red for blood, white for purity, and
j. dubbed with the king's sword
k. writes poetry
l. dances
m. trains in the home of a knight
n. rides into battle with knight
o. promises to come to the aid of his lord when called, and to defend the church, women, and orphans
p. receives the sword and spurs
q. cares for the knight's weapons
r. dresses knight for tournament
s. spars with the knight
t. carves
u. sings
v. lays weapons on the altar

## 2. Chivalry-code of Manners

Knights were guided in their conduct by a code of ethics known as chivalry. Chivalry promoted honesty, fairness in battle, and proper treatment of noblewomen. It set a high standard for the nobles of medieval times. Later, the concepts of chivalry gradually blended with the expectations of proper manners for the gentleman in western culture.

Discuss the following questions with your partner and then report to the whole class.
(1) What do you think might be included in the Code of Chivalry?

(2) If you could have written a Code of Chivalry, what would you change about it? Why?

(3) Why were knights in the Middle Ages portrayed as role models?

## 3. Writing

Who do you think can best represent the spirit of chivalry? And why?
Please write a composition on the topic "A Knight in My Eyes". Give at least two reasons for your choice.

**Read More**

### Text B  The Crusades

The Crusades were a series of military campaigns during the time of Medieval England against the Muslims of the Middle East. In 1076, the Muslims had captured Jerusalem—the holiest of holy places for Christians. Jesus had been born nearby Bethlehem and Jesus had spent most of his life in Jerusalem. He was crucified on Calvary Hill, also in Jerusalem. There was no more important place on Earth than Jerusalem for a true Christian, which is why Christians called Jerusalem the "City of God".

However, Jerusalem was also extremely important for the Muslims as Muhammad, the founder of the Muslim faith, had been there and there was great joy in the Muslim world when Jerusalem was captured. A beautiful dome, called the Dome of the Rock, was built on the rock where Muhammad was said to have sat and prayed and it was so holy that no Muslim was allowed to tread on the rock or touch it when visiting the Dome.

Therefore, the Christian fought to get Jerusalem back while the Muslims fought to keep Jerusalem. These wars were to last nearly 200 years.

Some history books do slightly vary with their dates regarding when the Crusades started. The problem seems to be on deciding whether the date a crusade was called for is the date it started or whether the date troops actually left for a crusade is the date it started.

| |
|---|
| The First Crusade: 1096 to 1099 |
| The Second Crusade: 1147 to 1149 |
| The Third Crusade: 1189 to 1192 |
| The Fourth Crusade: 1201 to 1204 |
| The Fifth Crusade: 1218 to 1221 |
| The Sixth Crusade: 1228 to 1229 |
| The Seventh Crusade: 1248 to 1254 |
| The Eighth Crusade: 1270 |

The First Crusade was an attempt to re-capture Jerusalem. After the capture of Jerusalem by the Muslims in 1076, any Christian who wanted to pay a pilgrimage to the city faced a very hard time. Muslim soldiers made life very difficult for the Christians and trying to get to Jerusalem was filled with danger for a Christian. This greatly angered all Christians.

In 1095, Pope Urban II called for a war against the Muslims so that Jerusalem was regained for the Christian faith. In his speech he said:

> Christians, hasten to help your brothers in the East, for they are being attacked. Arm for the rescue of Jerusalem under your captain Christ. Wear his cross as your badge. If you are killed your sins will be pardoned.

Those who volunteered to go to fight the Muslims cut out red crosses and sewed them on their tunics. The French word "croix" means cross and the word changed to "croisades" or "crusades". The fight against the Muslims became a Holy War.

The First Crusade had a very difficult journey getting to the Middle East. They could not use the Mediterranean Sea as the Crusaders did not control the ports on the coast of the Middle East. Therefore, they had to cross land. They traveled from France through Italy, then Eastern Europe and then through what is now Turkey. They covered hundreds of miles, through scorching heat and also deep snow in the mountain passes. The Crusaders ran out of freshwater and according to a survivor of the First Crusade who wrote about his experiences after his return, some were reduced to drinking their own urine, drinking animal blood or water that had been in sewage. Food was bought from local people but at very expensive prices.

Disease was common especially as men were weakened by the journey and drinking dirty water. Dysentery was common. Heatstroke also weakened many Crusaders. Disease and fatigue affected rich and poor alike.

By 1097, nearly 10,000 people had gathered at Constantinople ready for the journey to the Holy Land. There was no one person in charge of the First Crusade. Urban II had made Bishop Adbenar the leader but he preferred to let others do the work and make decisions. There were four separate proper Crusader armies in the First Crusade and also a large number of smaller armies. However, there was no proper command structure and with the problems of communications at that time, it is possible that a command structure with one person in charge was an impossibility.

The attack and capture of Jerusalem started in the summer of 1099. Jerusalem was well defended with high walls around it. The first attacks on the city were not successful as the Crusaders were short of materials for building siege machines. Once logs had arrived, two siege machines were built.

A monk called Fulcher was on the First Crusade. He wrote about the attack on the Holy City and he can be treated as an eye-witness as to what took place. Fulcher claimed that the Crusaders cut down anybody they could and that the streets of Jerusalem were ankle deep in blood. The rest of the Crusaders got into the city when the gates were opened. The slaughter continued and the Crusaders killed as they wished. Those Muslims who had their lives spared had to go round and collect the bodies before dumping them outside of the city because they stank so much. The Muslims claimed afterward that 70,000 people were killed and that the Crusaders took whatever treasure they could from the Dome of the Rock.

After the success of the Crusaders, the Kingdom of Jerusalem was created and its first king was Godfrey of Bouillon who was elected by other Crusaders. He died in 1100 and was succeeded by his brother Baldwin of Boulogne. However, the capture of Jerusalem did not end the Crusades as the Crusaders wanted to get rid of the Muslims from the whole region and not just Jerusalem. This desire led to the other Crusades.

*Questions for Reflection*
1. What were the Crusades? How many Crusades were there in history?
2. Why did Christians fight against Muslims in the Crusades?
3. What was the cause of the First Crusade? How did it get its name?
4. How would you describe the First Crusade? Please give details.

### Text C  The Black Death

In Medieval England, the Black Death was to kill 1.5 million people out of an estimated total of 4 million people between 1348 and 1350. No medical knowledge existed in Medieval England to cope with the disease. After 1350, it was to strike England another six times by the end of the century. Understandably, peasants were terrified at the news that the Black Death might be approaching their village or town.

The Black Death is the name given to a disease called the bubonic plague which was rampant during the fourteenth century. In fact, the bubonic plague affected England more than once in that century but its impact on English society from 1348 to 1350 was terrible. No amount of medical knowledge could help England when the bubonic plague struck. It was also to have a major impact on England's social structure which led to the Peasants Revolt of 1381.

The Black Death was caused by fleas carried by rats that were very common in towns and cities. The fleas bit into their victims literally injecting them with the disease. Death could be very quick for the weaker victims.

Its symptoms were described in 1348 by a man called Boccaccio who lived in Florence, Italy:

> The first signs of the plague were lumps in the groin or armpits. After this, livid black spots appeared on the arms and thighs and other parts of the body. Few recovered. Almost all died within three days, usually without any fever.

Written evidence from the time indicates that nearly all the victims died within three days though a small number did last for four days.

**Why did the bubonic plague spread so quickly?**

In towns and cities, people lived very close together and they knew nothing about contagious diseases. Also, the disposal of bodies was very crude and helped to spread the disease still further as those who handled the dead bodies did not protect themselves in any way.

The filth that littered streets gave rats the perfect environment to breed and increase their number. It is commonly thought that it was the rats that caused the disease. This is not true—the fleas did this. However, it was the rats that enabled the disease to spread very quickly and the filth in the streets of the towns and cities did not help to stop the spread of the disease.

Lack of medical knowledge meant that people tried anything to help them escape the disease. One of the more extreme was the flagellants. These people wanted to show their love of God by whipping themselves, hoping that God would forgive them for their sins and that they would be spared the Black Death.

The Black Death had a huge impact on society. Fields went unploughed as the men who usually did this were victims of the disease. Harvests would not have been brought in as the manpower did not exist. Animals would have been lost as the people in a village would not have been around to tend them.

Therefore, whole villages would have faced starvation. Towns and cities would have faced food shortages as the villages that surrounded them could not provide them with enough food. Those lords who lost their manpower to the disease, turned to sheep farming as this required fewer people to work on the land. Grain farming became less popular—this, again, kept towns and cities short of such basics as bread. One consequence of the Black Death was inflation—the price of food went up creating more hardship for the poor. In some parts of England, food prices went up by four times.

**How did peasants respond?**

Those who survived the Black Death believed that there was something special about them—almost as if God had protected them. Therefore, they took the opportunity offered by the disease to improve their lifestyle.

Feudal law stated that peasants could only leave their village if they had their lord's permission. Now many lords were short of desperately needed labor for the land that they owned. After the Black Death, lords actively encouraged peasants to leave the village where they lived to come to work for them. When peasants did this, the lord refused to return them to their original village.

Peasants could demand higher wages as they knew that a lord was desperate to get in his harvest.

So the government faced the prospect of peasants leaving their villages to find a better "deal" from a lord thus upsetting the whole idea of the Feudal System which had been introduced to tie peasants to the land. Ironically, this movement by the peasants was encouraged by the lords who were meant to benefit from the Feudal System.

To curb peasants roaming around the countryside looking for better pay, the government introduced the Statute of Labourers in 1351 that stated:

> No peasants could be paid more than the wages paid in 1346. No lord or master should offer more wages than paid in 1346. No peasants could leave the village they belonged to.

Though some peasants decided to ignore the statute, many knew that disobedience would lead to serious punishment. This created great anger amongst the peasants which was to boil over in 1381 with the Peasants Revolt. Hence, it can be argued that the Black Death was to lead to the Peasants Revolt.

Unit 6　The Middle Ages

## Questions for Reflection

1. What does the Black Death refer to? What was the cause of it? What were its symptoms?
2. Why did the epidemic spread so quickly?
3. What impact did the Black Death have on medieval society?
4. How did the peasants respond to the disease?

## Websites to Visit

https://www.history.com/topics/middle-ages (accessed Apr. 28, 2020)
This website provides a complete introduction to almost every social aspect of Medieval Europe.

http://www.timemaps.com/encyclopedia/medieval-europe-feudalism/ (accessed Apr. 28, 2020)
This website deals with the feudal system of Medieval Europe, focusing on western Europe.

## Movie to Watch

### King Arthur (2004)

*King Arthur* is an ambitious attempt to retell the legend of King Arthur and his Knights of the Round Table.

The film begins with the fall of the Roman Empire in 450 AD as Roman armies flee the British Isles. Arthur, a heroic knight and devoted Christian, is torn between his desire to travel to Rome to serve his faith and his loyalty to the land of his birth. As England falls into lawlessness, Arthur throws in his lot with a band of knights who hope to restore order to their fair and pleasant land and hopes to win freedom for his comrades. In time, Arthur and his men join forces with Merlin, a shaman whose band of renegade knights were often pitched in battle against Roman forces. Forming a united front as loyal Englishmen against the invading Saxon armies, Arthur, Merlin, and the brave and beautiful Guinevere are determined to unite a sovereign Britain under one army and one king.

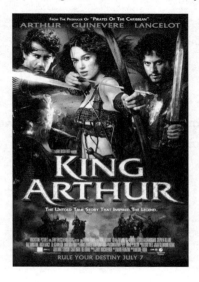

# Unit 7
## The Making of Renaissance

> The Renaissance is studded by the names of the artists and architects, with their creations recorded as great historical events.
> 
> —Arthur Erickson

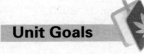
### Unit Goals

- To have a general understanding of the historical background of the Renaissance time
- To be able to account for the start of the Renaissance in Italy
- To learn the useful words and expressions that describe the Renaissance
- To improve language skills by learning this unit

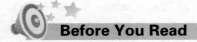
### Before You Read

**1. Test Your Knowledge**

How much do you know about Italy?

(1) Where is Italy located?

(2) What is this country famous for?

(3) What else do you know about this country?

**2. What do you know about the Renaissance?**

Have you ever heard of the term "Renaissance"? How much do you know about it? Please discuss the following questions with your partner.

(1) What does the term refer to?

(2) What is the meaning of the word?

(3) Name at least three famous Renaissance men that you know and tell the class what you know about them.

| Name | Occupation | Achievements |
|------|------------|--------------|
|      |            |              |
|      |            |              |
|      |            |              |

## Start to Read

### Text A  The Dawn of a New Age

At about 1450, European scholars became more interested in studying the world around them. Their art became truer to life. They began to explore new lands. The new age in Europe was eventually called "the Renaissance". Renaissance is a French word that means "rebirth". Historians consider the Renaissance to be the beginning of modern history.

The Renaissance began in northern Italy and then spread throughout Europe. Italian cities such as Naples, Genoa, and Venice became centers of trade between Europe and the Middle East. Arab scholars preserved the writings of the ancient Greeks in their libraries. When the Italian cities traded with the Arabs, ideas were exchanged along with goods. These ideas, preserved from the ancient past, served as the basis of the Renaissance. When the Byzantine Empire fell to Muslim Turks in 1453, many Christian scholars left Greece for Italy.

The Renaissance was much more than simply studying the work of ancient scholars. It influenced painting, sculpture, and architecture. Paintings became more realistic and focused less often on religious topics.

Rich families became patrons and commissioned great art. Artists advanced the Renaissance style of showing nature and depicting the feelings of people. In Britain, there was a flowering in literature and drama that included the plays of William Shakespeare.

> **Learning and the arts began to flourish during the Renaissance.**
> - Crusaders returned to Europe with a newfound understanding of the world.
> - The invention of the printing press encouraged literacy and helped to spread new ideas.
> - Wealthy families and the church had amassed enough wealth to become patrons.
> - The development of financial techniques such as bookkeeping and credit allowed merchants to prosper.

## Humanism

Many Renaissance scholars looked to the past for inspiration. They studied the classics—the works of the ancient Greeks and Romans. In the works of the classics, they found a spirit similar to theirs that valued innovation in this world rather than looking forward to the next world after death. A person who studied the classics was called a humanist. Humanists recreated classical styles in art, literature, and architecture. Humanists believed that by studying the classics, they could understand people and the world better.

The humanists emphasized the importance of human values instead of religious beliefs. Renaissance humanists were often devout Christians, but their promotion of secular, or non-religious values often put them at odds with the church.

Today we refer to the study of literature, philosophy and art as the humanities. The civilizations of Greece and Rome ended long ago, but they continue to influence us today.

## Gutenberg

A good cook can take leftovers and turn them into a delicious meal. Like a good cook, Johannes Gutenberg took what had already been discovered, and created a small invention that changed history.

Gutenberg created a machine that allowed him to move small blocks of letters in such a way that written material could be printed and mass-produced. Before the printing press, few people outside the clergy could read, but with inexpensive books, literacy spread through Europe.

Block printing existed long before Gutenberg. The Chinese had been carving wood blocks to print books as early as 868, but their process had one major drawback: a new set of woodcuts had to be made for each book. Producing one book was difficult; producing a variety of books was not practical.

Writing ink dates from about 2500 BC in Egypt and China. They took the soot from fires and mixed it with sap. Later civilizations used plant material for ink, particularly the dark blue indigo plant. Gutenberg used an oil-based printing ink that would last longer than other inks used in his time.

We do not know much about Gutenberg because he was not famous during his lifetime. We know that he was born in Germany at about 1400, and he worked as a goldsmith. In 1448, he developed engraved signatures for each number, letter, and punctuation mark. Gutenberg then built the molds to hold the signatures in place, and borrowed money to purchase a press. Gutenberg published the first mass-produced book: a 1,282 page *Bible*. To this day, more copies of the *Bible* have been printed than any other book.

Copies of Gutenberg's invention spread throughout Europe, but Gutenberg did not get rich from his invention. Patents did not yet exist, so anybody could build a printing press without compensating Gutenberg for his inspiration. Some religious and government officials denounced the invention of printing because they feared that it would spread bad ideas. But they were a minority. By 1500, there were 1,700 printing presses in Europe. The presses had already produced about 20 million volumes of 40,000 different books.

## City-states in Italy

During the Middle Ages, much of Italy was controlled by the Holy Roman Empire. As the emperors and popes fought for control, both were weakened. Several Italian cities formed states that were independent of both the empire and the church. Venice and Florence were two centers of power and wealth that became the cradle of the Renaissance.

Venice was founded in the fifth century by people fleeing from Attila the Hun. They settled on a group of islands on the northeastern edge of the Italian peninsula. Shipbuilding was the primary industry in Venice. During the Crusades, Venetian ships provided transportation to the Holy Land. By the 13th century, Venice was the most prosperous city in Europe. The city became rich by collecting taxes on all merchandise brought into its harbor. Venice built huge warships that protected the valuable cargo of its merchant ships from pirate raids. With the vast wealth from trade, many of the leading families of Venice competed with one another to build the finest palaces or support the work of the greatest artists.

Florence, the "city of flowers", was located in the hill country of north-central Italy. It prospered because of the wool industry. Sheep were raised in the rocky hill country of central Italy, and

Florence was a center of wool processing. During most of the Renaissance, wealthy merchants dominated Florence.

The merchants competed with one another by building grand palaces for themselves. The merchants were patrons of the arts. Patron comes from the Latin word for father. They hired artists to fill their homes with beautiful paintings and sculptures. Patrons bought rare books and paid scholars to teach their children. The money and encouragement of patrons together with that of the church, made the masterpieces of Renaissance art possible.

In the 15th century, the leading families of Florence decided they needed a strong person in charge to lead them against the growing threat of rival cities. They chose Cosimo de Medici, a wealthy banker, to take control of the government. Cosimo maintained the appearance of republican government, but he appointed his relatives and people he could control to important positions. When Cosimo died in 1464, his son and grandson continued his policies. The Medicis maintained control by exiling people who disagreed with them and encouraging other Italian cities to form alliances with Florence.

The best known of the Medicis was Cosimo's grandson, Lorenzo, who was known as "Lorenzo the Magnificent". Lorenzo was not only a shrewd banker and clever politician; he was also a scholar and a poet. Under Lorenzo's leadership, Florence became one of the most beautiful and prosperous cities in Italy, as well as a center of the Renaissance.

The people of Renaissance Florence, like most city-states of the era, were composed of four social classes. The nobles owned much of the land, and lived on large estates outside the city walls. They behaved according to the rules of chivalry and disdained the merchants.

The merchants were the newly rich, who gained wealth in industries like wool processing, boat making and banking. The merchants sought to protect their wealth by controlling the government and marrying into noble families. They became patrons of great artists in order to gain public favor. The middle class of Florence was composed of shopkeepers and professionals.

At the lowest level were the workers, who did not have job protection and were very dependent on their employers. Workers who violated rules could have their wages withheld or could be discharged from their jobs. Difficult as their lives were, however, these urban workers were better off than the peasants who lived in rural areas.

## Proper Nouns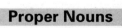

1. Renaissance 文艺复兴时期
2. Naples 那不勒斯(意大利城市)
3. Genoa 热那亚(意大利城市)
4. Venice 威尼斯(意大利城市)
5. Byzantine Empire 拜占庭帝国
6. William Shakespeare 威廉·莎士比亚(英国剧作家)
7. Johannes Gutenberg 约翰内斯·古登堡(印刷机的发明者)
8. block printing 雕版印刷
9. Attila the Hun 匈奴王阿提拉
10. the Holy Land 圣地,即耶路撒冷
11. Florence 佛罗伦萨 (意大利城市)
12. Medici family 美第奇家族,或译为梅第奇家族、梅迪契家族(佛罗伦萨13世纪到17世纪时期拥有强大势力的家族)
13. Cosimo de Medici 科西莫·美第奇
14. Lorenzo Medici 洛伦佐·美第奇

## After You Read

### Knowledge Focus

**1. Fill in the blanks with what you have read in the text. The first letter of the word is already given.**

  *a. The Dawn of A New Age*

   The Renaissance is the "r_____" of Europe, a period when scholars became more interested in studying the world around them, when art became more l_____, and when Europeans began to e_____ new lands. Arab s_____ preserved the writings of the ancient G_____ in their libraries. When t_____ from cities in northern Italy came into contact with Arabians, they exchanged i_____ as well as goods. Many Christian scholars moved to Italy from Greece after the Byzantine Empire fell to the T_____ in 1453.

   The Renaissance influenced p_____, sculpture, and a_____. Painting became more realistic and focused less often on r_____ topics. Rich families became p_____ by commissioning great arts. Artists advanced the Renaissance style of showing n_____ and depicting the f_____ of people.

### b. Humanism

Many Renaissance scholars were inspired by the c_____, the works of the ancient Greeks and Romans. Roman e_____ and Christian priests kept order in Europe for more than a millennium, but the scholars found a spirit in the ancient texts that valued i_____.

People who studied the classics were known as h_____. Humanists recreated ancient Greek and Roman styles in art, l_____, and architecture. Humanists believed they could understand people and the world better through an u_____ of the classics. The humanists emphasized the importance of s_____, or non-religious values, which often put them at odds with the c_____.

### c. Gutenberg

Johannes Gutenberg was a G_____ goldsmith who invented the p_____ press, a machine that allowed him m_____-produce written material. Gutenberg did not make any money for his invention because p_____ did not exist, so anyone could build a printing press without c_____ Gutenberg for his inspiration.

Gutenberg had not really invented anything. His genius was to combine or improve elements that already existed. B_____ printing had been invented by the Chinese more than f_____ centuries before the printing press, but Gutenberg used separate, movable blocks for each c_____ instead of a single wood-carved block for an entire page. The Egyptians and Chinese created i_____ from the soot of fires and mixed it with s_____. Later civilizations used p_____ material to generate ink, particularly the dark blue i_____ plant. Gutenberg improved on this by using an o_____ based ink.

Gutenberg's printing press was successful despite the o_____ of some government and religious leaders, who feared the invention would spread subversive i_____. By 1500, Gutenberg's inspiration spawned the printing press throughout Europe.

### d. City-states in Italy

The Renaissance began in trading cities in the northern part of the Italian p_____. Genoa, V_____, Pisa, and Florence were centers of power and wealth that became the c_____ of the Renaissance. Venice is a city of i_____ on the northeastern edge of the peninsula. The primary industry in Venice and Genoa during the Renaissance was s_____. Florence and Pisa p_____ because of the wool industry.

Wealthy m_____ in the Italian cities became patrons of the arts. They hired a_____ to fill their homes with beautiful paintings and s_____. They p_____ rare books and paid scholars to teach. The money and encouragement of the p_____, together with that of the c_____, made the masterpieces of Renaissance art possible.

**2. Discuss the following questions with your partner.**

(1) What does the Renaissance refer to? What is the meaning of the word "renaissance"?

(2) Where did the Renaissance begin? Why did it start there?
(3) Why did learning and the arts begin to flourish during the Renaissance?
(4) What is humanism? What did humanists in the Renaissance emphasize?
(5) Who is Johannes Gutenberg? What was his major achievement?
(6) What cities became the cradle of the Renaissance? Describe what you know about these cities.
(7) How did the Medici family influence the development of Florence?
(8) What social classes were found in the Renaissance Florence?

*Language Focus*
**1. Match the word in Column A with its corresponding meaning in Column B.**

| Column A | | Column B |
|---|---|---|
| (1) patron | (a) | an official right to be the only person or company allowed to make or sell a new product for a certain period of time |
| (2) secular | (b) | deep blue dye |
| (3) clergy | (c) | to force someone to leave their country, especially for political reasons |
| (4) goldsmith | (d) | a person who gives money or other support to a person, cause or activity |
| (5) patent | (e) | someone who sails on the seas, attacking other boats and stealing things from them |
| (6) indigo | (f) | someone who makes or sells things made from gold |
| (7) exile | (g) | the job or activity of recording the financial accounts of an organization |
| (8) pirate | (h) | to run fast (esp. of a horse) |
| (9) bookkeeping | (i) | not concerned with spiritual or religious affairs |
| (10) gallop | (j) | the official leaders of religious activities in organized religions |

**2. Fill in the blanks with the following words or expressions you have learned in the text.**

| amass | devout | at odds with | compensate | denounce |
| in charge | raid | withhold | alliance | discharge |

(1) The sanitation department is _____ of garbage disposal.
(2) I had expected to become more _____ as I grow older but somehow I haven't.
(3) Some of his colleagues envy the enormous wealth that he _____.
(4) The commandos carried out a daring _____ on the enemy.
(5) He is always _____ his father over politics.
(6) Patients were _____ from the hospital because the beds were needed by other people.
(7) The three smaller parties have forged a/an _____ against the government.

(8) We must _____ injustice and oppression.

(9) The prosecution was accused of _____ crucial evidence from the defense.

(10) She used her good looks to _____ for her lack of intelligence.

3. Fill in the blanks with the proper form of the word in the brackets.

(1) The Elizabethan age was a time of _____ (explore) and discovery.

(2) A suitable relative humidity is important for the _____ (preserve) of furniture.

(3) The politician was appointed as the Minister of _____ (financial).

(4) The _____ (allot) of direct taxes is decided on the basis of the state population.

(5) Running away is our _____ (instinct) reaction when we meet danger.

(6) You couldn't help but be aware of the _____ (peculiar) of the situation.

(7) She was an imaginative and _____ (innovation) manager.

(8) His best music was _____ (inspiration) by the memory of his mother.

(9) At no time has the country been more _____ (prosper) than at present.

(10) It was clear that they had not acted in _____ (violate) of the rules.

4. Fill in the blanks with the proper prepositions or adverbs that collocate with the neighboring words.

(1) I refuse to trade _____ that store ever again; they keep cheating us on the bill!

(2) Many people are looking _____ the new government to reduce unemployment.

(3) Their house is similar _____ ours, but ours has a bigger garden.

(4) This action is greatly _____ odds with his previous attitude.

(5) You are much more likely to get rich _____ hard work than _____ a lucky win.

(6) They could not settle _____ where to spend the holiday.

(7) The government imposed a heavy tax _____ luxury goods.

(8) The hall was filled _____ choking clouds of smoke.

(9) Many parents want their daughters to marry _____ a good family.

(10) The wretched peasant who has just died is better _____ than I am.

5. Error Correction: Each of the following sentences has at least one grammatical error. Identify the errors and correct them.

(1) Renaissance is a French word means "rebirth".

(2) The Renaissance was much more than simply study the work of ancient scholars. It influenced painting, sculpture, and architecture. Paintings became more realistic and focused little often on religious topics.

(3) In the works of the classics, they found a spirit similar to their that valued innovation in this world rather than look forward to the next world after death.

(4) As a good cook, Johannes Gutenberg took that had already been discovered, and created a small invention that changed history.

(5) Gutenberg used an oil-based printing ink that would last longer than any other inks used in his time.

(6) To this day, more copy of the *Bible* have been printed than any other books.

(7) The city became rich in collecting taxes on all merchandise bringing into its harbor.

(8) Along with the vast wealth from trade, many of the leading families of Venice competed with one others to build the finest palaces or support the work of the greatest artists.

(9) The people of Renaissance Florence, like most city-states of the era, composed of four social classes.

(10) Difficult although their lives were, however, the urban workers were better off than the peasants who lived in rural areas.

(11) Workers who violated rules could have their wages withhold or could discharge from their jobs.

## Comprehensive Work

### 1. Venice vs. Florence

Venice and Florence were among the most famous Italian cities in the Renaissance period. Please present the similarities and differences between the two cities according to what you have read in the text.

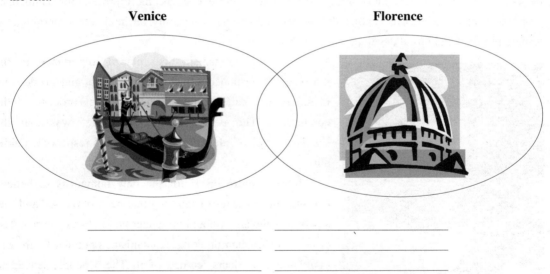

### 2. Writing

Choose one of the following topics. Write a paragraph of about 200 words to explain your answer to the question.

(1) Do you agree or disagree with the quote, "To each species of creature has been allotted a peculiar and instinctive gift. To horses galloping, to birds flying, comes naturally. To man only is given the desire to learn"? Defend your answer.

(2) Do you think art and music should be free and available to everyone, or should inventors like Gutenberg be compensated for their inspiration? Defend your answer.

### Read More

### Text B  Humanism of the Renaissance

Humanism (the philosophy that people are rational beings) became quite popular during the Renaissance. The dignity and worth of the individual were emphasized. This movement originated with the study of classical culture and a group of subjects known collectively as the "the humanities".

Humanism and the humanities disciplines included studies in speaking, grammar, poetry, ethics and history. The humanist preference was to study them as much as possible in their original classical texts (mostly Latin). The more traditional educational approach was that of scholasticism, which concentrates on logic, natural science and metaphysics.

The scholars from each philosophy often clashed with each other. The more traditional scholastic training prepared students to become doctors, lawyers and theologians. The new humanism believed that the focus on education should be broader and encompass more professions. Humanists proposed a more rounded education that placed the emphasis not only on intellectual learning, but also on physical and moral development.

This new humanism also placed importance in the individual's responsibilities of citizenship and leadership, including the participation in the political process in the community. The general humanism belief was that the scholastic type of education did not instill a respect for public duty.

It was controversial for the new humanists to believe that the ancient ways of thinking had been outgrown and that a person's thoughts should no longer be of abstract speculation or rely on Christian thinking. Humanism's popularity grew as more urban residents learned of it. These people tended to object to the traditional education system that was monopolized by the clergy and effectively excluded them. They could see that the new humanism could include them.

Humanism relied on flexible thinking and being open to all of the possibilities of life and less concerned with the thinking of the past (antiquity).

Francesco Petrarca (commonly known now as Petrarch) was born in 1304 near Florence and is known as the first great humanist. He was raised in Italy but traveled widely collecting ancient texts. One can see the urban emphasis in his teachings and his emphasis on the experiences of daily life like climbing mountains or traveling.

Petrarch was pulled between two worlds, the ideal world of antiquity and his desire to improve the current world. He believed he could learn to make the world a better place by studying classical literature. He, along with other humanists, admired the formal beauty of classical writing. He attempted to share the teachings of classical texts by studying them, and then, imitating them in Latin writings of his own.

After Petrarch, the humanist philosophy spread first through Italy, then into other parts of Europe. During the mid to late 14th century, a number of scholars in Florence followed Petrarch's lead and collected and studied ancient works. They lectured about them, imitated the style of the ancient works and the city of Florence became a center of humanistic learning.

As the movement grew, some extremist emerged. For the most part, humanists became experts in rhetoric and some town governments would frequently employ them to give humanistic style to their formal documents and to write official histories. Some of these humanists went to the extreme and became so pretentious and artificial that they would lose sight of their true objective and concentrate solely on the technique and detail of their work. Some of the extreme humanists had honed their style to such a pureness that they would only employ words used by the ancient Roman orator Cicero. It was this type of extremist humanists that caused some to accuse the humanists of being a frivolous pursuit. The detractors even accused the humanists of killing the Latin language by making it so isolated from their everyday life that it excluded everyone except the humanists themselves.

Other humanists used their study of classical writing to approach the world of politics. Florence had many humanists, led by historian Leonardo Bruni, become extremely patriotic. This was during a time when they were frequently attacked by Milan, a rival city-state. They applied classical teachings and used them to help solve their current problems. They found in the ancient Roman literature a love of country and then applied the patriotism to their current problems.

Some of the humanists broke from tradition and applied classical literature standards to their own language in everyday writing. This is the foundation for literary development in non-Latin writings and their intense patriotism allowed them to write about the city's history. Today, this gives us a modern historical perspective.

The study of texts was expanded by some humanists, during the 15th century, to include Greek. For the first time, Greek texts were read in the original language of Western Europe. The inclusion of Greek texts opened up new ideas for the humanists. One of the outcomes is the more precise understanding of Greek philosophy.

There was one Greek philosopher, Plato, who increasingly gained respect among the new humanists. A close follower of Plato was Marsilio Ficino, who persuaded the Florentine Academy, during the late 15th century, to take a more serious study of all of Plato's works. Ficino hoped that Plato would be the guide for new Western humanists thought, like Plato's student Aristotle had been for the traditional scholastic thinkers.

### Questions for Reflection

1. What is humanism? What does it emphasize?
2. What curriculum was included in the study of humanism? How did it differ from the traditional educational approach of scholasticism?
3. Who was the first great humanist? Why was he "pulled between two worlds"?
4. Which ancient philosopher was highly respected by new humanists? Why did the new humanists study his works?

### Text C  Johannes Gutenberg

Johannes Gutenberg (c. 1398 – 1468), German printer, is supposed to have been born in 1398 or 1399 at Mainz of well-to-do parents, his father being Friele zum Gensfleisch and his mother Elsgen Wyrich, whose birthplace "Gutenberg", was the name he adopted. The Germans, and most other people, contend that Gutenberg was the inventor of the art of printing with movable types.

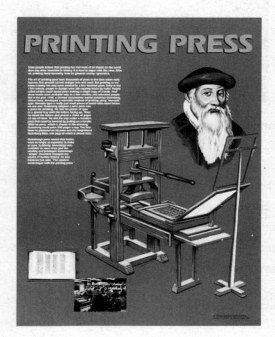

Gutenberg's father was a man of good family. Very likely the boy was taught to read. But the books from which he learned were not like ours; they were written by hand. A better name for them than books is "manuscripts", which means "hand-writings".

While Gutenberg was growing up, a new way of making books came into use, which was a great deal better than copying by hand. It was what is called block-printing. The printer first cut a block of hardwood the size of the page that he was going to print. Then he cut out every word of the written page upon the smooth face of his block. This had to be very carefully done. When it was finished the printer had to cut away the wood from the sides of every letter. This left the letters raised, as the letters are in books now printed for the blind. The block was now ready to be used. The letters were inked, paper was laid upon them and pressed down. With blocks, the printer could make copies of a book a great deal faster than a man could write them by hand. But the making of the blocks took a long time, and each block would print only one page.

Gutenberg enjoyed reading the manuscripts and block books that his parents and their wealthy friends had, and he often said it was a pity that only rich people could own books. Finally, he determined to contrive some easy and quick way of printing. Gutenberg did a great deal of his work in secret, for he thought it was much better that his neighbors should know nothing of what he was doing. He looked for a workshop where no one would be likely to find him. Gutenberg was now living in Strasbourg, and there was in that city a ruined old building where, long before his time, a number of monks had lived. There was one room of the building which needed only a little repair to make it fit to be used. So Gutenberg got the right to repair that room and use it as his workshop.

All his neighbors wondered what became of him when he left home in the early morning, and where he had been when they saw him coming back late in the twilight. Gutenberg did not care much what people had to say, and in his quiet room he patiently tried one experiment after another, often feeling very sad and discouraged day after day because his experiments did not succeed. At last, the time came when he had no money left.

He went back to his old home, Mainz, and there met a rich goldsmith and lawyer named Johann Fust (or Faust). Gutenberg told him how hard he had tried in Strasbourg to find some way of making books cheaply, and how he had now no more money to carry on his experiments. Fust became greatly interested and gave Gutenberg what money he needed.

First of all, it is thought that he made types of hardwood. Each type was a little block with a single letter at one end. Such types were a great deal better than block letters. The block letters were fixed. They could not be taken out of the words of which they were parts. The new types were movable so they could be set up to print one page, then taken apart and set up again and again to print any number of pages. But type made of wood did not always print the letters clearly and distinctly, so Gutenberg gave up wood types and tried metal types. This worked much better, and Gutenberg was progressing well toward the completion of the first book ever printed by movable type: the *Bible* in Latin.

Fust, however, was losing patience. He quarreled with Gutenberg and said that he was doing nothing but spending money. At last, he brought suit against him in the court, and the judge decided in favor of Fust. So everything in the world that Gutenberg had, even the tools with which he worked, came into Fust's possession.

Soon a Latin *Bible* was printed. It was in two volumes, each of which had three hundred pages, while each of the pages had forty-two lines. The letters were sharp and clear. They had been printed from movable types of metal. The news that books were being printed in Mainz went all over Europe. Before Gutenberg died, printing-presses like his were at work making books in all the great cities of the continent.

Between 1450 and 1455, the Gutenberg *Bible* was completed. Early documentation states that a total of 200 copies were scheduled to be printed on rag cotton linen paper, and 30 copies on velum animal skin. It is not known exactly how many copies were actually printed. Today, only 22 copies are known to exist, of which 7 are on velum.

If an entire Gutenberg *Bible* should become available on the world market, it would likely fetch an estimated 100 million dollars! Even an individual leaf (a single two-sided page) from the original Gutenberg *Bible* can fetch around $100,000. Gutenberg's work is the rarest and most valuable printed material in the world.

Johannes Gutenberg died in Mainz, Germany in 1468. Ironically, the inventor of the most important invention in history never profited from his invention and died in poverty, though the proceeds from the sale of just one single leaf from his *Bible* in today's market would have provided Gutenberg with enough money to live out his last years comfortably. He was buried in a Franciscan church, which was demolished and replaced with another church, which was also subsequently demolished. While Gutenberg sadly went without reward for producing the machine that changed the world, history recognizes him as holding this honor. Without his invention, the Protestant Reformation would not have been possible.

## *Questions for Reflection*

1. What kind of printing was used when Gutenberg was still a boy?
2. What happened when Gutenberg met Johann Fust?
3. What is the Gutenberg *Bible*? What do you know about it?
4. How did Gutenberg die?

## *Website to Visit*

http://www.history.com/topics/renaissance/renaissance (accessed Apr. 28, 2020)
This website offers a comprehensive study to almost all aspects of the Renaissance.

**Movie to Watch**

### Shakespeare in Love (1998)

*Shakespeare in Love* is a romantic comedy set in London in the late 16th century: Young playwright William Shakespeare struggles with his latest work *Romeo and Ethel, the Pirate's Daughter*. A great fan of Shakespeare's plays is the young, wealthy Viola who is about to be married to the cold-hearted Lord Wessex, but constantly dreams of becoming an actress. Women were not allowed to act on stage at that time (female roles were played by men, too), but dressed up as a boy, Viola successfully auditions for the part of Romeo. Soon she and William are caught in a forbidden romance that provides rich inspiration for his play.

The film won several of Academy Awards in 1999, including Best Picture, Best Actress (for Gwyneth Paltrow) and Best Supporting Actress (for Judi Dench).

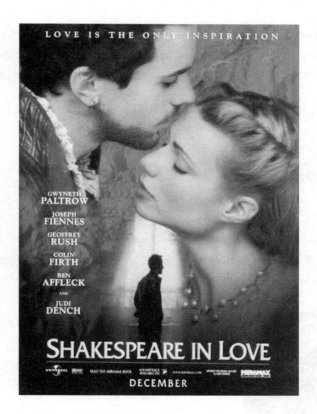

# Unit 8
## High Renaissance

> I have been impressed with the urgency of doing. Knowing is not enough; we must apply. Being willing is not enough; we must do.
> 
> —Leonardo da Vinci

### Unit Goals

- To be acquainted with Renaissance artists and their masterpieces
- To have a general understanding of the cultural legacy left by Renaissance artists
- To learn the useful words and expressions that describe Renaissance artists and their works
- To improve language skills by learning this unit

### Before You Read

**1. The Most Mysterious Woman in the World**

The woman in the following painting is regarded as one of the most mysterious women in the world. What do you know about her?

(1) What is the name of the painting?
_____

(2) Do you know anything concerning the identity/story of the woman in the painting?
_____

(3) Who is the author of the painting?
_____

(4) Have you ever read/heard of any mysteries related to the painting?
_____

## 2. William Shakespeare

William Shakespeare is widely regarded as the greatest playwright in the English language and the world's preeminent dramatist. Have you ever read any of William Shakespeare's plays? Complete the following form with what you know.

| William Shakespeare's Plays ||| 
|---|---|---|
| **Comedy** | **Tragedy** | **Historical Play** |
|  |  |  |
|  |  |  |
|  |  |  |
|  |  |  |

3. Form groups of three or four students. Try to find, on the Internet or in the library, more information about Renaissance art. Choose a topic that interests you most and prepare a five-minute classroom presentation.

## Start to Read

### Text A  Renaissance Art and Artists

Renaissance art is more lifelike than the art of the Middle Ages. The Renaissance patrons wanted art that showed joy in human beauty and life's pleasures. Artists studied perspective, or the differences in the way things look when they are close to something or far away. They painted in a way that showed these differences. As a result, their paintings seem to have depth.

The tradition of the Renaissance art has the following distinct features:

(1) Art broke away from the domination of the church. Artists who used to be craftsmen commissioned by the church to paint the design became a separate stratum like writers and poets doing noble and creative work.

(2) Themes of paintings changed from purely celestial realm focusing on the stories of the *Bible*, of God, Jesus and Mary to an appreciation of all aspects of nature and man. Even when the themes remained celestial, the heroes were given human qualities and given muscles and sinews of man. With the growth of cities and towns, they were asked to paint for fronts of private palaces, walls to perpetuate the glory and fame of notable people.

(3) The artists studied the ruins of Roman and Greek temples and put many of the principles of ancient civilization into their works. They began to be supported by individual collectors.

(4) Artists introduced in their works scientific theories of anatomy and perspective.

## Renaissance Artists

An artist from Florence named Giotto was one of the first to paint in this new style. Giotto lived more than a century before the beginning of the Renaissance, but his paintings show real emotion. The bodies look solid, and the background of his paintings shows perspective. The art produced during the Renaissance would build upon Giotto's style.

Perhaps the greatest of the Florentine artists was Leonardo da Vinci (1452 – 1519), one of the most versatile geniuses who ever lived. He was born in 1452 in the village of Vinci. His name means Leonardo of Vinci.

Leonardo personified the "Renaissance Man": he was a painter, architect, musician, mathematician, engineer, and inventor. He made notes and drawings of everything he saw. He invented a unique writing style—mirror writing—to record his secrets. He also invented clever machines, and even designed imitation wings that he hoped would let a person fly like a bird.

The illegitimate son of a notary and a peasant woman, Leonardo set up an artist's shop in Florence by the time he was twenty-five and gained the patronage of the Medici ruler of the city, Lorenzo the Magnificent. But if Leonardo had any weakness, it was his slowness in working and difficulty in finishing anything. This naturally displeased Lorenzo and other Florentine patrons, who thought an artist was little more than an artisan, commissioned to produce a certain piece of work of a certain size for a certain price on a certain date. Leonardo, however, strongly objected to this view because he considered himself to be no menial craftsman but an inspired creator. Therefore, in 1482 he left Florence for Milan where he was given freer rein in structuring his time and work.

The paintings of Leonardo da Vinci began what is known as High Renaissance in Italy. His approach to painting was that it should be the most accurate possible imitation of nature. Leonardo was like a naturalist, basing his work on his own detailed observations of a blade of grass, the wing of a bird, a waterfall. He obtained human corpses for dissection and reconstructed in drawing the minutest features of anatomy, the knowledge he carried over to his paintings. Leonardo worshiped nature, and was convinced of the essential divinity in all living things.

It is generally agreed that Leonardo's masterpieces are *The Virgin of the Rocks*, *The Last Supper*, and his portraits of *Mona Lisa* and *Ginevra da Benci*. *The Virgin of the Rocks* typifies not only his marvelous technical skill but also his passion for science and his belief in the universe as a well-ordered place. The figures are arranged geometrically, with every rock and plant depicted in accurate detail. *The Last Supper* is a study of psychological reactions. A serene Christ, resigned to his terrible fate, has just announced to his disciples that one of them will betray him. The artist succeeds in portraying the mingled emotions of surprise, horror, and guilt in the faces of the disciples as they gradually perceive the  meaning of their master's statement. The third and fourth of Leonardo's major triumphs, *Mona Lisa* and *Ginevra da Benci*, reflect a similar interest in the varied moods of the human soul.

Michelangelo Buonarroti of Florence was one of the greatest artists of all time. Like Leonardo, Michelangelo was a "Renaissance Man" of many talents. He was a sculptor, a painter, and an architect. When Michelangelo carved a statue of Moses, he included veins and muscles in the arms and legs.

Michelangelo was a devout Christian, and the church was his greatest patron. He designed the dome of St. Peter's Church in Rome. Nearby, Michelangelo's paintings cover the ceiling of the Sistine Chapel, the building where new popes have been selected for more than five hundred years. Michelangelo's painting illustrates the "Book of Genesis", with scenes that span from the Creation to the Flood. The project was very difficult. Working alone, Michelangelo had to lie on his back atop high scaffolding while he painted the vast ceiling.

Niccolo Machiavelli was one of the most influential writers of the Renaissance. He believed Italy could not be united unless its leader was ruthless. In 1513, he wrote *The Prince*, where he advised rulers to be kind only if it suited their purposes. Otherwise, he warned, it is better to be feared than loved.

> You must know there are two methods of fighting, the one by law, the other by force; the first method is of men, the second of beasts; but because the first is frequently not sufficient, one must have recourse to the second. Therefore it is necessary for a prince to understand how to use the methods of the beast and the man...
>
> A prince... ought to choose the fox and the lion; because the lion cannot defend himself against traps and the fox cannot defend himself against wolves. Therefore, it is necessary to be a fox to discover the traps and a lion to terrify the wolves. Those who rely simply on the lion do not understand this.
>
> —Niccolo Machiavelli, *The Prince* (1513)

**The Renaissance Spreads**

The rebirth of the Italian cities attracted visitors from all over Western Europe. Merchants and bankers hoped to make their fortunes in the Italian city-states. Artists and students sought knowledge and fame. When these travelers returned home, they brought Renaissance ideas with them. In time, the ideas of the Renaissance influenced people far from the Italian peninsula.

William Shakespeare is the best-known writer of the Renaissance. His plays mixed humor with drama, and showed the strengths and weaknesses of people. Audiences flocked to see his presentations of Roman emperors, British kings and queens, and Italian teenagers.

Pieter Bruegel was a Dutch painter who wanted to show people as they really were. Bruegel studied Italian art, but he developed his own style. Many of his paintings show peasants working, dancing, and eating.

The Renaissance created a culture which freed man to discover and enjoy the world in a way not possible under the medieval Church's dispensation. In this release lay the way of development of the modern world.

## Proper Nouns

1. perspective 透视画法
2. Giotto 乔托(文艺复兴时期意大利画家)
3. Leonardo da Vinci 列奥纳多·达·芬奇(文艺复兴时期画家)
4. *The Virgin of the Rocks*《岩间圣母》(达·芬奇代表画作之一)
5. *The Last Supper*《最后的晚餐》(达·芬奇代表画作之一)
6. *Mona Lisa*《蒙娜丽莎》(达·芬奇代表画作之一)
7. *Ginevra da Benci*《瓦本齐肖像》(达·芬奇代表画作之一)
8. Michelangelo Buonarroti 米开朗基罗·勃那罗蒂(文艺复兴时期画家、雕塑家)
9. Sistine Chapel 西斯廷教堂
10. "Book of Genesis"《圣经》中的《创世记》
11. Niccolo Machiavelli 尼科诺·马基雅维利(文艺复兴时期意大利政治家和诗人,是西方近代政治学说的奠基者)
12. Pieter Bruegel 皮耶特·布鲁格尔(也称老布鲁格尔,16世纪荷兰画家)

# After You Read

*Knowledge Focus*

**1. Match each fact below to its artist by writing an M or an L in each blank.**

M=Michelangelo　　　L=Leonardo da Vinci

(1) _____ He painted the Sistine Chapel.
(2) _____ He painted *Mona Lisa*.
(3) _____ He was known as the "Renaissance Man" because of his many skills.
(4) _____ He was interested in cutting up dead bodies to study anatomy.
(5) _____ Mirror writing kept his ideas a secret to others.
(6) _____ It took him several years to finish a painting while lying on his back.
(7) _____ He kept notebooks to record scientific observations.
(8) _____ He designed the dome of St. Peter's Church.
(9) _____ He painted *The Last Supper*.
(10) _____ He gained the patronage of the Medici ruler of the city.

**2. Fill in the blanks with what you have learned from the text.**

(1) Compared with the art of the Middle Ages, Renaissance art is more _____.
(2) _____ is the art of making some objects or people in a picture look further away than others.
(3) Themes of paintings in the Renaissance time changed from celestial realm to _____.
(4) _____ was one of the first artists to paint in the new Renaissance style.
(5) A Renaissance man is a person who _____. _____ and _____ are typical examples of the Renaissance man.
(6) Three of the most famous paintings by Leonardo da Vinci were _____, *Mona Lisa* and _____.
(7) _____ was famous for painting the ceiling of the Sistine Chapel.
(8) _____ was a Dutch painter who was good at showing peasant life in his paintings.

**3. Discuss the following questions with your partner.**

(1) How was Renaissance art different from the art of the Middle Ages?
(2) What were the themes of Renaissance art?
(3) What was the characteristic of Giotto's painting?
(4) Why was Leonardo da Vinci regarded as a "Renaissance Man"?
(5) What were the features of Leonardo da Vinci's paintings?
(6) What was Michelangelo famous for? Was he also a "Renaissance Man"?
(7) Who was Machiavelli? What was his major political view?
(8) What is the influence of Renaissance culture?

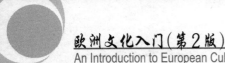

## Language Focus

**1. Fill in the blanks with the following words or expressions you have learned in the text.**

| perspective | commission | immensity | disown | personify |
|---|---|---|---|---|
| object | minute (a.) | flock (v.) | ruthless | resign |

(1) At sixteen, I was _____ to the fact that I'd never be a dancer.
(2) Justice is often _____ as a blindfolded woman holding a pair of scales.
(3) She is _____ to write a symphony.
(4) She showed a _____ determination to succeed in her career.
(5) The documentary showed an eye operation in _____ detail.
(6) _____ is the art of making some objects or people in a picture look further away than others.
(7) The business is conducted on a scale of unprecedented _____.
(8) Crowds of people _____ to see the Picasso exhibition.
(9) He _____ to the label "magician" which he is often given.
(10) It is a story set in the last century about a girl whose parents _____ her when she married a foreigner.

**2. Fill in the blanks with the proper form of the word in the brackets.**

(1) The writing of poems, stories or plays is often called _____ (create) writing.
(2) Children rarely show any _____ (appreciate) for what their parents do for them.
(3) The stamp _____ (collect) decided to get that rare stamp at all costs.
(4) An expert was needed to authenticate the original Vincent van Gogh painting from his _____ (imitate).
(5) There could be some _____ (psychology) explanation for his bad health.
(6) I felt a sense of _____ (betray) when my friends refused to support me.
(7) He is eminent both as a _____ (sculpture) and as a portrait painter.
(8) He used his _____ (influence) friends to help him get into the civil service.
(9) I'm taking four hundred pounds' worth of travelers' cheques—I think that should _____ (sufficient).
(10) She is the most _____ (progress) writer of the time.

**3. Fill in the blanks with the proper prepositions or adverbs that collocate with the neighboring words.**

(1) You should dress _____ a way that befits a woman of your position.
(2) He was late _____ a result of the heavy snow.
(3) You'd better not build your hopes _____ castles in the air.
(4) He tried to convince them _____ the safety of traveling by airplane.
(5) Hard work is the name of the game if you want to succeed _____ business.
(6) They have the ability to defend _____ hostile actions in outer space.

4. **Error Correction: Each of the following sentences has at least one grammatical error. Identify the errors and correct them.**

(1) Renaissance art is more lifelike than the Middle Ages.

(2) Artists who used to be craftsmen commissioning by the church to paint the design became a separate stratum like writers and poets doing noble.

(3) Even the themes remained celestial, the heroes were given human qualities and given muscles and sinews of man.

(4) Perhaps the great of the Florentine artists was Leonardo da Vinci, one of the versatilest geniuses who ever lived.

(5) But Leonardo had any weakness, it was his slowness in working and difficulty in finishing anything.

(6) Leonardo, strongly objected to this view because he considered himself to be no menial craftsman and an inspired creator.

(7) The paintings of Leonardo da Vinci began that is known as High Renaissance in Italy.

(8) The artist succeeds to portray the mingled emotions of surprise, horror, and guilt in the faces of the disciples.

(9) Michelangelo's painting illustrates the "Book of Genesis", with scenes span from the Creation to the Flood.

(10) In time, the ideas of Renaissance influenced people far from Italian peninsula.

(11) His plays were mixed humor with drama showed the strengths and weaknesses of people.

(12) *The Virgin of the Rocks* typifies not only his marvelous technical skill and his passion for science and his belief in the universe as a well-ordered place.

## Comprehensive Work

### 1. Renaissance Man

Leonardo da Vinci and Michelangelo were both called "Renaissance Man" because they were talented in many different fields. Discuss the following questions about "Renaissance Man" with your partner.

(1) What talents did Leonardo da Vinci and Michelangelo have respectively? Please fill in the following form with what you know about them.

| Leonardo da Vinci | | Michelangelo | |
|---|---|---|---|
| Skilled in... | Evidence | Skilled in... | Evidence |
|  |  |  |  |
|  |  |  |  |
|  |  |  |  |

(2) Please nominate your own choice for "Renaissance Man/Woman" of today. Explain why.

| Renaissance Man/Woman of Today  | |
|---|---|
| **My nomination:** _____ | |
| **He/She is skilled in...** | **Evidence/Proof** |
|  |  |
|  |  |
|  |  |
|  |  |

(3) Writing

Please write a composition on the topic of "Renaissance Man/Woman of Today". Give reasons/evidence to support your opinion.

**2. Sharing Ideas: Machiavelli**

Niccolo Machiavelli was one of the most influential writers of the Renaissance. Discuss the following topics with your classmates.

(1) Do you agree with Machiavelli that it is more important for a ruler to be feared than loved? Explain why.

_____

(2) What is the dictionary definition of Machiavellian? Name a famous person who you think fits this description.

_____

(3) When is it appropriate for a ruler to be a fox, and when is it appropriate to be a lion? In other words, when is it important to use your physical strength, and when is it important to use your wits?

_____

Unit 8  High Renaissance

### Text B  Mystery behind the *Mona Lisa*

Every year, six million visitors from the world travel across continents to the Musée du Louvre in Paris to gaze in wonder at Leonardo da Vinci's famous portrait, the *Mona Lisa*. An oil painting on poplar wood, the portrait took da Vinci four years (1503 – 1506) to complete. For centuries afterward, his talent and ingenuity sparked several debates and a multitude of theories in a global effort to uncover the mysteries hidden behind the *Mona Lisa*'s smile.

**Who is Mona Lisa?**

Many questions arose over the years as to the true identity of the lady in the portrait. The Italians call her La Gioconda, which means "the light-hearted woman". The French version, La Joconde, carries a similar meaning, provoking many thoughts and theories about *Mona Lisa*'s smile.

One popular theory suggests that the lady is the Duchess of Milan, Isabella of Aragon. Da Vinci was the family painter for the Duke of Milan for 11 years and could very well have painted the Duchess as the *Mona Lisa*. Other researchers have stated that the painting could depict a mistress of Giuliano de Medici, who reigned in Florence from 1512 to 1516. A more recent thought by Dr. Lillian Schwartz of Bell Labs is that the *Mona Lisa* is the feminine version of da Vinci himself. Through digital analysis, she discovered that da Vinci's facial characteristics and those of the *Mona Lisa* are perfectly aligned with one another.

Despite the above theories, it is currently widely accepted that the portrait depicts Lisa Gherardini, the third wife of a wealthy Florentine silk merchant named Francesco del Giocondo. In fact, the title Mona Lisa is discussed in da Vinci's biography, written and published by Giorgio Vasari in 1550. Vasari pointed out that Mona is commonly used in place of the Italian word Madonna, which could be translated into English as "Madam". Hence, the title Mona Lisa simply means "Madam Lisa".

**How does she smile?**

Mona Lisa's enigmatic smile has been the source of inspiration for many and a cause for desperation in others. In 1852, Luc Maspero, a French artist, jumped four floors to his death from a hotel room in Paris. His suicide note explained that he preferred death after years of struggling to understand the mystery behind Mona Lisa's smile. Today, visitors to the Musée du Louvre grapple with the same question: how does she smile?

Italians respond to this query by referring to a painting technique called sfumato, which was developed by da Vinci. In Italian, sfumato means "vanished" or "smoky", implying that the portrait is ambiguous and blurry, leaving its interpretation to the viewers' imagination. This technique uses a subtle blend of tones and colors to produce the illusion of form, depth, and volume.

Dr. Margaret Livingstone, a neuroscientist at Harvard, explains that the human eyes consist of two regions—the fovea, or central area, and the surrounding peripheral area. The fovea recognizes details and colors and reads the fine print, while the peripheral area identifies shadows, black and white, and motion. When a person looks at the *Mona Lisa*, the fovea focuses on her eyes, leaving the peripheral area on her mouth. Since peripheral vision is less accurate and does not pick up details, the shadows in Mona Lisa's cheekbones augment the curvature of her smile.

**Questions for Reflection**
1. What are the controversies concerning the identity of Mona Lisa?
2. Why did Luc Maspero, a French artist, jumped four floors to his death from a hotel room in Paris?
3. What is "sfumato"?
4. How does Dr. Livingstone explain the mysterious smile of Mona Lisa?

### Text C  William Shakespeare

William Shakespeare was born on April 23, 1564, in Stratford-on-Avon. The son of John Shakespeare and Mary Arden, he was probably educated at the King Edward IV Grammar School in Stratford, where he learned Latin and a little Greek and read the Roman dramatists. At eighteen, he married Anne Hathaway, a woman seven or eight years his senior. Together they raised two daughters: Susanna, who was born in 1583, and Judith (whose twin brother died in boyhood), born in 1585.

Little is known about Shakespeare's activities between 1585 and 1592. Robert Greene's *A Groatsworth of Wit* alludes to him as an actor and playwright. Shakespeare may have taught at school during this period, but it seems more probable that shortly after 1585 he went to London to begin his apprenticeship as an actor. Due to the plague, the London theaters were often closed between June 1592 and April 1594. During that period, Shakespeare probably had some income from his patron, Henry Wriothesley, earl of Southampton, to whom he dedicated his first two poems, "Venus and Adonis" (1593) and "The Rape of Lucrece" (1594). The former was a long narrative poem depicting the rejection of Venus by Adonis, his death, and the consequent disappearance of beauty from the world. Despite conservative objections to the poem's glorification of sensuality, it was immensely popular and was reprinted six times during the nine years following its publication.

In 1594, Shakespeare joined the Lord Chamberlain's company of actors, the most popular of the companies acting at Court. In 1599, Shakespeare joined a group of Chamberlain's Men that would form a syndicate to build and operate a new playhouse: the Globe, which became the most famous theater of its time. With his share of the income from the Globe, Shakespeare was able to purchase New Place, his home in Stratford.

While Shakespeare was regarded as the foremost dramatist of his time, evidence indicates that both he and his world looked to poetry, not playwriting, for enduring fame. Shakespeare's sonnets were composed between 1593 and 1601, though not published until 1609. That edition, *The Sonnets* of Shakespeare, consists of 154 sonnets, all written in the form of three quatrains and a couplet that is now recognized as Shakespearean. The sonnets fall into two groups: sonnets 1—126, addressed to a beloved friend, a handsome and noble young man, and sonnets 127—152, to a malignant but fascinating "Dark Lady", whom the poet loves in spite of himself. Nearly all of Shakespeare's sonnets examine the inevitable decay of time, and the immortalization of beauty and love in poetry.

In his poems and plays, Shakespeare invented thousands of words, often combining or contorting Latin, French and native roots. His impressive expansion of the English language, according to the *Oxford English Dictionary*, includes such words as: arch-villain, birthplace, bloodsucking, courtship, dewdrop, downstairs, fanged, heartsore, hunchbacked, leapfrog, misquote, pageantry, radiance, schoolboy, stillborn, watchdog, and zany.

Shakespeare wrote more than 30 plays. These are usually divided into four categories: histories, comedies, tragedies, and romances. His earliest plays were primarily comedies and histories such as *Henry VI* and *The Comedy of Errors*, but in 1596, Shakespeare wrote *Romeo and Juliet*, his second tragedy, and over the next dozen years he would return to the form, writing the plays for which he is now best known: *Julius Caesar, Hamlet, Othello, King Lear, Macbeth,* and *Antony and Cleopatra*. In his final years, Shakespeare turned to the romantic with Cymbeline, *A Winter's Tale,* and *The Tempest*.

Only eighteen of Shakespeare's plays were published separately in quarto editions during his lifetime; a complete collection of his works did not appear until the publication of the *First Folio* in 1623, several years after his death. Nonetheless, his contemporaries recognized Shakespeare's achievements. Francis Meres cited "honey-tongued" Shakespeare for his plays and poems in 1598, and the Chamberlain's Men rose to become the leading dramatic company in London, installed as members of the royal household in 1603.

Sometime after 1612, Shakespeare retired from the stage and returned to his home in Stratford. He drew up his will in January of 1616, which included his famous bequest to his wife of his "second best bed". He died on April 23, 1616, and was buried two days later at Stratford Church.

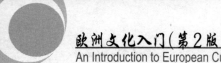

*Questions for Reflection*

Please make a timeline of Shakespeare's life according to what you read in the passage.

| A Chronological Timeline of Shakespeare's Life ||
|---|---|
| Year | Event |
| 1564 | |
| | He went to London to begin his apprenticeship as an actor. |
| 1593 | |
| 1594 | |
| | He wrote *Romeo and Juliet*. |
| 1612 | |
| 1616 | |

*Websites to Visit*

To know more about Leonardo da Vinci's paintings, please visit:
http://www.abcgallery.com/L/leonardo/leonardo.html (accessed Apr. 28, 2020)

For information concerning Shakespeare's plays, please visit:
http://shakespeare-online.com/plays/ (accessed Apr. 28, 2020)

For information about Michelangelo Buonarroti, please visit:
http://www.michelangelo.org/ (accessed Apr. 28, 2020)

*Movie to Watch*

### *The Da Vinci Code* (2006)

*The Da Vinci Code* is a 2006 feature film directed by Ron Howard, which is based on the bestselling 2003 novel *The Da Vinci Code* by Dan Brown.

Symbologist Robert Langdon is thrown into a mysterious and bizarre murder. Alongside Langon is the victim's granddaughter and cryptologist Sophie Neveu, who with Robert discovers clues within da Vinci's paintings. To further find the truth, Robert and Sophie travel from Paris to London, whilst crossing paths with allies and villains such as Sir Leigh Teabing and Silas. Wherever their path takes them, their discovery which is about to be revealed could shake the foundations of mankind.

# Unit 9
## The Reformation

> Reformation ends not in contemplation, but in action.
> —George Gillespie

### Unit Goals

- To understand how the Reformation and Counter-Reformation were carried out in Europe
- To be able to account for the influence of the Reformation on the European society
- To learn the useful words and expressions that describe the Reformation
- To improve language skills by learning this unit

### Before You Read

1. **Who is he?**
   Who is the man in the picture? What do you know about him?
   (1) Name
   
   _____
   
   (2) Title
   
   _____
   
   (3) Famous for
   
   _____
   
   (4) Something else you know about him
   
   _____

2. Form groups of three or four students. Try to find, on the Internet or in the library, more information about the Reformation. Choose a topic that interests you most and prepare a five-minute classroom presentation.

## Start to Read

### Text A  The European Reformation

The Reformation was a 16th century religious movement as well as a socio-political movement. It began as Martin Luther posted on the door of the castle church at the University of Wittenberg his *95 Theses*, inviting to debate on matters of practice and doctrine in the Church in 1517. This movement which swept over the whole of Europe was aimed at opposing the absolute authority of the Roman Catholic Church and replacing it with the absolute authority of the *Bible*. The reformers, priests, humanists and others denied that the church authorities and priests were the only authority in the interpretation of the *Bible* and believed in direct communication between the individual and God. To enable this direct communication, the reformists engaged themselves in translating the *Bible* into their mother tongues. The demands of the reformists also included that of simplifying rituals, abolishing heavy taxes levied on their countrymen and abolishing the indulgences, the centuries-old practice of paying money to replace the performance of the deed of penance.

The interests of the reformists covered a wide range, from wishing to see institutional reform of the Church, to making the *Bible* accessible to the common folks, to liberating national economy and politics from the interference of the Roman Catholic Church and carrying out wars in the interests of the peasants and revolution in the interests of the bourgeoisie.

**Martin Luther**

Martin Luther was the German leader of the Protestant Reformation. His doctrine marked the first break in the unity of the Catholic Church.

Martin Luther was a priest, a vicar and a professor of theology. His experiences in church matters and his study of the Scriptures led him to post on the door of the castle church at the University of Wittenberg his *95 Theses*, making open protests against the indulgences that had been in practice for centuries. He quoted the Scripture in support of his belief that men are redeemed by faith and not by the purchase of indulgences. This won sympathy among the exploited peasantry who had to yield a good part of their fruits of labor to the Church, as well as among the civil authorities who were forced to see their funds drained to the Roman Catholic Church for their worldly pleasures.

One of the doctrines of Martin Luther was that the *Bible* was the supreme authority and man was only bound to the law of the word of God, not the word of the clergy.

Before the Reformation, very few people in Europe read the *Bible*. Martin Luther, with his translation of the *New Testament* and later, the whole *Bible* into the vernacular, made the *Bible* accessible to every man, to the average churchgoer. This direct communication with God meant that the absolute control of the Catholic Church over the minds of the people was now losing ground. As Martin Luther declared that all believers were priests, so he preached that all occupations were holy, from the blacksmith at his forge to the potter at his wheel.

### Reformation in England

By the middle of the sixteenth century, all northern Europe was aroused in the Protestant Revolt. The ideas of Martin Luther had spread to as far as the Scandinavian kingdoms.

In England, there had been the influence of John Wycliffe. There also had been humanists who had talked freely of church reforms. On top of these was the fact that for four centuries in England there had been strong opposition to the Pope in Rome.

The split came when Henry VIII decided to ignore the authority of the Pope in his matrimonial affairs. Henry was first married to Catherine Aragon from Spain. She bored Henry several children but only one of them survived and this one was a daughter. Henry, however, desired to have a male heir and he asked the Pope for permission to divorce Catherine. Failing to obtain the approval of the Pope, Henry declared on his own that the marriage with Catherine invalid and married Anne Boleyn, Catherine's maid in waiting. When the Pope refused to recognize this marriage, British Parliament, in 1534, passed the *Act of Supremacy* which marked the formal break of the British with the papal authorities. The Parliament gave Henry an *Act of Succession*, recognizing the legality of the divorce and securing the Crown to Anne's children. On financial matters, it was made clear that revenues, instead of being paid to the Pope, would be paid to the crown. Above all, there was the establishment of the Church of England, or Anglican Church. The king, not the Pope, was now the head of the church.

Every English man was required to take the oath of Supremacy. Anybody who refused to do so would be charged with treason and subject to severe punishment. As for the church services, there were changes such as the use of English instead of Latin in the Lord's prayers and other parts of the service. And an English translation of the *Bible* was also adopted.

In England, therefore, the question of reform was not fundamentally one of belief or interpretation of the *Bible* but one of rejection of the supremacy of the Pope.

## Counter-Reformation

By late 1520, the Roman Catholic Church had lost its control over the church in Germany because the local church officials sided with the rebel princes in Germany. Meanwhile the movement against the Roman Catholic Church had swept over the whole of Europe, shaking the very foundation of the Roman Catholic Church.

The Roman Catholic Church did not stay idle. They mustered their forces, the dedicated Catholic groups, to examine the Church institutions and introduce reforms and improvements, to bring back its vitality. In time, the Roman Catholic Church did re-establish itself as a dynamic force in European affairs. This recovery of power is often called by historians the Counter-Reformation. The seed-bed for this Catholic Reformation was Spain with the Spanish monarchy establishing the Inquisition to carry out cruel suppression of heresy and unorthodoxy.

Faced with the growing threat, the papal authorities had to call a number of councils to introduce necessary reforms. Among them was the Council of Trent.

The sessions of the Council reaffirmed that the Church had the sole right to interpret the *Bible*. It was also stressed that Catholicism was a religion of infallible authority. There were such principles among the decrees as every bishop was required to take the oath of complete obedience to the Pope and reforms that were aimed at tightening the discipline of the clergy. The Catholic Reformation, that is Counter-Reformation afterwards, was to a great extent occupied with the principles and requirements laid down at the Council of Trent.

## Protestantism

Reformation movement broke the absolute authority of the Roman Catholic Church. In Europe, different denominations with the orthodox church began to appear one after another. Protestantism came into being. Liberal ideas took wing and as the countries in Europe went on their different ways to free themselves from the religious, political and economic control of the papal authorities, they each went on its way to nationhood and the way was thus prepared for capitalist development.

**Major branches within Christianity**

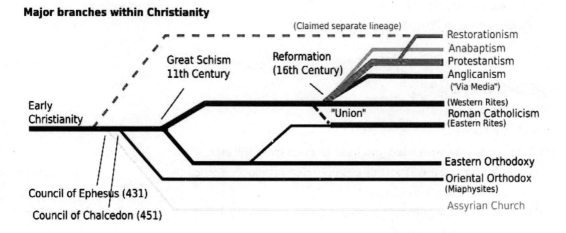

Before the Reformation, Europe was essentially feudal and medieval. It was under the absolute rule of the Roman Catholic Church and the Holy Roman Empire. The Roman Catholic Church was the international court to which all rulers and states were to be morally responsible for. Economically, peasants all over Europe had to pay a good amount of their gains to the Pope. In educational and cultural matters, the monopoly of the church was broken, and in religion, Protestantism brought into being different forms of Christianity to challenge the absolute rule of the Roman Catholic Church. In language, the dominant position of Latin had to give way to the national languages as a result of various translations of the *Bible* into the vernacular. In spirit, absolute obedience became outmoded and the spirit of quest, debate, was ushered in by the reformist.

In spite of the efforts of the Roman Catholic Church to kill this spirit, to maintain the established order and to check the political and economic advances of the European countries, Europe was to take a new course of development, a scientific revolution was to be underway and, capitalism was to set in with its dynamic economic principle.

## Proper Nouns

1. The Reformation 16世纪宗教改革运动
2. Martin Luther 马丁·路德(宗教改革运动倡导者)
3. the Catholic Church 天主教
4. John Wycliffe 约翰·威克里夫(英国宗教改革运动领导者)
5. Henry VIII 亨利八世(英国都铎王朝的第二位国王)
6. Catherine Aragon 阿拉贡的凯瑟琳(英国国王亨利八世的第一任王后)
7. Anne Boleyn 安妮·博林(英国国王亨利八世的第二任妻子,伊丽莎白一世的母亲)
8. *Act of Supremacy* 英国1534年颁布的《至尊法案》(法案宣布英国国王亨利八世不仅是世俗的最高统治者,也是宗教上的最高统治者,英国所有教会不再听从罗马教皇的指挥)
9. Anglican Church 英国圣公会
10. Council of Trent 特伦托会议
11. Protestantism 新教(基督教的一个分支)

## After You Read

***Knowledge Focus***

1. Fill in the blanks with what you have learned from the text.

   (1) The Reformation was a 16th-century religious movement led by _____. The beginning of the movement was marked by _____.

   (2) The Reformation aimed at opposing the absolute authority of _____ and replacing it with the absolute authority of _____.

(3) The demands of the reformists included that of simplifying _____, abolishing _____ levied on their countrymen and abolishing _____.

(4) Martin Luther was a _____ priest who made open protests against _____ and translated _____ from Latin to _____.

(5) When the Pope refused to recognize Henry VIII's marriage with Anne Boleyn, British Parliament, in 1534, passed _____ which marked the formal break of the British with the papal authorities.

(6) _____ recognized the legality of the divorce and secured the Crown to Anne's children.

(7) As a result of The English Reformation, _____ Church was established, and _____ became the head of the church.

(8) _____ reaffirmed that the Church had the sole right to interpret the *Bible*.

(9) As a result of the Reformation, different denominations of Christian Church began to appear, and _____ came into being.

(10) The influence of the Reformation could be felt in almost every social aspect. In spirit, _____ became outmoded and the spirit of _____ was ushered in by the reformist.

2. Discuss the following questions with your partner.
   (1) What is the Reformation? What marked the beginning of the Reformation?
   (2) Who was Martin Luther? What role did he play in the European Reformation?
   (3) What was the nature of the religious reformation in England? Was it a reform of belief or interpretation of the *Bible*?
   (4) What is the Council of Trent? How did it reinforce the power of the Roman Catholic Church?
   (5) What is the influence of the Reformation in Europe?

**Language Focus**

**1. Fill in the blanks with the following words or expressions you have learned in the text.**

| abolish | subordination | invalid | legality | side with |
| vitality | infallible | take wing | monopoly | usher in |

(1) I think bullfighting should be _____ because it is too cruel.
(2) The introduction of this new technology will _____ a new video and personal communications era.
(3) She claims that society is still characterized by male domination and female _____.
(4) She walked in the hills, letting her thoughts _____.
(5) No mathematician is _____; he may make mistakes, but he must not hedge.
(6) Tourism is important to the economic _____ of the region.
(7) Without the right date stamped on it, your ticket will be _____.
(8) It is safer to _____ the stronger party.

(9) The government is determined to protect its tobacco _____.

(10) The _____ of this action will be decided by the courts.

2. **Fill in the blanks with the proper form of the word in the brackets.**

   (1) The book is an _____ (authority) account of World War II.

   (2) The prime minister issued a _____ (deny) of the report that she is about to resign.

   (3) He is a man of _____ (individual).

   (4) She _____ (simple) the instructions so that the children could understand them.

   (5) This island is _____ (access) only by boat.

   (6) You've got to be firm, but at the same time you must be _____ (sympathy).

   (7) The capitalist system reposes on the _____ (exploit) of the laboring people.

   (8) I've applied for ten jobs, but all I've got is _____ (reject) letters.

   (9) I shall take on the work with humility and _____ (dedicate).

   (10) Britain's head of state is a constitutional _____ (monarchy).

3. **Fill in the blanks with the proper prepositions or adverbs that collocate with the neighboring words.**

   (1) Politicians should not engage _____ business affairs that might affect their political judgment.

   (2) The politician made a very poor showing in Parliament during the debate _____ the *National Labor Act*.

   (3) I'm ready to accept any job whatever, so long as it is _____ the interest of the people.

   (4) They are holding a rally to protest _____ the government's defense policy.

   (5) It's a fine scheme on paper, but will it work _____ practice?

   (6) The movie starts _____ 5 minutes and there's bound _____ be a long line.

   (7) If you mess up, you're _____ your own.

   (8) Taxis must conform to the rigorous standards laid _____ by the police.

   (9) The new government ushered _____ a period of prosperity.

   (10) The research project has only been _____ way for three months, so it's too early to evaluate its success.

4. **Error Correction: Each of the following sentences has at least one grammatical error. Identify the errors and correct them.**

   (1) Reformation was a 16-century religious movement as well as a socio-political movement.

   (2) This movement swept over the whole of Europe was aimed at opposing the absolute authority of the Roman Catholic Church.

   (3) To enable this direct communication, the reformists engaged in translating the *Bible* into their mother tongues.

   (4) The interests of the reformists covered a wide range, from wish to see institutional reform of the Church, to make the *Bible* accessible to the common folks.

(5) One of the doctrines of Martin Luther was the *Bible* was supreme authority.

(6) Martin Luther was priest, vicar and professor of theology.

(7) Before the Reformation, very a few people in Europe read *Bible*.

(8) This direct communication with God meant that the absolute control of Catholic Church on the minds of the people was now losing ground.

(9) Fail to obtain the approval of the Pope, Henry declared on his own that the marriage with Catherine invalid.

(10) The Parliament gave Henry an *Act of Succession*, recognize the legality of the divorce and securing Crown to Anne's children.

(11) Anybody who refused to do so would charge with treason and subject to severe punishment.

(12) In England, the question of reform was not fundamentally one of belief or interpretation of the *Bible* but also one of rejection of the supremacy of the Pope.

(13) Facing with the growing threat, the papal authorities had to call a number of councils to introduce necessary reforms.

(14) There were such principles among the decrees that every bishop was required to take the oath of complete obedience to the Pope and reforms that were aimed at tightening the discipline of the clergy.

## Comprehensive Work

### 1. Henry VIII and the Break with Rome

In 1534, King Henry made himself Supreme Head of the Church of England, breaking away from the Roman Catholic Church and the Pope in Rome. In this activity, you will answer the question—Why?

Sources suggest there were various reasons...

a. Number the reasons in the order of importance, explain what you think was Henry's MOST IMPORTANT reason for his break with Rome and why you choose it.

   (1) I think King Henry broke with Rome for the following reasons (in order of importance)
   _____

   (2) I think _____ is the most important reason, because
   _____

   (3) Compare your answer with your classmates, and try to convince them with evidence.

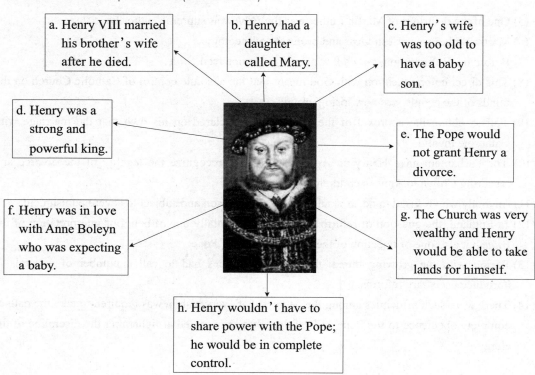

a. Henry VIII married his brother's wife after he died.

b. Henry had a daughter called Mary.

c. Henry's wife was too old to have a baby son.

d. Henry was a strong and powerful king.

e. The Pope would not grant Henry a divorce.

f. Henry was in love with Anne Boleyn who was expecting a baby.

g. The Church was very wealthy and Henry would be able to take lands for himself.

h. Henry wouldn't have to share power with the Pope; he would be in complete control.

b. Writing

There are many types of motives behind people's actions. What type of motive was Henry's number 1 reason for making himself head of the Church? Circle the choice that you think best accounts for Henry's motive in making himself head of the Church, and write a composition of about 200 words to illustrate your ideas.

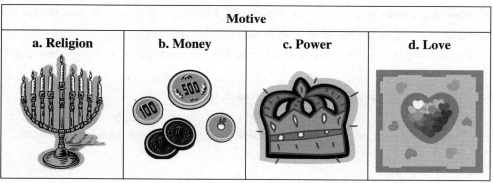

| Motive | | | |
|---|---|---|---|
| a. Religion | b. Money | c. Power | d. Love |

## 2. Martin Luther and His *95 Theses*

In October 1517, Martin Luther nailed a long list to the door of the Church at Wittenberg Castle. This list was later called *95 Theses*.

The following excerpts are taken from Luther's *95 Theses*. Read them carefully and answer the questions that follow.

5   The Pope has no power to let people off the punishments they must pay for their sins. He can only do so for penalties he or the Church has imposed.

21   Pardoners are mistaken when they say that by their indulgences a person is freed and saved from all punishment.

86   Why does not the Pope, whose riches are enormous, build the basilica of St. Peter with his own money instead of taking it from poor believers?

**Questions for Discussion**

(1) What did Luther criticize in these statements?

(2) Why did Luther condemn the Church for their wrongdoings?

(3) Why do you think Luther posted his list of arguments on the door of a church?

(4) Who do you think would support Luther's ideas?

(5) How would a man like Luther make his ideas known today?

**Read More**

### Text B   The Roman Catholic Church in 1500

The "rottenness" of the Roman Catholic Church was at the heart of Martin Luther's attack on it in 1517 when he wrote the *95 Theses*, thus sparking off the German Reformation.

In 1500 the Roman Catholic Church was all powerful in Western Europe. There was no legal alternative. The Catholic Church jealously guarded its position and anybody who was deemed to have gone against the Catholic Church was labeled a heretic and burnt at the stake. The Catholic Church did not tolerate any deviance from its teachings as any appearance of "going soft" might have been interpreted as a sign of weakness which would be exploited.

Its power had been built up over the centuries and relied on ignorance and superstition on the part of the populace. It had been indoctrinated into the people that they could only get to heaven via the church.

This gave a priest enormous power at a local level on behalf of the Catholic Church. The local population viewed the local priest as their "passport" to heaven and had been taught this from birth by the local priest. Such a message was constantly being repeated to ignorant people in church service. Hence keeping your priest happy was seen as a prerequisite to going to heaven.

This relationship between people and church was essentially based on money—hence the huge wealth of the Catholic Church. Rich families could buy high positions for their sons in the Catholic Church and this satisfied their belief that they would go to heaven and attain salvation. However, a peasant had to pay for a child to be christened (this had to be done as a first step to getting to heaven as the people were told that a non-baptized child could not go to heaven); he had to pay to get married and he had to pay to bury someone from his family in holy ground.

To go with this, he would be expected to give to the church via the collection at the end of each service (as God was omnipresent he would see if anyone cheated on him), he had to pay tithes (a tenth of his annual income had to be paid to the church which could be either in money or in kind such as seed, animals, etc.) and he was expected to work on church land for free for a specified number of days per week. The days required varied from region to region but if he was working on church land he could not be working on his own land growing food, etc. and this could be more than just an irritant to a peasant as he would not be producing for his family or preparing for the next year.

However unfair and absurd this might appear to someone now, it was the accepted way of life in 1500 as this was how it had always been and no one knew anything different and very few were willing to speak out against the Catholic Church as the consequences were too appalling to contemplate.

People were told that if they did not go to heaven, then the likelihood was that their souls had been condemned to Hell. Heresy was visibly punished with public burnings which they were expected to attend. John Huss was accused of heresy and granted safe passage to Constance in modern Switzerland to defend himself at trial. He never got his trial as he was arrested regardless of his guarantee of safe passage by the Catholic Church and burnt in public.

The Catholic Church also had three other ways of raising revenue.

Relics: These were officially sanctioned by the Vatican. They were pieces of straw, hay, white feathers from a dove, pieces of the cross, etc. that could be sold to people as the things that had been the nearest to Jesus on Earth. The money raised went straight to the church and to the Vatican. These holy relics were keenly sought after as the people saw their purchase as a way of pleasing God. It also showed that one had honored Him by spending his money on relics.

Indulgences: These were "certificates" produced in bulk that had been pre-signed by the Pope which pardoned a person's sins and gave his access to heaven. Basically, if he knew that he had sinned he would wait until a pardoner was in his region selling an indulgence and purchase one as the Pope, being God's representative on Earth, would forgive his sins and he would be pardoned. This industry was later expanded to allow people to buy an indulgence for a dead relative who might be in purgatory or Hell and relieve that relative of his sins. By doing this he would be seen by the Catholic Church of committing a Christian act and this would elevate his status in the eyes of God.

Pilgrimages: These were very much supported by the Catholic Church as a pilgrim would end up at a place of worship that was owned by the Catholic Church and money could be made by the sale of badges, holy water, certificates, etc. to prove one had completed his journey.

It was specifically the issue of indulgences that angered Martin Luther into speaking out against them—potentially a very dangerous thing to do.

**Questions for Reflection**

1. Why was the Roman Catholic Church so powerful in the 16th century?
2. For what reasons did ordinary people give money to the Church?
3. What would happen if a person did not follow the Catholic Church?
4. In what ways did the Church collect money?
5. What are indulgences?

### Text C  Driven to Defiance

> I would never have thought that such a storm would rise from Rome over one simple scrap of paper...
>
> —Martin Luther

Few if any men have changed the course of history like Martin Luther. In less than ten years, this fevered German monk plunged a knife into the heart of an empire that had ruled for a thousand years, and set in motion a train of revolution, war and conflict that would reshape Western civilization, and lift it out of the Dark Ages.

Luther's is a drama that still resonates half a millennium on. It is an epic tale that stretches from the gilded corridors of the Vatican to the weathered church door of a small South German town; from the barbarous pyres of heretics to the technological triumph of printing. It is the story of the birth of the modern age, of the collapse of medieval

feudalism, and the first shaping of ideals of freedom and liberty that lie at the heart of the 21st century.

But this is also an intensely human tale, a story that hurtles from the depths of despair to the heights of triumph and back again. This is the story of a man who ultimately found himself a lightning conductor of history, crackling with forces he could not quite comprehend or control.

For Luther, in a life full of irony, would find himself overwhelmed by his own achievements. As his followers sought to build a new and just Europe around him, he could only turn on them in frustration, declaring that his—and their—only goal should be Heaven.

Martin Luther stands as a hero, the man who built the bridge between the two halves of the last millennium, the Medieval and the Modern. His tragedy was that he would never find the courage to cross it himself.

Martin Luther was born into a world dominated by the Catholic Church, which holds spiritual dominion over all the nations of Europe. For the keenly spiritual Luther, the Church's promise of salvation is irresistible—caught in a thunderstorm, terrified by the possibility of imminent death, he vows to become a monk.

But after entering the monastery, Luther becomes increasingly doubtful that the Church can actually offer him salvation at all. His views crystallize even further with a trip to Rome, where he finds that the capital of Catholicism is swamped in corruption.

Wracked by despair, Luther finally finds release in the pages of the *Bible*, when he discovers that it is not the Church, but his own individual faith that will guarantee his salvation.

With this revelation, he turns on the Church, attacking its practice of selling Indulgences in the famous *95 Theses*. The key points of Luther's *95 Theses* were simple, but devastating: a criticism of the Pope's purpose in raising the money, "he is richer than Croesus, he would do better to sell St. Peters and give the money to the poor people..." and a straightforward concern for his flock, "indulgences are most pernicious because they induce complacency and thereby imperil salvation."

Luther was not only a revolutionary thinker, but he would also benefit from a revolutionary technology: the newly invented machinery of printing. A single pamphlet would be carried from one town to another, where it would be duplicated in a further print run of thousands. Within three months, all Europe was awash with copies of Luther's *95 Theses*.

Martin Luther had inadvertently chosen unavoidable conflict with what was the most powerful institution of the day, the Catholic Church.

## Questions for Reflection

1. What legacy did Luther leave for the centuries that follow? Why did he stand as a hero in European history?
2. Why did Luther become a monk, according to the passage?
3. What did Luther find on his trip to Rome?
4. How were Luther's ideas quickly spread to all of Europe?

## Websites to Visit

http://www.history.com/topics/reformation/reformation (accessed Apr. 28, 2020)
This website provides a detailed introduction to the Religious Reformation in Europe in the 16th century, including the causes, the spread, and the results and consequences.

http://www.luther.de/en/ (accessed Apr. 28, 2020)
On this website, you may find almost everything about Martin Luther, especially legends about him.

## Movie to Watch

### Luther (2003)

*Luther* is a biography of Martin Luther, the 16th-century priest who led the Christian Reformation and opened up new possibilities in exploration of faith.

The film begins with his vow to become a monk, and continues through his struggles to reconcile his desire for sanctification with his increasing abhorrence of the corruption and hypocrisy pervading the Church's hierarchy. He is ultimately charged with heresy and must confront the ruling cardinals and princes, urging them to make the Scriptures available to the common believer and lead the Church toward faith through justice and righteousness.

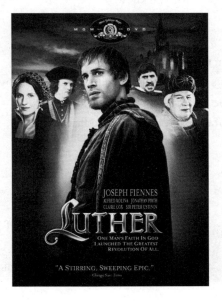

# Unit 10
## The Baroque Age

> The modern world, so far as mental outlook is concerned, begins in the seventeenth century.
>
> —Bertrand Russell

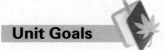
### Unit Goals

- To have a general understanding of the scientific achievements made in the 17th century
- To be familiar with the intellectual thoughts popular in the Baroque Age
- To learn the useful words and expressions that describe the Baroque Age
- To improve language skills by learning this unit

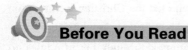
### Before You Read

**1. Who are they?**

In the 17th century, there emerged a great many physicists, astronomers, mathematicians and philosophers. Look at the following pictures and try to work out the answers according to each of the pictures. Fill in the blanks with what you know.

**Picture 1**

(1) The tower in the picture is called _____.
(2) On top of this tower, an experiment was carried out by a scientist called _____.
(3) How was the experiment carried out? _____
(4) The result of the experiment proved that _____.

**Picture 2**

(1) The man in the left picture is _____.

(2) He is pointing at the center of _____.

(3) He is most famous for his belief that _____.

**Picture 3**

(1) The man in the right picture is _____.

(2) He was most famous for _____.

(3) Share a story you know about him with your classmates.

2. Form groups of three or four students. Try to find, on the Internet or in the library, more information about the Baroque Age. Choose a topic that interests you most and prepare a five-minute classroom presentation.

## Start to Read

### Text A  The Age of Revolution

By the end of the sixteenth century, Europe was beginning to experience a decline in religious passions and a growing secularization that affected both the political and intellectual worlds. Some historians like to speak of the seventeenth century as a turning point in the evolution of a modern state system in Europe. The ideal of a united Christian Europe gave way to the practical realities of a system of secular states in which matters of state took precedence over the salvation of subjects' souls. By the seventeenth century, the credibility of Christianity had been so weakened through religious wars that more and more Europeans came to think of politics in secular terms.

One of the responses to the religious wars and other crises of the time was yearning for order. As the internal social and political rebellions and revolts died down, it became apparent that the privileged classes of society—the aristocrats—remained in control, although the various states exhibited important differences in political forms. The most general trend saw an extension of monarchical power as a stabilizing force. This development, which historians have called absolutism or absolute monarchy, was most evident in France during the flamboyant reign of Louis XIV.

But absolutism was not the only response to the search for order in the seventeenth century. Other states, such as England, reacted differently to the domestic crisis, and another very different system emerged where monarchs were limited by the power of their representative assemblies. Absolute and limited monarchy were the two poles of seventeenth-century state-building.

In addition to political, economic, and social crises, profound changes were also occurring in European intellectual life during the seventeenth century.

**The Scientific Revolution**

Between the early 1500s and the late 1600s, new ideas about the physical world brought sweeping changes to European philosophy and more broadly to Europeans' view of their place in the world. The "scientific revolution" entailed three changes: the emergence and confirmation of a heliocentric view of the universe, the development of a new physics that fits such a view, and the establishment of a method of inquiry.

The first major advance of modern science occurred in astronomy and Italy was the scene with Copernicus as the leading figure. Although he did not belong to the 17th century, Nicolaus Copernicus (1473 – 1543) was the immediate forerunner of modern science. Using logic and mathematics, Copernicus concluded that the long-held Ptolemaic system, which said that the Earth was the center of the universe, was wrong. He put forward his theory that the sun, not the Earth, is the center of the universe.

The first important astronomer after Copernicus to adopt his heliocentric theory was the German scientist Johannes Kepler (1571 – 1630). He was best known for his discovery of the three laws of planetary motion, the three laws being called Kepler's Laws published in 1609 and 1619. These laws supported, clarified and amended the Copernican system and turned the system from a general description of the sun and the planets into a precise mathematical formula. These three laws formed the basis of all modern planetary astronomy and led to Newton's discovery of the laws of gravitation.

Galileo Galilei (1564 – 1642) was also a great name in the physics of this period. His father, a Florentine, taught him Latin, Greek, mathematics and music. He also liked to draw and paint. At 17, he was sent to study medicine at the University of Pisa, but soon his interest and attention were drawn to physics and mathematics. A convinced Copernican, he was eager to use newly invented instruments to observe the heavenly bodies. He was the first to apply the telescope to the study of the skies. He even made a telescope for himself and used it to observe the stars with immense patience. What he saw in the sky with the help of the telescope proved that Ptolemy's geocentric system simply would not work and that Copernicus's powerful hypothesis had been right.

As a schoolboy, Isaac Newton (1642 – 1727) was reported as "idle" and "inattentive", often neglecting his duties in study but giving too much time to mechanical contrivances. His uncle, however, recognizing his talent, arranged for him to study at Trinity College, Cambridge. Four years later, he took his degree, and became a mathematics teacher. But Newton was not a very successful teacher. It is said that few students went to his lectures and fewer could understand him. Sometimes he had so few auditors that he read his lectures to the wall. However, as a scientist, Newton displayed his talents in many fields. As a mathematician, he invented calculus. In optics, he discovered that white light is composed of all the colors of the spectrum. Yet it was in the field of physics that Newton established his name as one of the most outstanding and influential figures in the history of natural science.

Of all his achievements in physics, his discovery of the law of the universal gravitation is the most important, which states that every body attracts every other with a force directly proportional to the product of their masses and inversely proportional to the square of the distance between them. To put it simply, the sun, the moon, the Earth, the planets, and all the other bodies in the universe move in accordance with the same basic force, gravitation. The law of gravitation is considered to be one of the most important discoveries in the history of science.

Newton's discoveries were summarized in his book *Mathematical Principles of Natural Philosophy*. In this work, Newton spelled out the mathematical proofs demonstrating his universal law of gravitation. And this work was the culmination of the theories of Copernicus, Kepler, and Galileo.

**A New Philosophy**

By the early 1600s, the increasingly "Copernican" sciences of mathematics and astronomy were changing quickly. At first, those changes were haphazard and very loosely related. As the practice of the new sciences became concentrated in Europe, however, several important thinkers began to produce not only new discoveries, but new principles of and goals for science, or natural philosophy.

The new methods were refined by two men in particular: the Englishman Sir Francis Bacon and the Frenchman René Descartes. Both men believed they lived in a new age of profound change and great opportunities for discovery. Both also believed that the bedrock of natural philosophy, the ideas of Aristotle, no longer met the needs of the times, and that a fresh approach would take European "moderns" well beyond the knowledge of the ancients. The methods they created were very different, but they together shaped the practice of natural philosophy in the later seventeenth century and left a deep mark on the evolution of modern science.

Sir Francis Bacon (1561 – 1626) was an extremely influential theorist of the new philosophy. Bacon's view, best expressed in his *Novum Organum (New Instrument)* of 1620, was that natural science could not advance unless it cast off the inherited errors of the past. The knowledge of ancient authorities was no longer the best guide to truth. To put it more cautiously, too much reverence for accepted doctrines could block discovery and full understanding. Using the "inductive method", philosophers would combine evidence from a huge number of particular observations to draw general

conclusions. Bacon also sought "useful knowledge", practical forms of understanding grounded in the detailed study of each part of the natural world. He argued that such knowledge was best gained through cooperation among researchers, and through carefully recorded experiments that could be repeated and verified.

Bacon's contemporary, the French philosopher René Descartes (1596 – 1650), agreed with him on two points. The first was the importance of questioning established knowledge. The second was that the value of ideas depended on their usefulness. Yet Descartes offered a completely different method for reaching useful knowledge. His first rule was to never to receive anything that he did not clearly know as a truth, and he found himself doubting everything until he accepted that the process of thought proved his own existence. Descartes made rationality the point of departure for his entire philosophical enterprise. His approach to the natural world is usually called the "deductive method".

Using new instruments and applying new mathematical techniques, scientists in the 17th century made many discoveries. These discoveries gave rise to a new confidence in the capacity of human reason alone to understand nature and so to improve human life—a confidence those who held to it declared to be a sign of the Enlightenment.

## Proper Nouns

1. Louis XIV 法国国王路易十四(法国专制主义的代表人物)
2. Enlightenment (欧洲18世纪的)启蒙运动
3. Nicolaus Copernicus 尼古拉·哥白尼(波兰天文学家)
4. Ptolemaic system (以古希腊天文学家托勒密命名的)托勒密学说(该学说认为地球是宇宙的中心)
5. Johannes Kepler 约翰内斯·开普勒(德国天文学家)
6. Galileo Galilei 伽利略·伽利雷(意大利天文学家)
7. Isaac Newton 艾萨克·牛顿(英国物理学家)
8. Trinity College 三一学院
9. Francis Bacon 弗朗西斯·培根(英国学者)
10. René Descartes 勒内·笛卡尔(法国思想家)
11. inductive method 归纳法
12. deductive method 演绎法

## After You Read

### Knowledge Focus

**1. Fill in the following blanks according to what you read in the text.**

(1) The two political responses to the religious wars in the 17th century were _____ and _____ . The former was best represented by _____ and the latter was represented by _____ .

(2) Copernicus put forward his theory that _____ is the center of the universe.

(3) _____ formed the basis of all modern planetary astronomy and led to Newton's discovery of the laws of gravitation.

(4) _____ was the first to apply the telescope to the study of the skies.

(5) In optics, Newton discovered that white light is composed of _____ .

(6) Of all Newton's achievements in physics, his discovery of _____ is the most important.

(7) _____ argued that knowledge was best gained through cooperation among researchers, and through carefully recorded experiments that could be repeated and verified.

(8) _____ approach to the natural world is usually called the "deductive method".

**2. Answer the following questions.**

(1) What were the two political responses to the religious wars and social crisis in Europe in the 17th century?

(2) What three changes were entailed in the term the "scientific revolution"?

(3) How did Kepler, Galileo and Newton contribute to the development of the Copernican theory?

(4) What similarities and differences existed between Bacon and Descartes in terms of their philosophical ideas?

**3. Explain the following terms in your own words.**

(1) Absolutism

(2) Limited monarchy

(3) Copernicus

(4) Sir Isaac Newton

### Language Focus

**1. Fill in the blanks with the following words or expressions you have learned in the text.**

| take precedence over | credibility | yearning | hover |
| entail | inquiry | inattentive | culmination |

(1) Because I live in a crowded city, I have this _____ for open spaces.
(2) Winning first prize was the _____ of years of practice and hard work.
(3) Such a large investment inevitably _____ some risk.
(4) _____ into the matter is pointless—no one will tell you anything.
(5) Business people often think that fluency and communication _____ grammar when speaking.
(6) He was wholly _____ to the needs of his children.
(7) Incidents like these began to undermine Angleton's _____.
(8) I heard the noise of a helicopter _____ overhead.

2. Fill in the blanks with the proper form of the word in the brackets.
   (1) The story of what had happened to her was barely _____ (credibility).
   (2) He _____ (precedence) his speech with a few words of welcome.
   (3) He suffered a second heart attack two days ago but his condition has now _____ (stable).
   (4) A _____ (physics) is a scientist who has special knowledge and training in physics.
   (5) We will send you written _____ (confirm) of our offer shortly.
   (6) The _____ (mathematics) is an impractical person who can't even boil an egg.
   (7) That girl is of _____ (proportion) build and is beautiful.
   (8) I find it necessary to use the utmost _____ (cautious) about my eye-sight.
   (9) His cool _____ (respond) suggested that he didn't like the idea.
   (10) _____ (rational), as a term, is related to the idea of reason.

3. Fill in the blanks with the proper prepositions or adverbs that collocate with the neighboring words.
   (1) _____ the end of next year, they will have finished work on the new stadium.
   (2) We mustn't give way _____ these unreasonable demands.
   (3) The figures are expressed _____ percentage terms.
   (4) Everyone is yearning _____ the weather to change, after this bitter winter.
   (5) In spite of the panic, she remained serene and _____ control.
   (6) I put _____ the hands of a clock when it is slow.
   (7) The board shall be composed _____ eight directors. Each director shall be appointed by his own side.
   (8) Payment will be proportional _____ the amount of work done.
   (9) He was always neatly and quietly dressed in accordance _____ his age and status.
   (10) War has left its mark _____ the country.

4. Error Correction: Each of the following sentences has at least one grammatical error. Identify the errors and correct them.
   (1) The ideal of a united Christian Europe gave way to the practical realities of a system of secular states which matters of state took precedence in the salvation of subjects' souls.

(2) By the seventeenth century, the credibility of Christianity was so weakened through religious wars that more and more Europeans came to think of politics in secular terms.

(3) The most general trend was seen an extension of monarchical power as a stabilizing force.

(4) This development, what historians have called absolutism or absolute monarchy, was most evident in France during the flamboyant reign of Louis XIV.

(5) A very different system emerged which monarchs were limited by the power of their representative assemblies.

(6) The first major advance of modern science was occurred in astronomy and Italy was the scene where Copernicus as the leading figure.

(7) Copernicus concluded that the long-held Ptolemaic system, that said that the Earth was the center of the universe, was wrong.

(8) But soon his interest and attention drew to physics and mathematics.

(9) The convinced Copernican, he was eager to use newly invented instruments to observe the heavenly bodies.

(10) That he saw in the sky with the help of the telescope proved that Ptolemy's geocentric system simply would not work and Copernicus's powerful hypothesis had been right.

(11) It was the field of physics that Newton established his name as one of the most outstanding and influential figures in the history of natural science.

(12) With the practice of the new sciences became concentrated in Europe, several important thinkers began to produce not only new discoveries, but new principles of and goals for science.

## Comprehensive Work

### 1. Bacon and Descartes

Francis Bacon and René Descartes are two famous philosophers in 17th-century Europe. Their philosophical ideas share similarities as well as differences.

Read the following two source cards. Which one is written by Francis Bacon and which one is written by Descartes? Explain why.

---

**Source A**

There are and can be only two ways of searching into and discovering the truth. The one flies from the senses and particulars to the most general axioms, and from these principles, the truth of which it takes for settled and immovable, proceeds to judgment and to the discovery of middle axioms. And this way is now in fashion. The other derives axioms from the senses and particulars, rising by a gradual and unbroken ascent, so that it arrives at the most general axioms last of all. This is the true way, but as yet untried.

### Source B

The first of these was to accept nothing as true which I did not clearly recognize to be so: that is to say, carefully to avoid precipitation and prejudice in judgments, and to accept in them nothing more than what was presented to my mind so clearly and distinctly that I could have no occasion to doubt it.

The second was to divide up each of the difficulties which I examined into as many parts as possible, and as seemed requisite in order that it might be resolved in the best manner possible.

The third was to carry on my reflections in due order, commencing with objects that were the most simple and easy to understand, in order to rise little by little, or by degrees, to knowledge of the most complex...

(1) I think Source A is probably written by _____, because _____.

(2) I think Source B is probably written by _____, because _____.

## 2. Writing

The followings are famous quotes from a great writer and philosopher of the 17th century. Read these quotations and answer the questions that follow.

☆ Knowledge is power.

☆ Virtue is like precious odours—most fragrant when they are incensed or crushed.

☆ Some books are to be tasted, others to be swallowed, and some few to be chewed and digested.

☆ Reading makes a full man, conference a ready man, and writing an exact man.

☆ Books must follow sciences, and not sciences books.

☆ Wives are young men's mistresses, companions for middle-age, and old men's nurses.

☆ There is no excellent beauty that hath not some strangeness in the proportion.

**Questions:**

(1) Who is the author of these quotations?

(2) What do you know about him?

(3) Choose one quotation and explain its meaning in your own words.

(4) Choose one quotation from the list as the topic of your composition. To what extent do you agree with this quotation? Write at least two reasons/examples to illustrate your idea.

## Read More

### Text B  Newton, the Apple, and Gravity

Nearly everyone has heard about Newton and an apple. But few people seem to know the story behind it! Technically, there is no actual documentation for this story, so it might contain exaggerations. But it is relatively well accepted.

Prior to this incident, Newton had invented something we now call the Calculus, and with it had mathematically proven that an "inverse square law" dependence, such as gravitation on distance, must act as though all the mass of an object (the Earth) is at the exact center of the Earth.

Newton was trying to think of some way of experimentally confirming what he had already calculated, that inverse square dependence. He was sitting out in a field, looking at the Moon in the sky overhead. He believed that the Moon was orbiting the Earth because of the gravitation of the Earth. He believed that the Moon would normally have gone straight off into space, but the Earth's gravitation caused it to "constantly fall" toward the Earth, making its path curved rather than straight. But he had not thought of any way to experimentally prove that!

By his time, science had fairly accurately calculated the radius of the Earth, just under 4,000 miles (6,400 km). It was also known that the Moon orbited the Earth at an average distance of just under 240,000 miles (384,000 km), about 60 times as far from the center of the Earth as he was.

When an apple fell from a tree near him, it suddenly dawned on him that the same Earth's gravitation that must be curving the Moon's path must also have made that apple accelerate toward the Earth in its fall!

His calculations had shown that the acceleration should not depend at all on the size or mass of the object. So, if that apple was out at the distance of the Moon, it should have the same acceleration as the Moon does, and would, therefore, also orbit the Earth.

He knew that an apple falls at "the acceleration due to gravity", 32 feet per second, what we call $g$. And that in the first second, that apple would fall very close to 16.1 feet (193″)* toward the Earth.

Then, if that apple was moved to a place 60 times as far away from the center of the Earth, and gravitation actually did depend on an inverse square relationship, then the apple out there should fall 1/3600th as far as it did from the tree. So he multiplied 16.1 feet by 1/3600 and got an expected falling distance in one second to be 0.0535 inch.

That meant that the Moon must "fall" 0.0535″ toward the Earth in a second (from an otherwise straight line. This is a really small curvature (less than 1/16″ over the 3,300 feet that the Moon moves every second). But it turns out that it is still pretty easy to confirm. If you draw a really big circle that represents the orbit of the Moon, and then look at a small part of that circle, the part that the Moon moves through in one second, then simple geometry can determine that small curvature (circle, chord, radius, etc.).

Interestingly, in this very simple calculation, the brilliant Newton apparently made a multiplication error regarding the radius of the Earth in inches! With this wrong value, there was no agreement in the results! Newton set aside this whole subject for six years! Around then, a new calculation of the radius of the Earth had been made (by Picard). Newton decided to try the calculation again, and he did it right this time, and the result was 0.0534″, a virtually perfect match. The inverse square law of gravitation was therefore proven. Also proven was the fact that the mass of the object, whether apple or Moon, did not affect the acceleration results.

As to this last statement, Newton later calculated that there actually is a tiny effect due to the mass. But it is an extremely tiny effect, for any practical sized objects, because the Earth is so big and massive!

There is also a tiny effect due to the differential gravitational effect of the Sun, which very slightly reduces the actual value for the Moon, which even explains that 0.0001″ discrepancy!

Now you know about Newton and the Apple!

\* *The sign "″" refers to arc second.*

## *Questions for Reflection*

1. How did Newton discover the law of gravitation?
2. What scientific discoveries have been made before Newton worked out the universal rule of gravitation?
3. Like Newton's story of apple, many scientific inventions or discoveries were triggered by accident. Do you happen to know any other similar stories? Share what you know with your classmates.

### Text C  Baroque Style

Baroque style is the style dominating the art and architecture of Europe and certain European colonies in the Americas throughout the 1600s, and in some places, until 1750. A number of its characteristics continue in the art and architecture of the first half of the 18th century, although this period is generally termed rococo and corresponds roughly with King Louis XV of France. Manifestations of Baroque art appear in virtually every country in Europe, with other important centers in the Spanish and Portuguese settlements in the Americas and in other outposts. The term baroque also defines periods in literature and music.

The origins of the word baroque are not clear. It may have been derived from the Portuguese *barocco* or the Spanish *barueco* to indicate an irregularly shaped pearl. The word itself does not accurately define or even approximate the meaning of the style to which it refers. However, by the end of the 18th century, baroque had entered the terminology of art criticism as an epithet leveled against 17th-century art, which many later critics regularly dismissed as too bizarre or strange to merit serious study. Writers such as the 19th-century Swiss cultural historian Jakob Burckhardt considered this style the decadent end of the Renaissance; his student Heinrich Wölfflin, in *Principles of Art History* (1915; translated into English in 1932), first pointed out the fundamental differences between the art of the 16th and 17th centuries, stating that "baroque is neither a rise nor a decline from classic, but a totally different art".

Baroque art encompasses vast regional distinctions. It may seem confusing, for example, to label two such different artists as Rembrandt and Gianlorenzo Bernini as baroque; yet despite differences, they shared certain baroque elements, such as a preoccupation with the dramatic potential of light.

Understanding the various forms of baroque art requires knowledge of its historical context. The 17th century could be called the first modern age. Human awareness of the world was continuously expanding. Many scientific discoveries influenced art; Galileo's investigations of the planets, for example, account for astronomical accuracy in many paintings of the time. The assertion of the Polish astronomer Copernicus that the planets did not revolve around the Earth was written by 1530, published in 1543, and only fully accepted after 1600. The realization that the Earth was not at the center of the universe coincided in art with the rise of pure landscape painting devoid of human figures. The active trade and colonization policies of many European nations accounted for numerous portrayals of places and peoples that were exotic to Europeans.

Religion determined many aspects of baroque art. The Roman Catholic church was a highly influential patron, and its Counter-Reformation, a movement to combat the spread of Protestantism, employed emotional, realistic, and dramatic art as a means of propagating the faith. The simplicity sought by Protestantism in countries such as the Netherlands and northern Germany likewise explains the severity of the architectural styles in those areas.

Political situations also influenced art. The absolute monarchies of France and Spain prompted the creation of works that reflected in their size and splendor the majesty of their kings, Louis XIV and Philip IV.

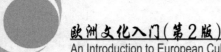

Among the general characteristics of baroque art is a sense of movement, energy, and tension (whether real or implied). Strong contrasts of light and shadow enhance the dramatic effects of many paintings and sculptures. Even baroque buildings, with their undulating walls and decorative surface elements, imply motion. Intense spirituality is often present in works of baroque art; in the Roman Catholic countries, for example, scenes of ecstasies, martyrdoms, or miraculous apparitions are common. Infinite space is often suggested in baroque paintings or sculptures; throughout the Renaissance and into the baroque period, painters sought a grander sense of space and truer depiction of perspective in their works. Realism is another integral feature of baroque art; the figures in paintings are not types but individuals with their own personalities. Artists of this time were concerned with the inner workings of the mind and attempted to portray the passions of the soul on the faces they painted and sculpted. The intensity and immediacy of baroque art and its individualism and detail—observed in such things as the convincing rendering of cloth and skin textures—make it one of the most compelling periods of Western art.

**Questions for Reflection**
1. What is Baroque style?
2. How was art influenced by the historical context of 17th-century Europe?
3. What are the characteristics of Baroque buildings?
4. How was Realism revealed in Baroque art?

**Websites to Visit**
The following websites provide further material and analysis into the social context of Europe in the 17th century.

For information about the Scientific Revolution:
http://www.clas.ufl.edu/users/rhatch/pages/03-Sci-Rev/SCI-REV-Home/ (accessed Apr. 28, 2020)

For information about Francis Bacon:
http://www.luminarium.org/sevenlit/bacon/ (accessed Apr. 28, 2020)

For information about René Descartes:
http://www.iep.utm.edu/d/descarte.htm (accessed Apr. 28, 2020)

**Movie to Watch**

*The Man in the Iron Mask* (1998)

As King Louis XIV prepares to rule France, he proves to be a cruel ruler. When he becomes responsible for sending a soldier, Raoul, to his death so he can have his love, Christine, Raoul's retired musketeer father and two other retirees work together to overthrow the king. Captain

D'Artagnan does not agree with his king but is loyal to him and refuses to be a part of the musketeers' plan. However, they learn that Louis has a secret good twin brother named Phillipe, who has been imprisoned in the castle and his face hidden behind an iron mask. Could Phillipe be a solution and safe haven to the people of France?

*The Man in the Iron Mask* is a film directed by Randall Wallace. Although a critical failure, scoring a 31% "Rotten" rating on Rotten Tomatoes, it was successful financially, and is notable for ending *Titanic*'s (also starring Leonardo DiCaprio) four-month stay at the summit of the U.S. box office.

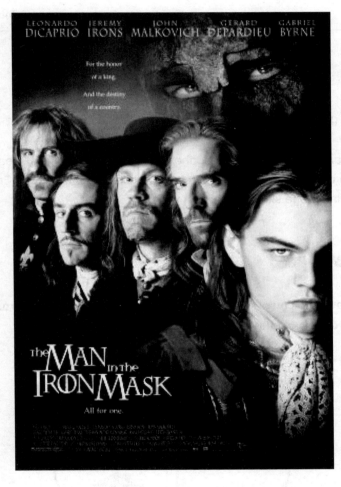

# Unit 11
## The Age of Enlightenment

> An excellent man, like precious metal, is in every way invariable; A villain, like the beams of a balance, is always varying, upwards and downwards.
>
> —John Locke

### Unit Goals

- To have a general understanding of the intellectual changes that characterized the 18th century
- To be familiar with important philosophers and their philosophical ideas
- To learn the useful words and expressions that describe the Age of Enlightenment
- To improve language skills by learning this unit

### Before You Read

1. Look at the following picture. What does it tell about the American government? Share what you know with your classmates.

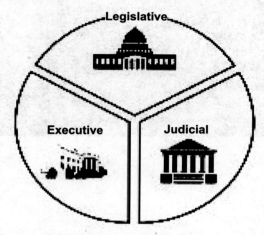

2. In the European Enlightenment, there emerged a great many intellectuals and philosophers. In the following cue cards, you will see descriptions of two philosophers. Try to guess who they are with the help of the cues.

Unit 11 The Age of Enlightenment

| Philosopher 1 |
|---|

- French poet, dramatist, historian and philosopher;
- He was an outspoken and aggressive enemy of every injustice such as tyranny, cruelty, but especially of religious intolerance;
- He was noted for his characteristic wit, satire and critical capacity.
- Famous quotes:
  - "Love truth, but pardon error."
  - "Liberty of thought is the life of the soul."
  - "I disapprove of what you say, but I will defend to the death your right to say it."

Answer: _____

| Philosopher 2 |
|---|

Answer: _____

- French philosopher, author, political theorist and composer;
- He favored a theory of social contract as the key to human freedom.
- Famous quotes:
  - "Man is born free, and everywhere he is in chains."
  - "The thirst after happiness is never extinguished in the heart of man."
  - "Nature made men happy and good, but society makes him evil and miserable."

3. **Form groups of three or four students. Try to find, on the Internet or in the library, more information about the Age of Enlightenment. Choose a topic that interests you most and prepare a five-minute classroom presentation.**

## Start to Read

### Text A  The Enlightenment

The Enlightenment was an intellectual movement originating in France, which attracted widespread support among the ruling and intellectual classes of Europe and North America in the 18th century. It characterizes the efforts by certain European writers and philosophers to use critical reason to free minds from prejudice, unexamined authority and oppression by Church or state. Therefore, the Enlightenment is also called the Age of Reason.

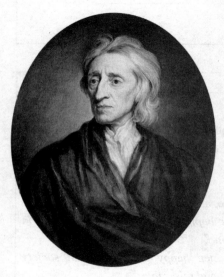

The eighteenth-century Enlightenment was a movement of intellectuals who dared to know. They were greatly impressed with the accomplishments of the Scientific Revolution, and when they used the word reason — one of their favorite words — they were advocating the application of the scientific method to an understanding of all life. If Isaac Newton could discover the natural laws regulating the world of nature, the intellectuals believed that they too, by using reason, could find the laws that governed human society. This belief, in turn, led them to hope that they could make progress toward a better society than the one they had inherited. Reason, natural law, hope, progress — these were buzzwords in the heady atmosphere of the eighteenth century.

The primary source of inspiration for the Enlightenment came from Isaac Newton and John Locke. Newton was frequently singled out for praise as the greatest and rarest genius in the history of science. Alexander Pope, a famous English poet declared: "Nature and Nature's Laws lay hid in Night; God said, 'Let Newton be', and all was Light." Enchanted by the grand design of Newtonian world-machine, the intellectuals of the Enlightenment were convinced that by following Newton's rules of reasoning, they could discover the natural laws that governed politics, economics, justice, religion, and the arts. The world and everything in it were like a giant machine.

John Locke's theory of knowledge had a great impact on eighteenth-century intellectuals. In his *Essay Concerning Human Understanding*, Locke argued that every person was born with a blank mind and our knowledge, then, is derived from our environment, not from heredity; from reason, not from faith. Locke's philosophy implied that people were molded by their environment, by the experiences that they received through their senses from their surrounding world. By changing the environment and subjecting people to proper influences, they could be changed and a new society created. And how should the environment be changed? Newton had already paved the way by showing how reason enabled enlightened people to discover the natural laws to which all institutions should conform. No wonder the philosophers were enamored of Newton and Locke. Taken together, their ideas seemed to offer the hope of a "brave new world" built on reason.

The intellectuals of the Enlightenment were known by the French term *philosophes*, although not all of them were French and few were philosophers in the strict sense of the term. They were literary people, professors, journalists, statesmen, economists, political scientists, and above all, social reformers. They came from both the nobility and the middle class, and a few even stemmed from lower-middle-class origins. The *philosophes* faced different political circumstances depending on the country in which they lived, but they shared common bonds as part of a truly international movement. They were called philosophers, but what did philosophy mean to them? The role of philosophy was to change the world, not just to discuss it. A spirit of rational criticism was applied to everything, including religion and politics.

Charles de Secondat, Baron de Montesquieu (1689 – 1755) was perhaps one of the most famous philosophers in the Enlightenment. Born in a French noble family, Montesquieu received a classical education and then studied law. His most famous work, *The Spirit of the Laws*, was published in 1748. This treatise was a comparative study of governments in which Montesquieu attempted to apply the scientific method to the social and political arena to ascertain the "natural laws" governing the social relationships of human being. Montesquieu distinguished three basic kinds of governments: republic, suitable for small states and based on citizen involvement; monarchy, appropriate for middle-sized states and grounded in the ruling class' adherence to law; and despotism, apt for large empires and dependent on fear to inspire obedience. Montesquieu used England as an example of the second category, and it was his praise and analysis of England's constitution that led to his most far-reaching and lasting contribution to political thought — the importance of checks and balances created by means of a separation of powers. He believed that England's system, with its separate executive, legislative, and judicial powers that served to limit and control each other, provided the greatest freedom and security for a state. The translation of his work into English two years after publication ensured its being read by American philosophers who incorporated its principles into the American constitution.

The Enlightenment belief that Newton's scientific methods could be used to discover the natural laws underlying all areas of human life led to the emergence in the eighteenth century of what we would call the social sciences. In a number of areas, *philosophes* arrived at natural laws that they believed governed human actions.

Adam Smith (1723 – 1790) in his famous *The Wealth of Nations*, published in 1776, made a clear statement of laissez-faire. Smith believed that the state should not interfere in economic matters; indeed, he gave to government only three basic functions: to protect society from invasion (army), to defend individuals from injustice and oppression (police), and to keep up public works, such as roads and canals, that private individuals could not afford. Thus, in Smith's view, the state should be a kind of "passive policeman" that remains out of the lives of individuals. In emphasizing the economic liberty of the individual, Adam Smith laid the foundation for what became known in the nineteenth century as economic liberalism.

## Proper Nouns

1. John Locke  约翰·洛克(英国思想家)
2. Montesquieu  孟德斯鸠(启蒙运动时期法国思想家)
3. Adam Smith  亚当·斯密(英国经济学家)

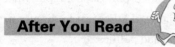

## After You Read

***Knowledge Focus***

**1. Match each of the following statements with a person that fits into its description.**

A. John Locke  　　　　　B. Newton
C. Montesquieu  　　　　D. Adam Smith

(1) _____ He believed that the world was like a giant machine that operated according to natural laws.

(2) _____ He was one of the leading philosophers of the Enlightenment period.

(3) _____ His advocating separation of powers had a great impact on the democratic politics of the US government.

(4) _____ He discovered the laws that regulate the world of nature.

(5) _____ He was a primary source of inspiration for the Enlightenment.

(6) _____ He argued that knowledge is derived from the environment, not from heredity.

(7) _____ He believed that the government should not interfere in economic matters.

(8) _____ He distinguished three basic kinds of governments: republic, monarchy, and despotism.

(9) _____ He held that the government should function as a "passive policeman".

(10) _____ He argued that people were shaped by the experiences they received through their senses from the surrounding world.

## Unit 11 The Age of Enlightenment

**2. Fill in the blanks with what you have learned from the text.**

(1) The Enlightenment was an _____ movement originating in_____, which attracted widespread support among_____ classes of Europe and North America in the 18th century. It is also called _____.

(2) In the Enlightenment, European writers and philosophers began to use_____ to free minds from prejudice, unexamined authority and oppression by_____.

(3) The favorite word of the European writers and philosophers in the Enlightenment was _____. They believed that by using it, they could find the laws that governed _____.

(4) _____ and_____ were the primary source of inspiration for the Enlightenment.

(5) In his *Essay Concerning Human Understanding*, _____ argued that our knowledge is derived from_____ and_____.

(6) The French term "philosophes" refers to _____.

(7) In *The Spirit of the Laws*, Montesquieu distinguished three basic kinds of governments: _____, _____, and _____. He believed that England's system, with its separate _____, _____, and _____ powers that served to limit and control each other, provided the greatest freedom and security for a state.

(8) Adam Smith made a clear statement of _____ in his famous work _____ published in 1776. He laid the foundation for what became known in the nineteenth century as _____.

**3. Discuss the following questions with your partner.**

(1) What characterized the Enlightenment period in 18th-century Europe?
(2) What intellectual developments led to the emergence of the Enlightenment?
(3) Who was the leading philosopher of the Enlightenment? What was his major contribution?
(4) What is laissez-faire? What did Adam Smith argue for in his book?

### Language Focus

**1. Fill in the blanks with the following words or expressions you have learned in the text.**

| | | | |
|---|---|---|---|
| buzzword | single out | enchant | heredity |
| subject... to | adherence | apt for | ascertain |

(1) Their emphasis is on the needs of the individual child rather than on_____ to a rigid curriculum.

(2) The ground is_____ the plow.

(3) The police have so far been unable to _____ the cause of the explosion.

(4) "Sensitivity" is the_____ in the beauty industry this fall.

(5) She was_____ four years of beatings and abuse.

(6) The audience was clearly _____ by her performance.

(7) Which would you＿＿＿＿ as the best?

(8) ＿＿＿＿ plays a role in some types of mental illness.

2. Fill in the blanks with the proper form of the word in the brackets.

(1) He is a man more noted for his＿＿＿＿(intellectual) than his charm.

(2) Every human being has the right to freedom from＿＿＿＿(oppress).

(3) How many＿＿＿＿(apply) did you have for the job?

(4) She was an＿＿＿＿(inspire) example to her followers.

(5) He is remembered for the ＿＿＿＿(noble) of his character.

(6) In a developing country, owning a car is a sign of＿＿＿＿(compare) wealth.

(7) The＿＿＿＿(emerge) of small Japanese cars in the 1970s challenged the US and European manufacturers.

(8) The government's＿＿＿＿ (interfere) in the strike has been widely criticized.

(9) For most citizens,＿＿＿＿ (liberal) means the freedom to practice their religious or political beliefs.

(10) Our English course places great ＿＿＿＿(emphasize) on conversational skills.

3. Fill in the blanks with the proper prepositions or adverbs that collocate with the neighboring words.

(1) The Industrial Revolution originates ＿＿＿＿ the invention of the steam engine.

(2) He is now working＿＿＿＿a new invention that will have a variety of applications ＿＿＿＿ industry.

(3) I can't help but be impressed＿＿＿＿the practicability of this education.

(4) The girl is singled＿＿＿＿ to represent the school.

(5) This offer is subject ＿＿＿＿ our final confirmation.

(6) The boredom of workers may stem ＿＿＿＿continuously having to perform a simple task.

(7) Sports clothes are not appropriate ＿＿＿＿a formal wedding.

(8) Look around at someone's life you admire. What do they do that you would like to incorporate ＿＿＿＿ your own life?

4. Error Correction: Each of the following sentences has at least one grammatical error. Identify the errors and correct them.

(1) Enlightenment was an intellectual movement originated in France.

(2) It was characterized by the efforts by certain European writers and philosophers to use critical reason to free minds from prejudice.

(3) This belief, in turn, led them to hope that they could make progress toward a better society than they had inherited.

(4) The world and everything in it like a giant machine.

(5) Locke argued that every person was born a blank mind and our knowledge derived from our

environment.

(6) By changing the environment and subjected people to proper influences, they could be changed and a new society created.

(7) Newton had already paved the way by showing how reason enabled enlightened people to discover the natural laws which all institutions should conform.

(8) Taking together, their ideas seemed to offer the hope of a "brave new world" built on reason.

(9) The role of philosophy was changing the world, not just to discuss it.

(10) A spirit of rational criticism applied to everything, including religion and politics.

(11) The translation of his work into English two years after publication ensured its reading by other American philosophers.

(12) The Enlightenment belief which Newton's scientific methods could be used to discover the natural laws led to the emergence of what we would call the social sciences.

(13) In emphasizing the economic liberty, Adam Smith laid the foundation for which became known as economic liberalism.

(14) In a number of areas, philosophers arrived at natural laws they believed governed human actions.

(15) This treatise was a comparative study of governments which Montesquieu attempted to apply the scientific method to the social and political arena.

## Comprehensive Work

**1. Sharing Ideas**

Read the following passage and answer the questions that follow.

> Let us then suppose the mind to be, as we say, white paper, void of all characters, without any ideas. How comes it to be furnished? Whence comes it by that vast store which the busy and boundless fancy of man has painted on it with an almost endless variety? Whence has it all the materials of reason and knowledge? To this I answer, in one word, from experience... our observation, employed either about external sensible objects or about the internal operations of our minds perceived and reflected on by ourselves, is that which supplies our understanding with all the materials of thinking.

**Questions for Discussion:**

1. Who is the author of the passage?

2. What is the main idea of this paragraph? Can you summarize it in your own words?

3. Do you agree with the author? To what extent do you agree? Please explain with examples.

## 2. Baron de Montesquieu's *The Spirit of the Laws*

Please read the following excerpts taken from Baron de Montesquieu's *The Spirit of the Laws* and rewrite them in your own words. Then circle the number on a scale of 1 to 5 corresponding with how much you agree or disagree with Montesquieu's quote, and explain why.

1. When the legislative and executive powers are united in the same person, or in the same body of magistrates, there can be no liberty; because apprehensions may arise, lest the same monarch or senate should enact tyrannical laws, to execute them in a tyrannical manner.

(1) Please rewrite the statement in your own words.
_____

(2) To what extent do you agree with this quote?

   1  2  3  4  5
  disagree   neutral   agree

2. The great advantage of representatives is their capacity of discussing public affairs. For this, the people collectively are extremely unfit, which is one of the chief inconveniences of a democracy.

(1) Please rewrite the statement in your own words.
_____

(2) To what extent do you agree with this quote?

   1  2  3  4  5
  disagree   neutral   agree

3. In a true state of nature, indeed, all men are born equal, but they cannot continue in this equality. Society makes them lose it, and they recover it only by the protection of laws.

(1) Please rewrite the statement in your own words.
_____

(2) To what extent do you agree with this quote?

   1  2  3  4  5
  disagree   neutral   agree

## 3. Writing

Choose one quote from Exercise 2. To what extent do you agree with the quote? Please write a composition on the topic you choose and explain in detail.

### Text B  Wolfgang Amadeus Mozart

Wolfgang Amadeus Mozart was born in Salzburg, Austria in 1756 and became a child prodigy at an incredibly early age.

His father Leopold Mozart was an accomplished musician, and his sister Maria Anna, born in 1751, had proved to inherit the musical talent of her father. By the time of her brother's arrival, she was already an accomplished harpsichordist. But her gifts were nothing compared to those rapidly displayed by her brother.

Almost as soon as he could reach the keyboards he was picking out tunes. The young Mozart would listen carefully to his sister's lesson, and as soon as it was over, he would sit at the keyboard and imitate perfectly the pieces he had just heard.

With tuition from his father, he was soon playing the violin with the proficiency of children three times his age. By the time he was six, he was composing minuets and other short pieces. The extraordinary thing was the innate sense of structure and balance that these pieces displayed. They were not childish doodling. He wrote his first symphony at nine years of age, and his first opera at twelve.

Music historians differ on whether Leopold Mozart nurtured his son's genius, or exploited it. The truth is probably a mixture of both. He took his two child prodigies on their first tour of Europe in January 1762, when Wolfgang had just turned six.

Everywhere they went, the audiences loved them. Wolfgang played the violin and the keyboard, and delighted everyone by playing at sight very complicated music by composers such as Johann Sebastian Bach, and Handel.

He embarked on a career as a professional musician and accompanied his father and sister to Munich, and then on to Vienna. They found the Austrian capital already buzzing with the news of the amazing Mozart children.

In 1769, Leopold again decided to take Wolfgang on tour, but this time to Italy, the home of opera. It was a great success, and Mozart continued touring off and on with his father until 1776, by which time he had written masses of string quartets, operas, symphonies, piano music, concertos, and a variety of other music.

Eventually, however, Leopold had to return to his role as a court musician in Salzburg and encouraged his son to accept a similar position. But Wolfgang had other ideas. He was not happy with the lack of musical opportunities in Salzburg, and much against his father's wishes, he quit and set off for Vienna in 1777. There he met Joseph Haydn who greatly admired his work, and the two became firm friends.

Whilst touring in Mannheim, he encountered and made friends with the Webber family who had two attractive daughters, Aloysia and Constanze. He fell in love with Aloysia, but unfortunately for him, she ran off with an actor. Some years later he met the Webber's again and this time fell in love with Constanze.

In 1782, they got married and were extremely happy until financial worries, and Wolfgang's health began to be a problem. The audiences who had feted him as a child had become indifferent. Burning the candle at both ends, he would often work late into the night with little or no sleep. But he also loved to mix with friends and enjoy himself, and both he and his wife were careless with money. When he died in 1791 after a fit of delirium at the tragically early age of 35, one of the greatest composers of all time was buried in a pauper's grave.

The notion that he might have been poisoned either by a jealous rival, Antonio Salieri, an Italian composer who ruled the roost in Vienna in Mozart's time, or as a result of a Masonic conspiracy, still has its advocates.

As a member of the secret brotherhood of Freemasons, he was able to make good use of his knowledge of their arcane rites in "The Magic Flute". The overture opens with grand chords from the brass instruments which parodies persons in high places, and matters of great import. While the lively action which follows hints of human comedy mixed with an air of mystery, and things unspoken.

This opera was an instant critical success when it opened in 1791, yet it failed to improve the fortunes of the impoverished composer.

But Mozart had been a prolific writer who, in his short life, had composed over 600 works. And all the ideas, melodies, rhythms and instrumentation would be carefully worked out in his head well before he transferred them to paper, the only part of his work he found tedious. Most of his greatest music was composed during the last ten years of his life. That is between the ages of 25 and 35.

His work belongs to the Classical period which came about in the latter half of the 18th century.

It was a time of order, simplicity, and refinement, and in marked contrast to the extravagant Baroque era that went before it.

Perhaps the most well known of his operas is "The Marriage of Figaro", a story of love and intrigue, as well as of comedy and sadness. It contains some of his most glorious music, as it also revolutionized the whole form and style of opera.

There is a long history in opera of women, both sopranos and contraltos, appearing in male roles. The traditional Italian name for this is "travesti", or "trouser" roles. And in this respect, Cherubino, the lovesick page boy in "The Marriage of Figaro", is probably the most famous of all "travesti" roles.

Mozart was probably the most comprehensively gifted musician who has ever lived. He could play both the violin and viola to soloist standard, and while there have been other prodigies, none have been able to reach Mozart's ability to combine a dazzling musical imagination with a total mastery of style and form, and matchless beauty of expression.

### Questions for Reflection

1. How was young Mozart influenced by the musical gifts of his families?
2. What musical tours did Mozart and his family take? Were they successful?
3. What difficulties did Mozart encounter in his late years?
4. Name at least two operas that Mozart wrote.
5. Why does the author believe that Mozart is probably the most comprehensively gifted musician who has ever lived?

## Text C  Women in the Enlightenment

The status of women during the Enlightenment changed drastically; surprisingly, much of the talk concerning individual liberties, social welfare, economic liberty, and education did not greatly affect the unequal treatment of women. In many ways, the position of women was seriously degraded during the Enlightenment. Economically, the rise of capitalism produced laws that severely restricted women's rights to own property and run businesses. While Enlightenment thinkers were proposing economic freedom and enlightened monarchs were tearing down barriers to production and trade, women were being forced out of a variety of businesses throughout Europe. In 1600, more than two-thirds of the businesses in London were owned and administered by women; by 1800, that number had shrunk to less than ten percent.

While the Enlightenment greatly changed the face of education, the education of women simultaneously expanded in opportunity but seriously degraded in quality. In the sixteenth and seventeenth centuries, education was available only to the wealthiest women, while education was available, in theory at least, to most men. But the education that these selected women received was often fairly equivalent in content and quality to the best education available to men. The Enlightenment, however, stressed the absolute importance of education for moral development and

the ideal operation of society. So education was extended to the women of the upper and middle classes; however, Enlightenment thinkers also believed that the various intellectual disciplines, such as science and philosophy, were meant only for men. These subjects, then, were closed off to women. Instead, women were offered training in "accomplishments", that is, various skills that contribute to the moral development and the "display" quality of a wife: music, drawing, singing, painting, and so on. So while men were learning the new sciences and philosophies, all that was offered to women in education was decorative "accomplishments".

The economics of pre-industrial Europe were primarily based on family economies; the individual household was the fundamental unit of economic production. Within this unit, most of the necessities of life were produced by members of the family. These family economies were, by and large, sustenance economies. In this environment, there was no place for individuals living outside of a family. If someone lived individually, he or she was regarded as a criminal or beggar or worse. For both men and women, then, there really was no alternative, socially or economically, to living within a family.

Women began to function as productive laborers within this family economy at the age of six or seven (sometimes earlier). In agricultural communities, this meant, usually, light farm labor, and in an artisan's family, this meant taking part in the business itself. Women in artisan families were very often trained in the artisanal skills of the family; as they grew up, they became more vital and important to the functioning of the business. On the farm, however, women's labor was considerably less valued, and women almost always left home between the ages of eleven and fourteen to either work on another farm or become a servant in a household.

Very few women could marry without a dowry. If a woman was part of a family, the family would usually make up the dowry. If she was on her own, which was the most typical fate of rural women, then she had to save enough money to pay her own dowry. This dowry went to the husband and was invested in the family economy, whether agricultural or artisanal. That is, the woman was required to invest in the household economy before she could join it.

In general, women's lives were oriented around the economy of the household rather than family. Both the marriage and the children took second place to production within the family economy; this was absolutely vital, for a bad year in the family economy could mean starvation.

Nevertheless, the new urban economies of pre-industrial Europe created low-level, low-wage jobs in various industries. For both men and women, this work was brutish, harsh, cruel, and actually paid less than sustenance wages. While most women stayed within the family economy, several displaced women found themselves as the central labor force of pre-industrial industries. In an illustration by William Hogarth, we see a hemp factory where women are beating hemp into ropes. The labor is obviously difficult and the shop steward of the factory can be seen hovering over the main character with a whip.

We know little of women's communities for the general run of the European population. Women's lives, in general, consisted of unceasing labor. In the middle and upper classes, however, women's communities began to develop a new and revolutionary life. The works of the *philosophes* began to filter into women's communities and undoubtedly shaped women's self-concepts; in fact, much of the activity of the *philosophes* was sponsored by women and women's communities. While women found that the presses were closed off to them, they still had an immense amount of influence over the currents and contents of the philosophical movement. A seed was being planted; women's communities were demanding a more central intellectual role in European life. This seed would blossom into the revolutionary feminist works at the end of the century: Mary Wollstonecraft's *Vindication of the Rights of Woman* and Olympe de Gouges' *Declaration of the Rights of Women*.

## Questions for Reflection

1. What is the general position of women in the 18th century?
2. Why does the author say that "all that was offered to women in education was decorative 'accomplishments'"?
3. What is the major function of women in the Enlightenment period?

## Websites to Visit

http://www.thoughtco.com/a-beginners-guide-to-the-enlightenment-1221925 ( accessed Apr. 28, 2020)
This website provides a comprehensive introduction to the development of the European Enlightenment.

http://www.classicalarchives.com/mozart.html (accessed Apr. 28, 2020)
This website provides students with chances to listen to almost all works of Mozart. You may also find a very brief introduction about Mozart's life and music.

## Movie to Watch

### Amadeus (1984)

*Amadeus* is a 1984 drama directed by Miloš Forman. Based on Peter Shaffer's stage play *Ama-*

deus, the film is based very loosely on the lives of Wolfgang Amadeus Mozart and Antonio Salieri, two composers who lived in Vienna, Austria, during the latter half of the 18th century.

The film was nominated for 53 awards and received 40, including 8 Academy Awards (including Best Picture), 4 BAFTA Awards, 4 Golden Globes, and a DGA Award. In 1998, *Amadeus* was ranked the 53rd best American movie by the American Film Institute on its *AFI's 100 Years 100 Movies* list.

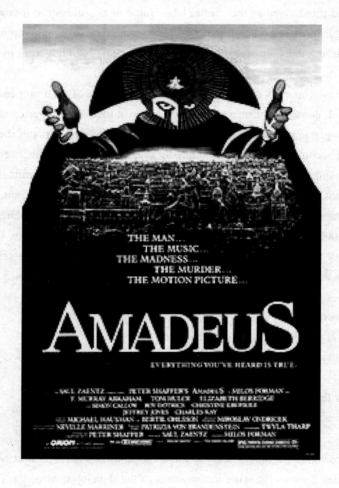

# Unit 12
## The French Revolution

> Men are moved by two levers only: fear and self-interest.
> There is only one step from the sublime to the ridiculous.
> — Napoléon Bonaparte

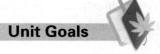
### Unit Goals

- To learn the historical development of the French Revolution
- To understand the causes and influence of the French Revolution
- To learn the useful words and expressions that describe the French Revolution
- To improve language skills by learning this unit

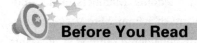
### Before You Read

1. Study and discuss the following picture. What event is described in the painting? Who are these people and what are they doing? What is the message that the painting was intended to convey?

2. Form groups of three or four students. Try to find, on the Internet or in the library, more information about the French Revolution. Choose a topic that interests you most and prepare a five-minute classroom presentation.

# An Introduction to European Culture (Second Edition)

## Start to Read

### Text A  The French Revolution

In 1789, one European out of every five lived in France. Many Europeans considered France the center of European culture. It followed that a revolution in France would immediately command the attention of Europe and assume international significance. Yet the French Revolution attracted and disturbed men and women for much more important reasons. Both its philosophical ideals and its political realities mirrored attitudes, concerns, and conflicts that had occupied the minds of educated Europeans for several decades. When the revolutionaries pronounced in favor of liberty, they spoke not only with the voice of the eighteenth-century *philosophes*, but with that of the English aristocracy in 1688 and the North American revolutionaries of 1776.

They also raised issues that resonated across Europe. Absolutism was increasingly the bane of a wide spectrum of thoughtful opinion. Aristocrats across Europe and the colonies resented monarchical inroads on their ancient freedoms. Members of the middle class, many of whom were very successful, chafed under a system of official privilege that they increasingly considered outmoded. Peasants fiercely resented what seemed to them the never-ceasing demands of the central government on their limited resources. Nor were resentments focused exclusively on absolutist monarchs. Tensions existed as well between country and city dwellers, between rich and poor, over-privileged and under-privileged, slave and free. The French Revolution marked part of a crisis that shook all of late eighteenth-century Europe and its colonies, bringing revolutionary movements to the British Empire, to Belgium and the Netherlands, and to South America. The age of revolution restructured the nations of the West.

The opening of the age or revolution came in the North American colonies. The American Revolution of 1776 was one of the last in a series of conflicts over colonial control of the New World, conflicts that had wracked England and France throughout the eighteenth century. It also became one of the first crises of the old regime at home. The New World was where the fears and aspirations were first dramatized, where extralegal associations of common citizens defied acts of a sovereign power, where abstract ideas of political philosophy were substantiated in the actions of ordinary men. Among "enlightened" Europeans, the success with which citizens of the new nation had thrown off British rule and formed a republic based on Enlightenment principles was the source of tremendous optimism. Change would come. Reform was possible. The costs would be modest.

If the American Revolution first dramatized Europeans' "fear and aspirations", the events in France deepened them. The French Revolution proved a more radical project, though it did not necessarily begin that way. It became immeasurably more costly—protracted, complex, and violent. It aroused much greater hopes and consequently, in many cases, bitter disillusionment. It raised issues that would not be settled for half a century.

## The French Revolution: An Overview

In Charles Dickens's *A Tale of Two Cities* (1859), the source of many popular images of revolution, the French upheaval blurs into a frightening picture of bloodthirsty crowds watching a guillotine. The picture is memorable but misleading. The "French Revolution" is a shorthand term for a complex series of events between 1789 and 1799. (Napoléon ruled from 1799 to 1814—1815.) To simplify, those events can be divided into three stages. In the first stage, running from 1788 to 1792, the struggle was constitutional and relatively peaceful. An increasingly bold elite articulated its grievances against the king. Like the American revolutionaries, elites refused taxation without representation, attacked "despotism", or arbitrary authority, and offered an Enlightenment-inspired program to rejuvenate the nation. Reforms, many of them breathtakingly wide ranging, were instituted—some accepted or even offered by the king, and others passed over his protests. The peaceful, constitutional phase did not last. Unlike the American Revolution, the French Revolution did not stabilize around one constitution or one set of political leaders for many reasons. Reforms met with resistance, dividing the country. The threat of change in France created international tensions. In 1792, these tensions exploded into war and the monarchy fell, to be replaced with a republic. The second stage of the Revolution, which lasted from 1792 to 1794, was one of crisis and consolidation. A ruthlessly centralized government mobilized all the country's resources to fight the foreign enemy as well as counterrevolutionaries at home, to destroy traitors and the vestiges of the Old Regime. The Terror, as this policy was called, did save the republic, but it exhausted itself in factions and recriminations. In the third phase, from 1794 to 1799, the government, still at war with Europe, drifted into the corruption and almost inevitably into military rule under Napoléon. Napoléon continued the war until his final defeat in 1815.

## A Chronology of Major Events in French Revolution

| | |
|---|---|
| May 5, 1789 | A meeting of the Estates-General was called by Louis XVI in Versailles to discuss and approve a new tax plan. |
| June 17, 1789 | The Third Estate proclaimed itself "The National Assembly". A few liberal nobles and many clergymen joined the movement of the Third Estate. Tennis |

|  |  |
|---|---|
|  | Court Oath: After being locked out of their meeting room, deputies of the Third Estate assembled on a tennis court and swore not to separate until a consti-tutional regime was established. |
| July 7 – 13, 1789 | The National Assembly appointed a committee of thirty members to draft a constitution, proclaiming itself the Constituent National Assembly, with full authority and power to decree laws; their primary task to draw up and adopt a constitution. |
| July 14, 1789 | The storming and fall of the Bastille. |
| August 4, 1789 | The end of feudalism and serfdom in France was announced by The National Assembly. |
| August 27, 1789 | *The Declaration of the Rights of Man* was issued by The National Assembly. |
| October 5, 1789 | The women of Paris invaded Versailles. Parisians, led by a large number of women, marched upon Versailles and forced the royal family back to Paris, where they took up residence at the Tuileries. Louis XVI was considered by many a "Prisoner" in Paris. The Assembly, still in Versailles, declared, in the spirit of constitutional monarchy, its inseparability from the king. |
| 1790 | *The Civil Constitution of the Clergy* was passed. |
| 1791 | *The Constitution of 1791* was adopted. |
| June 20, 1791 | Louis XVI and his family were arrested while trying to flee from France. |
| April 20, 1792 | France declared war on Austria. |
| September 1792 | The First meeting of the National Convention was held. |
| December 1972 | Commencement of the trial of Louis XVI. |
| January 21, 1793 | Louis XVI was sentenced to the guillotine. |
| August 1793 | A National Draft was issued calling for all able-bodied men to enlist in the army. |
| September 1793 – July 27, 1794 | The Reign of Terror court sentenced 20,000 to 40,000 people to death. The National Convention arrested Robespierre. |
| 1795 | A new Constitution was adopted. |
| 1799 | The fall of the Directory heralds the end of the French Revolution. |

## Proper Nouns

1. Charles Dickens 查尔斯·狄更斯(英国作家)
2. Louis XVI 路易十六(法国国王)
3. Versailles 凡尔赛宫
4. The Third Estate 第三等级(指平民阶层)
5. the Bastille 巴士底狱

# After You Read

*Knowledge Focus*

1. **Decide whether the following statements are true or false according to what you read in the text.**
   (1) (　) France was the center of Europe prior to the French Revolution.
   (2) (　) The liberal ideas of French revolutionaries were borrowed not only from the eighteenth-century *philosophes*, but also from the North American revolutionaries.
   (3) (　) Before the French Revolution, the only social class that supported absolutism was the aristocrats.
   (4) (　) American Revolution was the first of a series of conflicts over colonial control of the New World.
   (5) (　) Compared with the American Revolution, the French Revolution seemed to be more radical.
   (6) (　) The image of the French Revolution in Dickens's novel is frightening, yet misleading.
   (7) (　) The beginning of the French Revolution was violent and radical.
   (8) (　) In the second phase of the French Revolution, the monarchy fell and a centralized government was established.

2. **Compare the French Revolution with the American Revolution of 1776. What are the similarities and differences?**

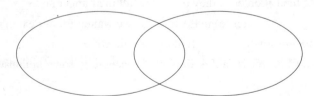

3. **Discuss the following questions with your partner.**
   (1) Why did the French Revolution immediately command the attention of the whole Europe?
   (2) What was the French society like before the revolution? What resentment did French people have towards the government?
   (3) How was the French Revolution influenced by the American Revolution of 1776?
   (4) What does the term "French Revolution" refer to? How many stages did it include?
   (5) Draw a brief outline of the development of the French Revolution.

**Language Focus**

**1. Fill in the blanks with the following words or expressions you have learned in the text.**

| stabilize | articulate | blur | in favor of | resonate |
| arbitrary | rejuvenate | dramatize | a spectrum of | aspiration |

(1) In the discussion, he spoke _____ reducing defense expenditures.
(2) The noise of the bell _____ through the building.
(3) Counseling covers _____ behavior problems.
(4) She was filled with the _____ to succeed in life.
(5) Don't believe everything she tells you; she tends to _____.
(6) As she drifted into sleep, the doctor's face began to _____ and fade.
(7) Many people are opposed to the new law, but have had no opportunity to _____ their opposition.
(8) I have no idea of what is in fashion, so my choice is quite _____.
(9) He has decided to _____ the team by bringing in a lot of new, young players.
(10) In China, the policy of one child per family was introduced to _____ the country's population.

**2. Fill in the blanks with the proper form of the word in the brackets.**

(1) Residents are fed up with the _____ (disturb) caused by the nightclub.
(2) At no point in his life should a _____ (revolution) lie back and take life easy.
(3) One by one these northern states expressed their desire for _____ (consolidate) with the union.
(4) Instead of discussing their problems, they bottled up all their anger and _____ (resent).
(5) You could feel the _____ (tense) in the room as we waited for our exam results.
(6) The new house he bought was _____ (colony) architecture.
(7) _____ (sovereignty) power is said to lie with the people in some countries, and with a ruler in others.
(8) There was a note of _____ (optimistic) in his voice as he spoke about the company's future.
(9) I have not seen them since that _____ (memory) evening when the boat capsized.
(10) There is a lot of _____ (resist) to the idea of a united Europe.

**3. Fill in the blanks with the proper prepositions or adverbs that collocate with the neighboring words.**

(1) I took the job _____ necessity because we had no money left.
(2) There were 16 votes _____ favor of my suggestion, and 15 against.
(3) She's one of those guests who does nothing _____ complain.
(4) The celebration will run _____ next Monday.
(5) He'd been harboring a grievance _____ his boss.
(6) The boss decided to pass _____ his slight mistakes.

(7) Every failure simply has to be replaced _____ another attempt.
(8) During the Second World War, Germany was _____ war with almost all the countries in the world.

4. **Error Correction: Each of the following sentences has at least one grammatical error. Identify the errors and correct them.**
   (1) In 1789, one European of every five lived in France.
   (2) It was followed that a revolution in France would immediately command the attention of Europe and assume international significance.
   (3) French Revolution attracted and disturbed men and women for many important reasons.
   (4) Members of the middle class, many of who were very successful, chafed under a system of official privilege.
   (5) Peasants fiercely resented it seemed to them the never-ceasing demands of the central government on their limited resources.
   (6) The French Revolution marked part of a crisis shook all of late eighteenth-century Europe and its colonies.
   (7) American Revolution of 1776 was one of last in a series of conflicts over colonial control of the New World.
   (8) The success that citizens of the new nation had thrown off British rule and formed a republic was the source of tremendous optimism.
   (9) The French Revolution was proved a more radical project.
   (10) It raised issues what would not be settled for half a century.
   (11) As the American revolutionaries, elites refused taxation without representation.
   (12) Reforms were met with resistance, dividing the country.
   (13) In 1792, these tensions exploded into war and the monarchy fell, being replaced with a republic soon.
   (14) The Terror, like this policy was called, saved the republic.
   (15) The government, still at war with Europe, was drifted into the corruption and almost inevitably into military rule under Napoléon.
   (16) The "French Revolution" is a shorthand term for a complex series of event between 1789 and 1799.

## Comprehensive Work
### 1. The Causes of the French Revolution (I)
The cartoon in the following was produced in the 1780s and is a comment on the social situation in France at that time. It can be used to help explain the causes of the French Revolution of 1789.
(1) Label the three figures in the cartoon by writing in the spaces provided.

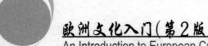

- Peasant
- Priest
- Noble

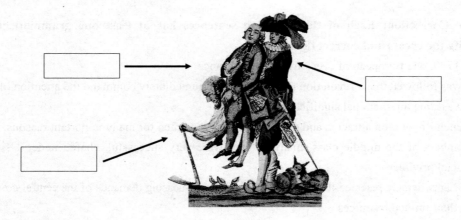

(2) Explain how the cartoon can be used to describe the causes of the French Revolution.

_____

## 2. The Causes of the French Revolution (II)

Many documents in the eighteenth century reflected possible reasons for the French Revolution as well. Study the following source cards and answer the questions that follow.

| Source A | Yearly Incomes Compared |
|---|---|

Archbishop of Paris 50,000 livres.

Marquis de Mainvillette 20,000 livres.

Prince de Conti 14,000 livres.

A Paris parish priest 10,000 livres.

A typical village priest 750 livres.

A master carpenter 200 livres.

(The livre was replaced by the franc in 1795. In the 1780s, there were about 4 livres to £1).

| Source B | An Englishman's View of French Peasants, 1787 – 1790 |
|---|---|

I was joined by a poor woman who complained of the times. Her husband had only a morsel of land, one cow and a poor horse. But they had to pay 20kg of wheat and three chickens as feudal dues to one lord, and 60kg of oats, one chicken and five pence to another, along with very heavy taxes to the king's tax collectors: "The taxes and feudal dues are crushing us."

—Arthur Young, *Travels in France*, 1792

Unit 12　The French Revolution

> **Source C**　　　　　**The People Should Have Power, 1775**
>
> Man is born free. No man has any natural authority over others; force does not give anyone that right. The power to make laws belongs to the people and only to the people.
> 　　　　　—Jean-Jacques Rousseau, A pamphlet, banned by the French government in 1775

**Questions for Discussion:**

(1) How does the author of Source B describe the lives of French peasants?

___

(2) Study Sources A and B together. Do these sources explain why poor people in France resented the rich? Explain your answer with the sources.

___

(3) Rousseau (Source C) was an influential writer at that time. Along with other writers like Voltaire, he wanted France to have a more democratic form of government. Who would be most influenced by his words and why?

___

(4) The pamphlet which source C came from was banned in 1775. Why do you think it was banned? Which members of French society would want it to be banned?

___

**3. Writing**

(1) Work on an extended piece of writing titled: "What Was Wrong with the French Society in 1789?" Refer to Sources A – C in the above exercise, use keywords and your own knowledge in your answer.

(2) Design a poster to encourage members of the Third Estate to campaign for a fairer way. Include on your poster the reasons why people were resentful of the rich.

> JOIN THE FIGHT FOR A FAIRER WAY

## Read More

### Text B  The Storming of the Bastille

There are few more iconic buildings than the Bastille of Paris, France. The storming of the Bastille by enraged commoners on July 14, 1789 was the spark that began the long and violent struggle to overthrow the ancient aristocratic regime, and triggered the eventual birth of modern democracy.

### A dark history

For all its iconic status today, the Bastille does not exist in a physical sense — it was torn down by the orders of the National Assembly two days after its storming. Today, the July Column, at one corner of the Place de la Bastille, commemorates the site where the prison once stood. Despite its destruction, however, the Bastille lives on, immortalized in countless paintings, plays and other works of literature, where it has become a symbol for the freedom of French people from repression.

The Bastille has, throughout much of its history, been a symbol of royal privilege and oppression. Internment in the Bastille was the king's business, and many of the prisoners were the victims of the king's arbitrary judgments or transient whims. It began life as the fortress Bastille Saint-Antoine, built as part of the defensive system of the city. By the 18th century, it was simply known as the Bastille, and was appropriated by Louis VIII as a convenient prison for state prisoners. The practice continued through the reign of Louis XVI, until the Revolution put an end to the aristocracy.

Despite popular imagination, the Bastille was not particularly reprehensible, as far as prisons go. Internment here was generally reserved for heretics and political dissidents, though there were, of course, the more common criminals present. They were treated reasonably well under the circumstances. Noble prisoners had their own, fairly spacious cells, which they decorated with their own furniture. They were free to mix, play games and exercise in the open spaces of prison. They had their own servants, had guests and even threw parties—Cardinal de Rohan once had dinner for 20 in his cell. Of course, the commoners lived less graciously than their blue-blooded fellow prisoners, but not remarkably so.

### The reason for the popular resentment

The Bastille's black reputation did not actually stem from the physical conditions of the prisoners, which were rather outstanding by the standards of the barbaric penal system of the time. It became the focus of popular resentment because it was a tangible sign of the king's power over the helpless populace. The 18th century was a time of great unrest among the peasants and the commoner merchants, who resented the aristocrat's cruel, arbitrary rule. All power rested in the hands of the king, and any threat was ruthlessly removed. Writers who criticized the nobility, political agents who upset the status quo, religious preachers who called for a change in the government, were all taken and imprisoned in the Bastille, and the people deeply resented their suppression.

By the time of Louis XVI, revolutionary popular sentiment was overwhelmingly strong, particularly as the country was then suffering famine and a financial crisis, neither of which were being addressed by the king. The entire nation was a powder keg in need of a spark and Paris soon provided it.

## The revolutionaries take the Bastille

On 12th July, a series of oppressive moves to control the restive populace, ill-timed political decisions and a rumor that Swiss and German battalions were about to descend on the city to massacre the citizens prompted mobs to take to the streets.

The storming of the Bastille was almost an incidental action. The mobs were looking for more arms, having already raided a number of depots around the city. The garrison stationed in the Bastille consisted of a small number of Swiss mercenaries armed with large quantities of arms. The rioters decided they would take the Bastille, and on the morning of 14th July, gathered in front of the prison.

The take-over began civilly enough, with the usual exchange of delegates, negotiations, offers and counter-offers. In charge of the Bastille was Governor de Launay, son of the previous supervisor and actually born in the Bastille. He was, from all accounts, determined not to surrender, but as the crowd grew impatient with the negotiations and his own garrison pressed for a quick solution, things quickly got out of hand.

The restless rioters began trying to get into the fortress, and even numerous shots from the defenders could not dissuade them, though they paid with their lives for their stubbornness. It was an unequal battle, with the defenders holding the upper hand until a detachment of soldiers (who would later form the National Guard) joined on the rioter's side, bringing with them cannons and more arms. It was at this point the defenders began to weaken, as they realized the rioters were beginning to prepare for a full-scale siege. They convinced de Launay to capitulate, despite his intention to blow up the Bastille rather than surrender. At the end of the day, ninety-eight revolutionaries were dead, and only one defender.

### The aftermath of the takeover

The attackers succeeded in taking control of the Bastille's arms and from then on, the power of the aristocracy was increasingly transferred to the hands of the triumphant commoners. Louis XVI made what concessions he could to the people, but the increasingly revolutionary mood of the time ultimately resulted in the end of aristocratic rule and the beginning of democracy. The revolutionary fever would soon spread, first to the already rebellious American colonies, and from there onwards around the world. It was the beginning of a worldwide shift in the fundamental structure of society, and those who died in the storming were only the first of millions who would later die around the world as the new order came into power.

One of the first casualties of this climatic change was de Launay. After his surrender, he was dragged through the streets in a storm of abuse, and subjected to an increasingly unpleasant discussion of his fate. After one particularly vicious suggestion from a man named Desnot, de Launay cried "Enough! Let me die!" and kicked Desnot in the groin. He was immediately stabbed to death, and his head sawn off and paraded on a spike.

Incidentally, contrary to the later romanticization of the episode, the revolutionaries did not release hundreds of grateful prisoners. There were only seven people incarcerated at the time: four forgers, two lunatics and a deviant aristocrat. The storming would, however, prove enormously useful to the revolutionaries for its propaganda value, as it became a symbolic act of rebellion against oppression. This episode would become commemorated as the pivotal moment in the birth of democracy and the modern French nation, and is now celebrated on July 14th as Bastille Day, the French national holiday.

*Questions for Reflection*

1. Does the Bastille still exist today? Why is it regarded as an iconic building in French history?
2. What did the Bastille symbolize? Why did it become the focus of popular resentment in the 18th century?
3. Please give an account of how the Bastille was taken by the revolutionaries.
4. What happened after the Bastille was taken?

## Text C  The Reign of Terror

To ensure the accomplishment of the Revolution, the rulers of France resorted to bloody authoritarianism that has come to be known as the Terror. Although the Convention succeeded in 1793 in drafting a new democratic constitution based on male suffrage, it deferred its introduction because of a wartime emergency. Instead, the Convention prolonged its own life year after year, and increasingly delegated its responsibilities to a group of twelve leaders, or the Committee of Public Safety.

Foremost among the political leadership were Jean-Paul Marat, Georges Jacques Danton, and Maximilien Robespierre, the latter two members of the Committee of Public Safety. Jean-Paul Marat was educated as a physician, and by 1789 had already earned enough distinction in that profession to be awarded an honorary degree by St. Andrews University in Scotland. Marat opposed nearly all of his moderate colleagues' assumptions, including their admiration for Great Britain, which Marat considered corrupt and despotic. Soon made a victim of persecution and forced to take refuge in unsanitary sewers and dungeons, he persevered as the editor of the popular news sheet, *The Friend of the People*. Exposure to the infection left him with a chronic skin disease, from which he could find relief only through frequent bathing. In the summer of 1793, at the height of the crisis of the revolution, he was stabbed in his bath by Charlotte Corday, a young royalist, and became a revolutionary martyr.

Georges Jacques Danton, like Marat, was a popular political leader, well known in the more plebian clubs of Paris. Elected a member of the Committee of Public Safety in 1793, he had much to do with organizing the Terror. As time went on, however, he wearied of ruthlessness and displayed a tendency to compromise that give his opponents in the Convention their opportunity. In April 1794, Danton was sent to the guillotine.

The most famous and perhaps the greatest of the radical leaders was Maximilien Robespierre. Born of a family reputed to be of Irish descent, Robespierre was trained for the law and speedily achieved modest success as a lawyer. His eloquence, and his consistent, or ruthless, insistence that leaders respect the "will of the people" eventually won him a following in the Jacobin Club. Later he became president of the National Convention and a member of the Committee of Public Safety. Though he had little to do with starting the Terror, he was nevertheless responsible for enlarging its scope. He came to justify ruthlessness as necessary to revolutionary progress.

The two years of the Terror brought a stern dictatorship in France. Pressed by foreign enemies, the Committee faced opposition from both the political right and left at home. In June 1793, responding to the need for absolute political control, leaders of the "Mountain", a party of radicals allied with Parisian artisans, purged moderates from the Convention. Rebellions broke out in the provincial cities of Lyon, Bordeaux, and Marseilles, ruthlessly repressed by the Committee and its local representatives. The government also faced counterrevolution in the west. The peasantry there resented the government's assault on its religious institutions. The government's attempts to conscript troops into the revolutionary armies fanned long-smolder-

ing resentments into open rebellion. By the summer, the peasant forces in the west posed a serious threat to the Convention. Determined to stabilize France, whatever the cost, the Committee dispatched commissioners into the countryside to suppress the enemies of the state.

During the period of the Terror, from September 1793 to July 1794, the most reliable estimates place the number of executions as high as twenty-five to thirty thousand in France as a whole, fewer than twenty thousand of whom were condemned by the courts. In addition, approximately five hundred thousand were incarcerated between March 1793 and August 1794. Few victims of the Terror were aristocrats. Many more were peasants or laborers accused of hoarding, treason, or counterrevolutionary activity. Anyone who appeared to threaten the republic, no matter what his or her social or economic position, was at risk. When the Abbé Sieyès was asked what he had done to distinguish himself during the Terror sometime later, he responded dryly, "I lived."

**Questions for Reflection**

1. Who were the most famous political leaders in the Reign of Terror?
2. Fill in the following form with the information you read from the passage about the three political leaders.

| Name | Famous for... |
|---|---|
| Jean-Paul Marat | |
| Georges Jacques Danton | |
| Maximilien Robespierre | |

3. Describe the social condition of France during the Reign of Terror.

**Websites to Visit**

https://www.history.com/topics/france/french-revolution (accessed Apr. 28, 2020)
This website has been designed to elaborate on many aspects of the French Revolution. It covers the causes of the revolution, rise of the Third Estate, *Declaration of the Rights of Man and of the Citizen*, etc.

http://chnm.gmu.edu/revolution/ (accessed Apr. 28, 2020)
With 12 topical essays, 250 images, 350 text documents, 13 songs, 13 maps and a timeline, this website provides you with a good chance to explore the French Revolution.

*Movie to Watch*

### A Tale of Two Cities (1958)

 *A Tale of Two Cities* is a 1958 film of Charles Dickens' novel *A Tale of Two Cities*. It starred Dirk Bogarde and Dorothy Tutin, and was directed by Ralph Thomas.

 British barrister Sydney Carton lives an insubstantial and unhappy life. He falls under the spell of Lucie Manette, but Lucie marries Charles Darnay. When Darnay goes to Paris to rescue an imprisoned family retainer, he becomes entangled in the snares of the brutal French Revolution and is jailed and condemned to the guillotine. But Sydney Carton, in love with a woman he cannot have, comes up with a daring plan to save her husband...

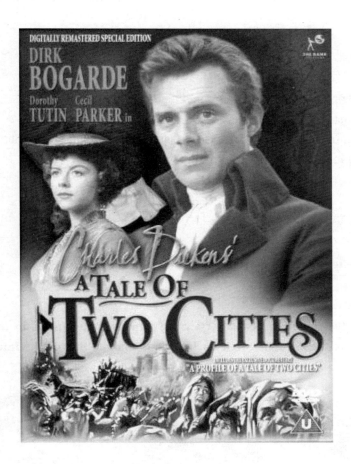

# Unit 13
## Romanticism

> To say the word Romanticism is to say modern art—that is, intimacy, spirituality, color, aspiration towards the infinite, expressed by every means available to the arts.
>
> —Charles Baudelaire, French poet

### Unit Goals

- To be familiar with the cultural characteristics of Romanticism
- To appreciate the literary works of Romantic writers
- To learn the useful words and expressions that describe the Romantic Age
- To improve language skills by learning this unit

### Before You Read

1. What is Romanticism? What do you know about Romanticism?

_____

2. Do you know the following people? They are famous writers/poets in the Romantic era. Choose one from the list and search for information about him on the Internet. Share your findings with your classmates.

Goethe

Percy Bysshe Shelley

William Wordsworth

# Start to Read

## Text A  Romanticism

When a person hears the word Romanticism, his first thought may be of romance storybooks or novels or illustrated books depicting romantic art. A few individuals, however, may connect the root of the word to a certain city on the Tiber. Despite the apparent connection between the words, Romanticism has little to do with romance, nor did the Romantic Movement originate in any country that speaks of romance-related legends.

The Romantic Movement started in Germany and England in the late 18th century, and it ended with the death of Goethe and Sir Walter Scott in 1832. The Romantic Movement followed the neoclassicism school of art and was in many ways a rebellion against the tenets of neoclassicism. The artists and writers who worked when the neoclassicism school held sway saw the universe as an orderly place that the humankind could control. Nature existed so that mankind could tame it and harness its power  rather than the other way around. The prevailing philosophy of neoclassicism was that with the use of order and reason, the universe could ultimately be understood and that the individual was merely part of the greater whole. Although the official date marking the end of the Romantic period is given to be 1832, authors in the USA and some painters in Europe went on to continue the tradition beyond the day.

Instead of embracing the ideas of their predecessors, the artists of the Romantic period saw an individual as a heroic entity capable of achieving great things through sheer force of will. The individual was still a part of the universe, but the creativity an individual possessed could propel him/her to great heights. What made the individual unique was his/her ability to use imagination as a creative force. One poet who wrote during the age of Romanticism expressed pity for people with no spark of imagination in them.

It may seem strange that the greatest example of individual power during this period is not one of the many artists and authors working during the Romantic period, but

Napoléon Bonaparte. The name of Bonaparte may not be popular today, but he started out as a lowly soldier and rose to become an emperor through his own abilities. This feat makes him the perfect example of the self-made man that the Romantic movement idealized. Certainly, the victories Napoléon managed to achieve required a special type of strategic creativity.

The authors and artists also broke with the neoclassicism school by changing the way nature was viewed in works of art. Only one single unifying philosophy connected how every author and artist of the Romantic period viewed nature. Rather than being considered as something to be harnessed and controlled, nature was viewed as a good thing that served as a source of inspiration.

Modern schools of literature and art have demoted the individual from the supreme place he enjoyed in the Romantic school, suggesting instead that an artist cannot help but be influenced by his surrounding environment. This web of influence includes other artists, painters and writers with whom a person producing any work of art is familiar. It holds true for the Romantic writers as well. Since Romanticism was a rebellion against the artistic school that preceded it, it could not help but be influenced by the rejection of the ideals of neoclassicism. Romantic period authors interpreted their ideals in such a way that strange dichotomy developed in the writings of the period. Many authors chose real settings and real characters, but others chose fantastic backgrounds or unbelievable events that their protagonists needed to overcome. A few writers skillfully interwove elements of the fantastic and the believable.

Neoclassicism, which started during the Age of Enlightenment, was marked with a "turn away" from superstition. Applying the principles of rational thought was the beginning of solving all of mankind's problems. Emotion was not eliminated by neoclassical artists, but emotion was often viewed as a hindrance. Further, turning away from the previous school, the artists of the Romantic period felt that emotion was a necessary and vital part of life and that emotion and imagination often came up with solutions that reasoning alone could not achieve. In the worlds that the Romantic authors created, a single person could change the world, but he did so through utilizing his creative power, imagination and understanding his emotions rather than regarding them as a hindrance.

Although Romanticism ended nearly two centuries ago, many of its ideals still live on. The individual may see less importance in the artwork of today where the voice of an author is believed to be controlled by his surroundings, but the idea of a person being able to change the world through his abilities and ideas lives on.

Romanticism may no longer be the school of prevailing literature and artistic thought, but its effects are alive and prevalent. Perhaps, this is because it started as a grassroots movement and the authors and artists did not view themselves as innately superior to the common man, and many of the movement's ideals survive in both modern art and society.

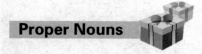
**Proper Nouns**

1.Romanticism 浪漫主义

2. Goethe 歌德(Johann Wolfgang von Goethe, 德国诗人)
3. Sir Walter Scott 沃尔特·司各特爵士(英国19世纪历史小说家和诗人)
4. Napoléon Bonaparte 拿破仑·波拿巴(法国革命家)

### After You Read

*Knowledge Focus*

1. Decide whether the following statements are true or false according to what you read in the text.

   (1) (　) Romanticism is connected with romance or romance related legends.
   (2) (　) The beginning of the Romantic Movement was marked by the works of Goethe and Sir Walter Scott.
   (3) (　) The Romantic Movement was seen as a rebellion against the neoclassicism in many respects.
   (4) (　) An important characteristic of Romanticists is their use of imagination.
   (5) (　) Napoléon Bonaparte can be seen as a great example of the self-made man that Romantic movement idealized.
   (6) (　) In the eyes of the Romanticists, nature was viewed as a source of inspiration.
   (7) (　) According to the passage, Romantic writers would be inevitably influenced by the ideas of neoclassicism.
   (8) (　) Emotion was abandoned by neoclassical artists, but seen as necessary by Romantic authors.

2. Compare Neoclassicism with Romanticism. What are the similarities and differences?

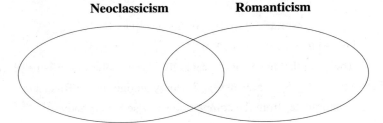

3. Discuss the following questions with your partner.

   (1) What is Romanticism? Does the term have anything to do with romance?
   (2) According to Romanticists, what is the role of the individual in the universe?
   (3) Why was Napoléon Bonaparte viewed as a great example of the Romanticist?
   (4) What is the influence of Neoclassicism on the work of Romantic artists?
   (5) Please summarize the influence of Romanticism.

**Language Focus**

**1. Fill in the blanks with the following words or expressions you have learned in the text.**

| sheer | propel | demote | hold sway | harness |
|---|---|---|---|---|
| ultimately | end with | interweave | prevailing | hindrance |

(1) The English alphabet begins with "A" and _____ "Z".
(2) Among English playwrights, few would deny that Shakespeare _____.
(3) We can _____ the power of the wind to make electricity.
(4) Everything will _____ depend on what is said at the meeting with the directors next week.
(5) I have never considered my disability a _____, but other people have.
(6) He persuaded them to join him by the _____ magnetism of his personality.
(7) His addiction to drugs _____ him towards a life of crime.
(8) Product buy-back is a _____ payment term at present.
(9) The captain was _____ to sergeant for failing to fulfill his duties.
(10) She has created an intriguing story by skillfully _____ fictional and historical events.

**2. Fill in the blanks with the proper form of the word in the brackets.**

(1) He told us a _____ (romantic) about a prince who married a poor girl.
(2) Too rigid parental control fosters _____ (rebel) of children.
(3) His _____ (hero) feats made him a legend in his own time.
(4) Many students tend to _____ (ideal) the life in college.
(5) Their bombs are always placed in _____ (strategy) positions to cause as much chaos as possible.
(6) He gave an _____ (inspiration) reading of his own poems.
(7) He never asked her to marry him out of fear of _____ (reject).
(8) It is _____ (believe) that the event repeated itself years later in the same place.
(9) I am shocked at the _____ (prevalent) of bribery among these officials.
(10) Their _____ (eliminate) from the completion surprised everybody.

**3. Fill in the blanks with the proper prepositions or adverbs that collocate with the neighboring words.**

(1) Mathematics has a lot to do _____ IQ tests, as it is well proven that children good at numbers tend to have a stronger reasoning faculty.
(2) The film ends _____ the death of the heroine.
(3) You are going in the wrong direction. It's the other way _____.
(4) It was a shooting star that propelled me _____ astronomy in the first place.
(5) I've got some work to do but I should be _____ in an hour if you can wait.
(6) It's difficult to break _____ old habits.

178

(7) I believe those principles hold true _____ everyone, everywhere.

(8) No one has come up _____ a convincing explanation of why dinosaurs die _____.

**4. Error Correction:** Each of the following sentences has at least one grammatical error. Identify the errors and correct them.

(1) Romantic Movement ended the death of Goethe and Sir Walter Scott in 1832.

(2) The Romantic Movement was followed the neoclassicism school of art and was in many ways a rebellion against the tenets of neoclassicism.

(3) The artists and writers worked when the neoclassicism school held sway saw the universe as an orderly place that the humankind could control.

(4) Nature existed such that mankind could tame it and harness its power rather than other way around.

(5) It made the individual unique was his/her ability to use imagination as a creative force.

(6) One poet wrote during the age of Romanticism expressed pity for people with no spark of imagination in them.

(7) This feat makes him the perfect example of the self-made man what the Romanticism movement idealized.

(8) The authors and artists also broke with the Neoclassicism school in changing the way nature was viewed in works of art.

(9) Only one single unifying philosophy connected every author and artist of the Romantic period viewed nature.

(10) Romanticism suggests that an artist cannot help but influenced by his surrounding environment.

(11) This web of influence include other artists, painters and writers whom a person producing any work of art is familiar.

(12) Romantic period authors interpreted their ideals in such a way as strange dichotomy developed in the writings of the period.

(13) To apply the principles of rational thought was the beginning of solving all of mankind's problems.

(14) The artists of the Romantic period felt that emotion was necessary and vital part of life.

(15) Romanticism may not longer be the school of prevailing literature and artistic thought, but its effects are alive and prevalent.

## Comprehensive Work

### 1. A Romantic Poem

The following poem was written by William Wordsworth, one of the most famous poets in the Age of Romanticism. Read the poem and discuss with your partner how the poem reflects the characteristic features of the Romantic Movement.

## I Wandered Lonely As a Cloud

I wandered lonely as a cloud
That floats on high o'er vales and hills
When all at once I saw a crowd,
A host, of golden daffodils;
Beside the lake, beneath the trees,
Fluttering and dancing in the breeze.

Continuous as the stars that shine
And twinkle on the milky way,
They stretched in never-ending line
Along the margin of a bay:
Ten thousand saw I at a glance,
Tossing their heads in a sprightly dance.

The waves beside them danced; but they
Out-did the sparkling waves in glee:
A poet could not but be gay,
In such jocund company:
I gazed—and gazed—but little thought
What wealth the show to me had brought:

For oft, when on my couch I lie
In vacant or in pensive mood,
They flash upon that inward eye
Which is the bliss of solitude;
And then my heart with pleasure fills,
And dances with the daffodils.

**Questions for Discussion:**

(1) Give two examples of poetic language (metaphor, simile, personification).

Example 1:
_____

Example 2:
_____

(2) Pick two quotes from this poem that illustrate the "romantic" style. Tell why you picked that quote and how the quote illustrated a romantic style.

_____

## 2. A Case Study: *The Bullfight*

The following painting was made by Goya, a Spanish Romantic painter. Study the painting carefully and discuss the questions that follow.

**Questions for Discussion:**

(1) What do you see in this painting?

_____

(2) How do you feel about it?

_____

(3) What characteristics of this painting make it a "romantic painting"? Please be specific.

_____

## 3. Writing

Romanticism and Neoclassicism are two major schools of thought popular in the 18th century. Please compare Romanticism and Neoclassicism. Write a composition of about 200 words on the similarities and differences of the two schools of thought.

## Read More

### Text B  The Sorrows of Young Werther

**PREFACE**

I have carefully collected whatever I have been able to learn of the story of poor Werther, and here present it to you, knowing that you will thank me for it. To his spirit and character you cannot refuse your admiration and love; to his fate you will not deny your tears.

And you, good soul, who suffer the same distress as he endured once, draw comfort from his sorrows; and let this little book be your friend, if, owing to fortune or through your own fault, you can not find a dearer companion.

**BOOK I**

MAY 4.

How happy I am that I am gone! My dear friend, what a thing is the heart of man! To leave you, from whom I have been inseparable, whom I love so dearly, and yet to feel happy! I know you will forgive me. Have not other attachments been specially appointed by fate to torment a head like mine? Poor Leonora! And yet I was not to blame. Was it my fault, that, whilst the peculiar charms of her sister afforded me an agreeable entertainment, a passion for me was engendered in her feeble heart? And yet am I wholly blameless? Did I not encourage her emotions? Did I not feel charmed at those truly genuine expressions of nature, which, though but little mirthful in reality, so often amused us? Did I not—but oh! What is man, that he dares so to accuse himself? My dear friend, I promise you I will improve; I will no longer, as has ever been my habit, continue to ruminate on every petty vexation which fortune may dispense; I will enjoy the present, and the past shall be for me the past. No doubt you are right, my best of friends, there would be far less suffering amongst mankind, if men—and God knows why they are so fashioned—did not employ their imaginations so assiduously in recalling the memory of past sorrow, instead of bearing their present lot with equanimity. Be kind enough to inform my mother that I shall attend to her business to the best of my ability, and shall give her the earliest information about it. I have seen my aunt, and find that she is very far from being the disagreeable person our friends allege her to be. She is a lively, cheerful woman, with the best of hearts. I explained to her my mother's wrongs with regard to that part of her portion which has been withheld from her. She told me the motives and reasons of her own conduct, and the terms on which she is willing to give up the whole, and to do more than we have asked. In short, I cannot write further upon this subject at present; only assure my mother that all will go on well. And I have again observed, my dear friend, in this trifling affair, that misunderstandings and neglect occasion more mischief in the world than even malice and wickedness. At all events, the two latter are of less frequent occurrence.

In other respects, I am very well off here. Solitude in this terrestrial paradise is a genial balm to my mind, and the young spring cheers with its bounteous promises my oftentimes misgiving heart. Every tree, every bush, is full of flowers; and one might wish himself transformed into a butterfly, to float about in this ocean of perfume, and find his whole existence in it.

The town itself is disagreeable; but then, all around, you find an inexpressible beauty of nature. This induced the late Count M to lay out a garden on one of the sloping hills which here intersect each other with the most charming variety, and form the most lovely valleys. The garden is simple; and it is easy to perceive, even upon your first entrance, that the plan was not designed by a scientific gardener, but by a man who wished to give himself up here to the enjoyment of his own sensitive heart. Many a tear have I already shed to the memory of its departed master in a summer-house which is now reduced to ruins, but was his favorite resort, and now is mine. I shall soon be master of the place.

The gardener has become attached to me within the last few days, and he will lose nothing thereby.

MAY 10.

A wonderful serenity has taken possession of my entire soul, like these sweet mornings of spring which I enjoy with my whole heart. I am alone, and feel the charm of existence in this spot, which was created for the bliss of souls like mine. I am so happy, my dear friend, so absorbed in the exquisite sense of mere tranquil existence, that I neglect my talents. I should be incapable of drawing a single stroke at the present moment; and yet I feel that I never was a greater artist than now. When, while the lovely valley teems with vapor around me, and the meridian sun strikes the upper surface of the impenetrable foliage of my trees, but a few stray gleams steal into the inner sanctuary, I throw myself down among the tall grass by the trickling stream; and, as I lie close to the earth, a thousand unknown plants are noticed by me; when I hear the buzz of the little world among the stalks, and grow familiar with the countless indescribable forms of the insects and flies, then I feel the presence of the Almighty, who  formed us in his own image, and the breath of that universal love which bears and sustains us, as it floats around us in an eternity of bliss; and then, my friend, when darkness overspreads my eyes, and heaven and earth seem to dwell in my soul and absorb its power, like the form of a beloved mistress, then I often think with longing. Oh, I could describe these conceptions, could impress upon paper all that is living so full and warm within me, that it might be the mirror of my soul, as my soul is the mirror of the infinite God! O my friend—but it is too much for my strength—I sink under the weight of the splendor of these visions!

**Questions for Reflection**
1. Why am "I" so happy?
2. Describe what kind of people "she" is in the author's eyes.
3. Please comment on the writing style of the passage.

## Text C  The Romantic Painting

Romantic painting, which flourished in late eighteenth- and early nineteenth-century Europe, was characterized by its search for the dramatic, the heroic, the unconventional and the mysterious. In its life-affirming mode, it celebrated the feats of the individual mind and will. Gros' *General Bonaparte at the Bridge of Arcole* (1797) depicts its conquering hero as a man of action, his elaborate sashes and unfurling flag expressing the extraordinariness, inner intensity and iron will of the hero. Nothing could be further from the earlier ancient régime concept of "subjects" as (largely powerless) servants of the monarch and of the state.

Romantic painting celebrated individuality and enterprise and seemed to promise a significant break with the past. Due to the precarious developments of these revolutionary times, however, the ideal of the hero was always on a knife-edge, haunted by the fear of loss. Important state commissions such as Gros' *Napoléon Visiting the Field of the Battle of Eylau* (1808) celebrated the victor's heroic feats while at the same time drawing attention to the bloodshed and suffering of war. Would the new order really fulfill its promise? In its less life-affirming manifestations, Romantic painting was concerned with impossible or lost dreams and hidden desire.

As political turmoil in Europe gave way to a more stable, if bourgeois, state of affairs, artists inherited an interest in the individual mind that expressed itself through an increasing emphasis on inwardness. For painters and sculptors, this posed a particular problem. How could one express the inner workings of the mind, inherently an invisible phenomenon, in a medium constituted by the visual? One possible way forward was to express the visual images conjured up by the imagination, particularly in dreams. While most eighteenth-century artists and theorists had conceived of the imagination as a creative synthesis of inherited tradition with newly observed sights in nature or reality (think, for example, of Joshua Reynolds' endless variations on classical formulae in his society portraits), the Romantics saw the capacity of the imagination as boundless.

There was also an unprecedented emphasis on religious or spiritual vision and a general faith that the inner  (rather than outwardly heroic) life could be given visible form. Just as events on the political stage had broken the mold, so the imagination could find endless new ways of seeing things and "see" things previously unseen. Originality and unconventionality were highly prized, even if more conservative critics or members of the viewing public were not yet ready for this. The Enlightenment's ideal of art as a school of morals gave way to a culture of liberation and was fully reawakened only much later, in the Victorian era. The world of the subconscious and supra-rational was in vogue, in the grimacing fairies of Fuseli's *Titania and Bottom* (c.1790), the madmen and witches depicted by Goya and the vision of Hell in Blake's *Capaneus the Blasphemer*.

Blake was part of an important strain of Romantic art that attempted to place the concerns of mortals within the larger scale of the divine. This was another example of the quest of Romanticism to reach beyond the plainly visual to the unseen. His *Capaneus* (guilty of over-reaching pride and ambition) is consumed by the flames of divine wrath, his solid mortal body on the point of dissolution.

Other artists explored ways of dissolving recognizable forms and shapes in order to transcend the normal limits of our vision, reason and experience. Caspar David Friedrich literally dissolved his landscapes in mist and fog so that they unleashed the creative powers of the viewer's imagination. The effect is evident in his *Monk by the Sea* (1809 – 1810), *Abbey in the Oak Forest* (1809 – 1810) and *Wanderer above the Sea of Fog* (c. 1818). Turner immersed himself in the representation of evanescent light effects and swirling mists, to the point of near-annihilation of the visible. Constable represented rainbows, sunshine and storm clouds as motifs that illuminated paintings while obscuring fine detail. While earlier eighteenth-century artists had striven to respect classical ideals of order, proportion, balance and legibility, some Romantic artists celebrated obscurity. Friedrich's landscapes were often symmetrical in effect while subverting this symmetry with a fog of uncertainty.

The clearly-outlined forms of Neoclassicism often gave way to looser brushwork that suggested rather than defined forms (although such changes were not uniform, as the work of Ingres demonstrates). Sketchiness, haziness and incompleteness became desirable and undermined the traditional emphasis on a precise and uniform "finish" or paint surface advocated by the academies. The content and possible meanings of paintings became less clearly signaled, as viewers were thrown back on their own subjective resources.

This loss of certainty was related to a changing response to the Enlightenment's concept of the sublime. Theorized by Burke in his *A Philosophical Enquiry into the Origin of Our Ideas of the Sublime and Beautiful* (1757), the sublime was defined as a state of mind provoked by certain qualities in the objects and phenomena we observe: this state of mind was terror. Stimulants of the sublime included objects of great size that threatened our capacity to take them in all at once, objects or living creatures of great power and extreme darkness and obscurity. The Enlightenment mindset had welcomed this opportunity to catalog and define yet another aspect of our mental capacities and generally regarded the sublime as a source of aesthetic delight (it could please and thrill us as long as we were not in any real danger when contemplating it) and human pride: our minds were challenged by it but were also inspired to raise themselves to new heights of perception.

A perfect example of the Enlightenment sublime can be seen in the detailed watercolors of Caspar Wolf, with their neatly framed, if massive, Alpine caverns and waterfalls. The Romantics were less optimistic about our capacity to rise to the challenge of the sublime and often saw it as a threat of annihilation. Friedrich's precipices seem to position the viewer in unstable, uncertain viewpoints; Turner's waterfalls and abysses threaten to engulf us completely. In Romantic paintings, such features are more likely to appear to burst the frame and appear less subject to rational or human control. (In fact, of course, such effects were often carefully stage-managed.)

Romantic art helped to form our modern conception of what it means to be an artist. We now take it for granted that the artist is someone of rich, unlimited creativity and exceptional individuality. So accustomed are we to this notion that it can take precedence over the need to assess an artist's work by means of any "objective" or more widely shared criteria. To some present-day observers, this cheapens art by excusing all in the name of originality. It is perhaps worth recalling, however, that many Romantic artists were gifted draftsmen skilled in producing the fine lines required of a Neoclassical composition or a drawing from nature. Turner was a skilled technician of color pigments and effects. Delacroix, painter of a dramatic orgy of death and sex in his *The Death of Sardanapalus* (1827 – 1828), had a strong allegiance to classical traditions of painting bequeathed by Renaissance art.

The "liberation" of Romantic artists was more than an undisciplined descent into self-indulgence. It was fuelled, to a considerable degree, by the demands of a public anxious for color and escapism in an age which produced a violent revolution, entrepreneurial industrialism and the rise of a middle-class existence recognizable today and challenged, more recently, in the "liberated" sixties.

## Questions for Reflection

1. What was the focus of Romantic painting?
2. What was the problem that confronted most painters and sculptors in the 18th century?
3. What is the Enlightenment's concept of sublime? How was the sublime expressed in art?

## Websites to Visit

https://www.famousauthors.org/top-10-greatest-romance-authors-of-all-time (accessed Apr. 28, 2020)
This website provides a list of the 10 greatest Romantic authors of all time.

http://www.artsz.org/artists/romanticism/ (accessed Apr. 28, 2020)
This website explains to you in simple language what Romantic art is. By analyzing some sample paintings, you can have a clearer understanding of the characteristics of Romanticism in oil painting.

## Movie to Watch

**William Wordsworth (1996)**
—The Famous Authors Series

This documentary film follows the career of the eighteenth-century Romantic poet William Wordsworth. Known for his love of nature, his humanitarianism and his identification with the common people, Wordsworth translated these beliefs into his expressive poetry. He and his close friend and poetry colleague Samuel Coleridge pioneered the literary style known as English Romanticism and together published *Lyrical Ballads*, a collection of both poets' works. Among Wordsworth's most beloved poems are *The Excursion* and *The Prelude*. This documentary uses portraits, paintings, documents, maps, and other archival material to tell the story of this socially minded writer.

# Unit 14
## Realism

> It is not the language of painters but the language of nature which one should listen to... The feeling for the things themselves, for reality, is more important than the feeling for pictures.
>
> —Vincent van Gogh

### Unit Goals

- To learn the major intellectual developments in the Age of Realism
- To appreciate realistic writings and art
- To learn the useful words and expressions that describe the Age of Realism
- To improve language skills by learning this unit

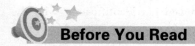
### Before You Read

1. What do you know about Charles Dickens? Have you ever read any of his works?

   Study the names of the following books. Tick (√) the ones that were written by Charles Dickens.

| Hard Times | | Great Expectations | |
|---|---|---|---|
| Vanity Fair | | Tess of the d'Urbervilles | |
| Sense and Sensibility | | The Count of Monte Cristo | |
| A Tale of Two Cities | | A Farewell to Arms | |
| The Old Curiosity Shop | | David Copperfield | |
| The Scarlet Letter | | Oliver Twist | |

2. Study the following picture. What is the message conveyed by the picture? List three words/ phrases that are associated with the picture. After you finish, compare your answer with your classmates.

Associated words/phrases:
(1) _____
(2) _____
(3) _____

3. Form groups of three or four students. Try to find, on the Internet or in the library, more information about Realism. Choose a topic that interests you most and prepare a five-minute classroom presentation.

## Start to Read

### Text A  Science and Culture in an Age of Realism

Between 1850 and 1870, two major intellectual developments were evident: the growth of scientific knowledge, with its rapidly increasing impact on the Western worldview, and the shift from Romanticism, with its emphasis on the inner world of reality, to Realism, with its focus on the outer, material world.

**A New Age of Science**

By the mid-nineteenth century, science was having a greater and greater impact on European life. The Scientific Revolution of the sixteenth and seventeenth centuries had fundamentally transformed the Western worldview and fostered a modern, rational approach to the study of the natural world. Even in the eighteenth century, however, these intellectual developments had remained the preserve of an educated elite and resulted in few practical benefits. Moreover, the technical advances of the early Industrial Revolution had depended little on pure science and much more on the practical experiments of technologically oriented amateur inventors. Advances in industrial technology, however, fed an interest in basic scientific research, which in turn, in the 1830s and afterward, resulted in a rash of basic scientific discoveries that were soon transformed into technological improvements that affected all Europeans.

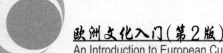

The development of the steam engine was important in encouraging scientists to work out its theoretical foundations, a preoccupation that led to the study of thermodynamics, the science of the relationship between heat and mechanical energy. The laws of thermodynamics were at the core of nineteenth-century physics. In biology, the Frenchman Louis Pasteur postulated the germ theory of disease, which had enormous practical applications in the development of modern, scientific medical practices. In chemistry, the Russian Dmitri Mendeleyev in the 1860s classified all the material elements then known on the basis of their atomic weights and provided the systematic foundation for the periodic law. The Briton Michael Faraday discovered the phenomenon of electromagnetic induction and put together a primitive generator that laid the groundwork for the use of electricity, although economically efficient generators were not built until the 1870s.

The steadily increasing and often dramatic material benefits generated by science and technology led Europeans to a growing faith in the benefits of science. The popularity of scientific and technological achievements produced a widespread acceptance of the scientific method, based on observation, experiment, and logical analysis, as the only path to objective truth and objective reality. This, in turn, undermined the faith of many people in religious revelation and truth. It is no accident that the nineteenth century was an age of increasing secularization, particularly evident in the growth of materialism or the belief that everything mental, spiritual, or ideal was simply an outgrowth of physical forces. Truth was to be found in the concrete material existence of human beings, not as Romanticists imagined in revelations gained by feeling or intuitive flashes. The importance of materialism was strikingly evident in the most important scientific event of the nineteenth century, the development of the theory of organic evolution according to natural selection. On the theories of Charles Darwin could be built a picture of humans as material beings that were simply part of the natural world.

**Realism in Literature and Art**

The literary Realists of the mid-nineteenth century were distinguished by their deliberate rejection of Romanticism. The literary Realists wanted to deal with ordinary characters from actual life rather than Romantic heroes in unusual settings. They also sought to avoid flowery and sentimental language by using careful observation and accurate description, an approach that led them to eschew poetry in favor of prose and the novel. Realists often combined their interest in everyday life with a searching examination of social questions.

The leading novelist of the 1850s and 1860s, the French Gustave Flaubert (1821 – 1880), perfected the Realist novel. His *Madame Bovary* (1857) was a straightforward description of barren and sordid provincial life in France. Emma Bovary, a woman of some vitality, is trapped in a marriage to a drab provincial doctor. Impelled by the images of romantic love she has read about in novels, she seeks the same thing for herself in adulterous affairs. Unfulfilled, she is ultimately driven to suicide, unrepentant to the end of her lifestyle. Flaubert's contempt for bourgeois society was evident in his portrayal of middle-class hypocrisy and smugness.

William Thackeray (1811 – 1863) wrote the prototypical Realist novel in Britain: *Vanity Fair*, published in 1848. Subtitled *A Novel Without a Hero*, the book deliberately flaunted Romantic conventions. Perhaps the greatest of the Victorian novelists was Charles Dickens (1812 – 1870), whose realistic novels focusing on the lower and middle classes in Britain's early industrial age became extraordinarily popular. His descriptions of the urban poor and the brutalization of human life were vividly realistic.

In art, too, Realism became dominant after 1850, although Romanticism was by no means dead. Among the most important characteristics of Realism is a desire to depict the everyday life of ordinary people, whether peasants, workers, or prostitutes; an attempt at photographic realism; and an interest in the natural environment. The French became leaders in Realist painting.

Gustave Courbet (1819 – 1877) was the most famous artist of the Realist school. In fact, the word *Realism* was first coined to describe one of his paintings. Courbet revealed in a straightforward portrayal of everyday life. His subjects were factory workers, peasants, and the wives of saloon keepers. One of his famous works, *The Stonebreakers*, painted in 1849, shows two men engaged in the exhausting work of breaking stones to build a road. This representation of human misery was a scandal to those who objected to his "cult of ugliness". To Courbet, no subject was too ordinary, too harsh, or too ugly.

Jean-François Millet (1814 – 1875) was preoccupied with scenes from rural life, especially peasants laboring in the fields, although his Realism still contained an element of Romantic sentimentality. In *The Gleaners*, Millet's most famous work, three peasant women gather grain in a field, a centuries-old practice that for Millet showed the symbiotic relationship between humans and nature. Millet made landscapes and country life important subjects for French artists, but he too was criticized by his contemporaries for the crude subject matter and unorthodox technique.

## Proper Nouns

1. Louis Pasteur 路易斯·巴斯德(法国微生物学家,化学家)
2. Dmitri Mendeleyev 德米特里·门捷列夫(俄国化学家,化学元素周期律的发现者)
3. Michael Faraday 迈克尔·法拉第(英国物理学家,化学家,电磁学的奠基人)
4. Charles Darwin 查尔斯·达尔文(英国生物学家,著有《物种起源》)
5. Gustave Flaubert 居斯塔夫·福楼拜(法国批判现实主义作家)
6. William Thackeray 威廉·萨克雷(英国作家,代表作为长篇小说《名利场》)
7. Gustave Courbet 居斯塔夫·库尔贝(法国画家,写实主义美术的代表)
8. Jean-François Millet 让–弗朗索瓦·米勒(法国巴比松派画家)

## After You Read

### Knowledge Focus

**1. Fill in the blanks with what you read from the text.**

(1) The two major intellectual developments between 1850 and 1870 were _____ and _____.

(2) The development of _____ encouraged scientists to work out its theoretical foundations.

(3) The Scientific method, based on _____, _____, and logical analysis, was believed to be the only path to objective truth.

(4) In the Age of Realism, truth was to be found in the concrete _____ of human beings.

(5) Realist writers often sought to avoid _____ and _____ language by using careful _____ and accurate _____.

(6) In art, Realism is characterized by a desire to depict the everyday life of _____, an attempt at photographic realism, and an interest in _____.

**2. Match the names in Column A with their corresponding descriptions in Column B.**

| Column A | Column B |
| --- | --- |
| (1) Gustave Flaubert | a. A biologist who postulated the germ theory of disease |
| (2) Charles Darwin | b. The author of *Vanity Fair* |
| (3) Dmitri Mendeleyev | c. A Frenchman who wrote *Madame Bovary* |
| (4) Gustave Courbet | d. A French painter who painted *The Stonebreakers* |
| (5) Michael Faraday | e. The creator of the periodic table of elements |
| (6) Charles Dickens | f. A biologist who was famous for his theory of evolution |
| (7) Jean-François Millet | g. An English chemist and physicist who contributed to the fields of electromagnetism |

(8) Louis Pasteur        h. A Victorian writer who focuses on the lower and middle classes in Britain's early industrial age in his works

(9) William Thackeray    i. A painter who was famous for his depiction of scenes from rural life

## Language Focus

**1. Fill in the blanks with the following words or expressions you have learned in the text.**

| a rash of | intuitive | foster | sentimental | generate |
| postulate | amateur | preoccupation | impel | vital |

(1) I'm trying to _____ an interest in classical music in my children.
(2) The competition is open to both _____ and professional photographers.
(3) There have been _____ robberies in the last two months.
(4) His main _____ at that time was getting enough to eat.
(5) It was the Greek astronomer, Ptolemy, who _____ that the Earth was at the center of the universe.
(6) The new development will _____ 1500 new jobs.
(7) Men are often regarded as less _____ than women.
(8) The dog was bouncing with health and _____.
(9) The President's speech _____ the nation to greater efforts.
(10) He has a _____ attachment to his birthplace.

**2. Fill in the blanks with the proper form of the word in the brackets.**

(1) It's a _____ (theory) possibility, but I don't suppose it will happen.
(2) The prime minister has said that the government is committed to the _____ (preserve) of the country's national interests.
(3) Science means _____ (system) knowledge possessed as a result of practice and study.
(4) The inspectors were impressed by the speed and _____ (efficient) of the new system.
(5) There's no _____ (logical) in the decision to reduce staff when orders are the highest for years.
(6) The judge had a reputation for complete _____ (objective).
(7) I can't explain how I knew—I just had an _____ (intuitive) that you'd been involved in an accident.
(8) I was surprised to hear that Johnson had been divorced by his wife on the grounds of _____ (adulterous).
(9) The _____ (portray) of the characters in the novel is lifelike.
(10) The politician is _____ (hypocrisy), caring about himself but never about others.

3. **Fill in the blanks with the proper prepositions or adverbs that collocate with the neighboring words.**
   (1) The integrated circuit has had a very significant impact _____ digital system development.
   (2) All the approaches _____ the palace were guarded by troops.
   (3) An excessive dosage of this drug can result _____ injury to the liver.
   (4) The magician transformed the frog _____ a prince.
   (5) Responsibility without control is _____ the core of management.
   (6) Her gestures and movements were distinguished _____ a noble and stately grace.
   (7) It is an essential principle that we must combine theory _____ practice.
   (8) This is _____ no means a good way to solve the problem.
   (9) A large proportion of people are engaged _____ the production of goods.
   (10) The State Department was preoccupied _____ a meeting of the Armistice Commission.

4. **Error Correction: Each of the following sentences has at least one grammatical error. Identify the errors and correct them.**
   (1) The technical advances of the early Industrial Revolution had depended few on pure science and much more on the practical experiments of technologically oriented amateur inventors.
   (2) Advances in industrial technology fed an interest in basic scientific research, it in turn resulted in a rash of basic scientific discoveries.
   (3) In chemistry, the Russian scientist classified all the material elements then know on the basis of their atomic weights.
   (4) The steadily increasing and often dramatic material benefits generating by science and technology led Europeans to a growing faith in the benefits of science.
   (5) It is no accident the nineteen century was an age of increasing secularization.
   (6) Truth was to be found in the concrete material existence of human beings, not like Romanticists imagined in revelations gained by feeling or intuitive flashes.
   (7) The literary Realists of the mid-nineteenth century distinguished by their deliberate rejection of Romanticism.
   (8) They also sought to avoid flowery and sentimental language by using careful observation and accurate description, the approach that led them to eschew poetry in favor of prose and the novel.
   (9) Impelling by the images of romantic love she has read about in novels, she seeks the same thing for herself in adulterous affairs.
   (10) Perhaps the greatest of the Victorian novelists was Charles Dickens, his realistic novels focusing on the lower and middle classes became extraordinarily popular.
   (11) Among the most important characteristics of Realism are a desire to depict the everyday life of ordinary people.
   (12) I have never seen neither angels nor goddesses, so I am not interested in painting them.
   (13) This representation of human misery was a scandal to those objected to his "cult of ugliness".

(14) Jean-François Millet preoccupied with scenes from rural life, especially peasants laboring in the fields.

## Comprehensive Work

### 1. Romanticism vs. Realism

(1) Form groups of three or four. Discuss with each other on the differences and similarities of Romanticism and Realism. You may use the following diagram for help.

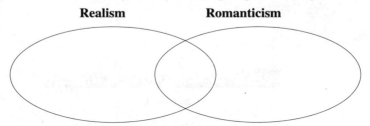

(2) Based on the discussion above, write a composition of about 200 words on the DIFFERENCES between Romanticism and Realism.

### 2. Realistic Painting: *The Stonebreakers*

**The Stonebreakers by Gustave Courbet, 1849**

*The Stonebreakers* by Gustave Courbet is regarded as one of the most famous Realistic paintings in the 19th century. Study the painting carefully and answer the questions that follow.

**Questions for Discussion:**

(1) What do you see in this painting?

(2) How do the people in the painting look? Describe their appearances in detail.

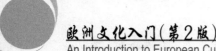

(3) What kind of life do you think they live?

(4) How do you feel when you see the painting?

(5) What characteristics of this painting make it a "Realistic painting"? Please be specific.

### Text B  A Tale of Two Cities
### Chapter I
### The Period

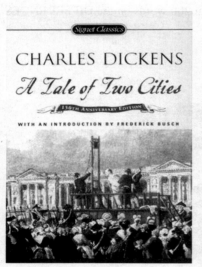

It was the best of times, it was the worst of times, it was the age of wisdom, it was the age of foolishness, it was the epoch of belief, it was the epoch of incredulity, it was the season of Light, it was the season of Darkness, it was the spring of hope, it was the winter of despair, we had everything before us, we had nothing before us, we were all going direct to Heaven, we were all going direct the other way—in short, the period was so far like the present period, that some of its noisiest authorities insisted on its being received, for good or for evil, in the superlative degree of comparison only.

There were a king with a large jaw and a queen with a plain face, on the throne of England; there were a king with a large jaw and a queen with a fair face, on the throne of France. In both countries it was clearer than crystal to the lords of the State preserves of loaves and fishes, that things in general were settled for ever.

It was the year of Our Lord one thousand seven hundred and seventy-five. Spiritual revelations were conceded to England at that favored period, as at this. Mrs. Southcott had recently attained her five-and-twentieth blessed birthday, of whom a prophetic private in the Life Guards had heralded the sublime appearance by announcing that arrangements were made for the swallowing up of London and Westminster. Even the Cock-lane ghost had been laid only a round dozen of years, after rapping out its messages, as the spirits of this very year last past (supernaturally deficient in originality) rapped out theirs. Mere messages in the earthly order of events had lately come to the English Crown and People, from a congress of British subjects in America: which, strange to relate, have proved more important to the human race than any communications yet received through any of the chickens of the Cock-lane brood.

France, less favored on the whole as to matters spiritual than her sister of the shield and trident, rolled with exceeding smoothness downhill, making paper money and spending it. Under the guidance of her Christian pastors, she entertained herself, besides, with such humane achievements as sentencing a youth to have his hands cut off, his tongue torn out with pincers, and his body burned alive, because he had not kneeled down in the rain to do honor to a dirty procession of monks which passed within his view, at a distance of some fifty or sixty yards. It is likely enough that, rooted in the woods of France and Norway, there were growing trees, when that sufferer was put to death, already marked by the Woodman,

Fate, to come down and be sawn into boards, to make a certain movable framework with a sack and a knife in it, terrible in history. It is likely enough that in the rough outhouses of some tillers of the heavy lands adjacent to Paris, there were sheltered from the weather that very day, rude carts, bespattered with rustic mire, snuffed about by pigs, and roosted in by poultry, which the Farmer, Death, had already set apart to be his tumbrils of the Revolution. But that Woodman and that Farmer, though they work unceasingly, work silently, and no one heard them as they went about with muffled tread: the rather, forasmuch as to entertain any suspicion that they were awake, was to be atheistical and traitorous.

In England, there was scarcely an amount of order and protection to justify much national boasting. Daring burglaries by armed men, and highway robberies, took place in the capital itself every night; families were publicly cautioned not to go out of town without removing their furniture to upholsterers' warehouses for security; the highwayman in the dark was a City tradesman in the light, and, being recognized and challenged by his fellow-tradesman whom he stopped in his character of "the Captain", gallantly shot him through the head and rode away; the mall was waylaid by seven robbers, and the guard shot three dead, and then got shot dead himself by the other four, "in consequence of the failure of his ammunition?" after which the mall was robbed in peace; that magnificent potentate, the Lord Mayor of London, was made to stand and deliver on Turnham Green, by one highwayman, who despoiled the illustrious creature in sight of all his retinue; prisoners in London gaols fought battles with their turnkeys, and the majesty of the law fired blunderbusses in among them, loaded with rounds of shot and ball; thieves snipped off diamond crosses from the necks of noble lords at Court drawing-rooms; musketeers went into St. Giles's, to search for contraband goods, and the mob fired on the musketeers, and the musketeers fired on the mob, and nobody thought any of these occurrences much out of the common way. In the midst of them, the hangman, ever busy and ever worse than useless, was in constant requisition; now, stringing up long rows of miscellaneous criminals; now, hanging a housebreaker on Saturday who had been taken on Tuesday; now, burning people in the hand at Newgate by the dozen, and now burning pamphlets at the door of Westminster Hall; to-day, taking the life of an atrocious murderer, and to-morrow of a wretched pilferer who had robbed a farmer's boy of sixpence.

All these things, and a thousand like them, came to pass in and close upon the dear old year one thousand seven hundred and seventy-five. Environed by them, while the Woodman and the Farmer worked unheeded, those two of the large jaws, and those other two of the plain and the fair faces, trod with stir enough, and carried their divine rights with a high hand. Thus did the year one thousand seven hundred and seventy-five conduct their Greatnesses, and myriads of small creatures—the creatures of this chronicle among the rest—along the roads that lay before them.

*Questions for Reflection*
1. What was the attitude of British and French nobility concerning the future of their rule?
2. In France, what was a common punishment for not kneeling to honor monks?
3. What was the crime situation in England at this time?

## Text C  Charles Darwin

Darwin is the first of the evolutionary biologists, the originator of the concept of natural selection. His principal works, *The Origin of Species by Means of Natural Selection* (1859) and *The Descent of Man* (1871) marked a new epoch. His works were violently attacked and energetically defended, then; and, it seems, yet today.

Charles Darwin (1809 – 1882) was born in Shrewsbury, England. He was the fifth of six children born to Robert Darwin (1766 – 1848) and Susannah Wedgwood-Darwin (1765 – 1817). Susannah died when Charles was only eight years old. Charles was the grandson of two very prominent men of the time, Erasmus Darwin (1731 – 1802) and Josiah Wedgwood (1730 – 1795). Erasmus, who died several years before Charles was even born, was a dedicated evolutionist. Erasmus' pre-Charles Darwin evolutionary writings include *Zoonomia, or, the Laws of Organic Life* (1794 – 1796, a two-volume work). Consider this excerpt from his posthumous poem *Temple of Nature* (1802): "Organic life beneath the shoreless waves was born and nurs'd in ocean's pearly caves / First forms minute, unseen by spheric glass, move on the mud, or pierce the watery mass / these, as successive generations bloom, new powers acquire and larger limbs assume / whence countless groups of vegetation spring, and breathing realms of fin and feet and wing."

## Education

Charles Darwin entered Shrewsbury School as a boarding student in 1822. He left three years later, at the age of 16, called by his father to study medicine with his elder brother, Erasmus, at Edinburgh University. Repelled by the horror of early 19th-century surgery, Darwin dropped out of Edinburgh in 1827 and enrolled in Christ College, Cambridge University, studying to be a clergyman in the Church of England. Charles earned his Bachelor's Degree in Theology in 1831. During his tenure as a student at Cambridge, Darwin befriended botanist and mineralogist John Stevens Henslow (1796 – 1861), one of his professors. It was Henslow who recommended Darwin to Captain Robert FitzRoy (1805 – 1865) of the HMS Beagle, who was in need of a naturalist. In August of 1831, Darwin received an invitation to serve as a naturalist aboard the Beagle. Darwin accepted and set sail on a fateful five-year voyage (1831 – 1836).

## Voyage Aboard the HMS Beagle

It was the research Charles Darwin did while aboard the HMS Beagle that formed the basis for his classic work, *The Origin of Species by Means of Natural Selection, or the Preservation of Favoured Races in the Struggle for Life* (*Origin of Species*), published in 1859. His voyage took him to the Coasts of South America, where it is thought he contracted Chagas' Disease. Darwin was inflicted with intestinal illness and chronic fatigue until his death in 1882. Before Darwin set sail, Henslow recommended that he take Sir Charles Lyell's *Principles of Geology, Being an Attempt to Explain the Former Changes of the Earth's Surface, by Reference to Causes Now in Operation* (1830 – 1833, a three- volume work). Darwin took the first volume of *Principles of Geology* with him on his voyage and he had the second mailed to him while he was at sea. Lyell's book did two things in Darwin's mind. First, it undermined the

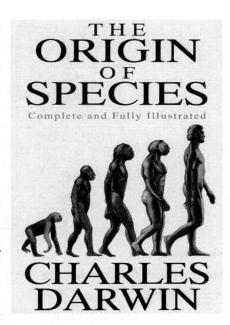

*Bible's* Genesis account (Lyell's work was diametrically opposed to the Biblical account). Second, it gave Darwin the time scale necessary to accommodate the idea that all life had evolved gradually. And so, Darwin, who began as a minister in the Church of England, ended up one of its most influential opponents. Lyell's *Principles of Geology*, with its geologic timescale, was his turning point.

## *Origin of Species* and Natural Selection

Charles Darwin returned to England in 1836. In 1839, he was elected a Fellow of the Royal Society and, five days later, married to his cousin Emma Wedgwood, who bore him 10 children. In 1842, Darwin began drafting his *Origin of Species*. Darwin's work was heavily influenced by Lyell's *Prin-*

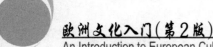

ciples of Geology and Thomas Malthus' *An Essay on the Principle of Population* (1798). *Origin of Species* was ultimately published in 1859.

Darwin did not invent the evolutionary worldview. He simply brought something new to the old philosophy: a plausible mechanism called "natural selection". In his *Origin of Species*, Darwin proposed natural selection as the mechanism by which all life could have descended from a common ancestor (Darwin defined evolution as "descent with modification"). However, today we know that natural selection is a deficient mechanism, even in light of genetic mutation. In fact, with the tremendous advances we have made in molecular biology, biochemistry and genetics over the past fifty years, Darwin's theory has become "a theory in crisis".

**Questions for Reflection**

Complete the following form with the information you read from the text above.

### A Chronology of Darwin's Life

| Year | Major Event |
| --- | --- |
| 1809 | |
| 1822 | |
| 1827 | |
| 1831 | |
| 1831 – 1836 | |
| 1839 | |
| 1842 | |
| 1859 | |
| 1882 | |

**Websites to Visit**

https://www.cliffsnotes.com/literature/t/a-tale-of-two-cities/a-tale-of-two-cities-at-a-glance (accessed Apr. 28, 2020)

This website provides a book summary and analysis of Charles Dickens' *A Tale of Two Cites*.

https://www.biography.com/scientist/charles-darwin (accessed Apr. 28, 2020)

To know more information about Charles Darwin, you can refer to the above website. It provides you with almost everything you want to know about this great biologist.

**Movie to Watch**

### Oliver Twist (2005)

Oliver Twist is an orphan, who is soon kicked out of the orphanage and thrown into a terrible home. The bad treatment Oliver receives forces him to run off to London. There, he is soon picked up by the Artful Dodger and taken to Fagin. Fagin treats Oliver well, but is it the life Oliver really wants?

*Oliver Twist* is a 2005 film directed by Roman Polanski. It is based on the novel *Oliver Twist* by Charles Dickens.

# Unit 15
## Modernism and Other Contemporary Trends

> Skill without imagination is craftsmanship and gives us many useful objects such as wickerwork picnic baskets. Imagination without skill gives us modern art.
> —Tom Stoppard
>
> What distinguishes modern art from the art of other ages is criticism.
> —Octavio Paz

### Unit Goals

- To develop a general understanding of Modernism and its influence in contemporary culture
- To recognize and identify key contemporary works in art and literature
- To learn the words and phrases that describe the artistic development of the 20th century
- To improve language skills by learning this unit

### Before You Read

1. A series of great events which took place in the 20th century has exerted great influence on the development of human society. Study the following pictures. What event does each picture describe? What do you know about these events?

# Unit 15  Modernism and Other Contemporary Trends

2. **How much do you know about the scientific and cultural development of the 20th century? Please take this quiz.**

   (1) Who is the 20th-century Austrian physician and neurologist, whose analysis of the unconscious opened up a new school of psychology?
       a. Karl Marx.              b. Jean-Paul Sartre.
       c. Sigmund Freud.          d. Bertrand Russell.

   (2) What is the Freudian term originating from a Greek tragedy, in which an ancient King unknowingly killed his father and married his mother?
       a. Narcissus complex.      b. Oedipus complex.
       c. Golgi complex.          d. Electra complex.

   (3) Who is the author of *Mrs. Dalloway* and *To the Lighthouse*?
       a. Virginia Woolf.         b. Joseph Conrad.
       c. D. H. Lawrence.         d. James Joyce.

   (4) Which of the following is NOT written by Ernest Hemingway?
       a. *For Whom the Bell Tolls*.   b. *The Sun Also Rises*.
       c. *The Snows of Kilimanjaro*.  d. *The Rainbow*.

   (5) This school of art is marked by the expression of reality by means of distortion to communicate one's inner vision. The artists of this school used bright colours to bring out their pessimistic views on life. This school art is called_____.
       a. Futurism.               b. Surrealism.
       c. Expressionism.          d. Dadaism.

   (6) Black humor, which is the laughter at tragic things, is best represented in _____.
       a. *Ulysses*.              b. *Catch-22*.
       c. *The Old Man and the Sea*.   d. *On the Road*.

   (7) Who discovered the X-rays?
       a. Marie Curie.            b. Rutherford.
       c. Rontgen.                d. Einstein.

(8) What is the term which was used by Ernest Hemingway to refer to the young men who survived the war physically but were afterward spiritually and morally adrift?

    a. Angry Young Men.　　　　b. Lost Generation.

    c. Nouveau Roman.　　　　　d. Beat Generation.

(9) The painter of this painting, *Dora Maar au Chat* (1941), is _____. His paintings best represented _____.

    a. Vincent van Gough, Impressionism.

    b. Henri Matisse, Fauvism.

    c. Pablo Picasso, Cubism.

    d. Salvador Dali, Surrealism.

(10) Who is the director of the Hollywood movie *Godfather* and its sequel *Godfather II*?

    a. Woody Allen.　　　　　　b. Oliver Stone.

    c. Francis Coppola.　　　　　d. Steven Spielberg.

## Start to Read

### Text A  Modernism Defined

Modernism was a complex and diverse international movement in all the creative arts, originating about the end of the 19th century. It provided the greatest creative renaissance of the 20th century. It was made up of many facets, such as symbolism, surrealism, cubism, expressionism, futurism, etc.

Modernism has been called "the tradition of the new". It was characterized by a conscious rejection of established rules, traditions and conventions. It strove to reflect 20th century's social and political changes, its dangers and anxieties, its rapid growth in technological and psychological knowledge. It provided fresh ways of looking at man's position and function in the universe.

Modernism has also been called the "dehumanization of art". It pushes into the background traditional humanistic notions of the individual and society. Yet, it is not divorced from the past. It restates, in new terms, the same questions about existence and human nature found in 19th-century works of art and literature.

Modernism has also become the synonym of revolution in form. Not any of the previous periods in history has ever seen so many experiments in form and style. The term "modernist" is usually reserved for more experimental and innovative modern works, those that view experience in new ways and adopt new forms. For instance, in Modernist literature, rather than a conventional picture of reality, one finds many perspectives shaped and distorted to suggest a special, personal view.

As a wide-ranging and deep-seated movement, Modernism was not merely a mixture of various kinds of literary and artistic experiments within Western society, but a result of long-term historical and social developments and a process for cultural, ideological, literary and artistic reformation. It was more than a matter of methodology or technique, but a thorough and serious revaluation of all traditional forms of art and literature, a reflection on human values and moral codes and a full demonstration of all the cultural potential and possibilities. In all, it was a milestone of cultural progress and monument to Western civilization.

## Historical Context

Great changes occurred between the last three decades of the 19th century and the first three of the 20th century, which accelerated political, economic, social and intellectual development. Politically, the bourgeoisie had consolidated its ruling status and furthered its overseas expansion; economically, the capitalist way of production had given rise to scientific progress and an increase of productive forces. As to social conditions, various kinds of class contradictions became more sharpened, especially the clashes among the major capitalist countries and the struggles between the proletariat and the bourgeoisie. Social turmoil and crises struck Western countries as well as the whole world, creating a continuous tension.

## Major Achievements of Modernism

With the rapid development in economic and social fields, intellectual crisis appeared in art, literature and other cultural areas where people had begun to suffer from an atmosphere of spiritual drought, a sense of depression, a lack of expectations and consequent displeasure. Many of the Modernist writers focused on what seemed irrational representation of their dissatisfaction and exposure of the weakness of human nature. This was how symbolism, futurism, imagism and expressionism were born, as creative techniques and ideological trends in the Modernist movement.

Ideologically **symbolism** was at least partly based on Schopenhauer's pessimism and affected by Bergson's intuitionalism. Its representatives denied the overstated significance of rational knowledge and logical thinking and believed that man could turn to mystic and intuitional powers to go beyond common physical phenomena to find insight into some absolute image beyond the material world. They insisted that artists should ignore the reality around them and using intuitional power, express those idealistic beauties in abstract images. The tone of such work was always

characterized by pain, frustration and sorrow. The most frequent themes almost always were death and what was most often depicted was dusk, autumn, fallen leaves, tolls at the grave and burned-out candles etc., like those of Baudelaire and Rimbaud.

**Futurism** originally came from Italy, based itself on Nietzsche's philosophy, adverted the radical nationalism and will of power, and later echoed by Mussolini's fascism. The futurists denied the importance of past cultural heritage, eulogized modern urban life and the bourgeois machine-age civilization as presented by Filippo Marinetti. Artistically they adverted formalism and claimed to destroy the existing form of written words and all past cultural existences such as libraries and museums. They used mathematical symbols to create a special kind of telegram-and-cipher typed document, calling such works "future art". Initially, they welcomed the Russian Revolution and writers such as Mayakovsky who promoted a modified version of futurism in Russia for a time.

**Imagism** is related to Bergson's intuitionalism and French symbolism. It holds that the image is the essence of intuitional language and the artist's mission is to catch images in life by intuitional power. These views were first submitted by Thomas Ernest Hulme (1883 – 1917) from England and developed by Ezra Pound and T. S. Eliot before it became a new form of classicism which seemed so difficult and abstract to follow and therefore did not last long as a movement. Ezra Pound's enthusiasm for the new translations of Chinese poetry and the Japanese "haiku" form, also contributed to Imagism.

**Expressionism** came into fashion first among a group of German painters and then spread to other forms of art and literature. It claimed that the central concern of modernist art and literature should be to represent the social crisis and man's alienation. This movement first appeared in the early 20th-century painting and soon was adopted by drama and fiction. Quite a number of distinguished dramatists took up this mode and the most notable ones were Eugene O'Neill (1888 – 1953) in the US and Bertolt Brecht (1898 – 1956) in Germany as well as August Strindberg (1849 – 1912) in Sweden, all of whom demonstrated a sense of the profound crisis of contemporary capitalist society. Similarly, Kafka's story *Metamorphosis* and other novels like *The Trial* and *The Castle* incorporate the theme of man's alienation, marking an important milestone in modernist fiction. The characters in modernist fiction, based on the representation of alienation, spiritual wounding and abnormally twisted minds, reflect the modern world's chaotic social order, indifferent human relations, pessimism and all its dark moods.

## Proper Nouns

1. Arthur Schopenhauer 亚瑟·叔本华 (德国哲学家)
2. Henri Bergson 亨利·柏格森 (法国哲学家)
3. Charles Baudelaire 夏尔·波德莱尔 (法国诗人及散文家)
4. Arthur Rimbaud 阿尔蒂尔·兰波 (法国诗人)
5. Friedrich Nietzsche 弗里德里希·尼采 (德国哲学家)
6. Benito Mussolini 贝尼托·墨索里尼 (法西斯主义的创始人,意大利法西斯党魁)
7. Filippo Marinetti 菲利波·马里内蒂 (意大利诗人,"未来主义"流派创始人)
8. Mayakovsky 马雅可夫斯基 (苏联立体未来主义的代表人物,诗人、剧作家)
9. Thomas Ernest Hulme 托马斯·欧内斯特·休姆 (英国意象派的先驱人物)
10. Ezra Pound 埃兹拉·庞德 (美国诗人,意象派运动主要发起人)
11. T. S. Eliot T. S. 艾略特 (美国诗人)
12. Eugene O'Neill 尤金·奥尼尔 (美国现代剧作家)
13. Bertolt Brecht 贝尔托·布莱希特 (德国现代剧场改革者,剧作家及导演)
14. August Strindberg 奥古斯特·斯特林堡 (瑞典戏剧家,小说家)
15. Franz Kafka 弗兰兹·卡夫卡 (奥地利小说家)

## After You Read

### Knowledge Focus

1. Look up in the dictionary. Define the following "-ism", and try to give their Chinese equivalents.

| Term | Chinese equivalent | Definition |
| --- | --- | --- |
| Symbolism | | |
| Surrealism | | |
| Cubism | | |
| Expressionism | | |
| Futurism | | |
| Intuitionalism | | |
| Fascism | | |
| Formalism | | |
| Imagism | | |
| Classicism | | |

2. Discuss the following questions with your partner.
   (1) What is Modernism? Please define the term.
   (2) Why is Modernism called "the tradition of the new"?
   (3) How is Modernism a synonym of revolution in form?
   (4) Please describe the historical background in which Modernism emerged and developed.
   (5) What are the major trends in the Modernist movement?
   (6) What are the frequent themes of Symbolism?
   (7) What is "future art"?
   (8) What are the characteristics of Expressionism?

3. Compare Symbolism, Futurism, Imagism, and Expressionism. Use what you have learned from the text to complete the following form.

|  | Origin | Characteristics | Themes | Representative Artists |
|---|---|---|---|---|
| Symbolism |  |  |  |  |
| Futurism |  |  |  |  |
| Imagism |  |  |  |  |
| Expressionism |  |  |  |  |

**Language Focus**

1. Fill in the blanks with the following words or expressions you have learned in the text.

| divorce | turmoil | facet | embody |
| eulogize | strive | turmoil | synonym |

   (1) She has so many _____ to her personality.
   (2) In her writing she _____ for a balance between innovation and familiar prose forms.
   (3) How can you _____ the issues of environmental protection and overpopulation?
   (4) This pioneering spirit is a _____ for individualism.
   (5) But he seemed to me at this moment to _____ the life-hope of the British nation.
   (6) In the _____ resulting from the collision, the arrested man broke loose and ran off.
   (7) Inflation is likely to _____ this year, adding further upward pressure on interest rates.
   (8) Critics everywhere _____ her new novel.

2. Fill in the blanks with the proper form of the word in the brackets.
   (1) She's regained _____ (conscious), but she's not out of the woods yet.
   (2) There is now a mood of deepening _____ (pessimistic) about the economy.
   (3) Religious values can often differ greatly from _____ (humanism) morals.

(4) The drug is still at the _____ (experiment) stage.
(5) After years of state control, the country is now moving towards cultural _____ (pluralistic).
(6) The prison riots _____ (sharp) the debate about how prisons should be run.
(7) He dared his grandfather's _____ (pleasure) when he left the family business.
(8) She traced her _____ (rational) fear of birds back to something that had happened to her as a child.
(9) She has shown no _____ (abnormal) in intelligence or in disposition.
(10) All these changes to the newspaper _____ (alienation) its traditional readers.

3. Fill in the blanks with the proper prepositions or adverbs that collocate with the neighboring words.
   (1) The novelist characterizes his heroine _____ capricious and passionate.
   (2) His articles are fixed _____ form and monotonous _____ content.
   (3) The first three rows of the hall are reserved _____ special guests.
   (4) Her disappearance gave rise _____ the wildest rumors.
   (5) He seems to be lacking _____ common sense.
   (6) This year's sales figures go _____ all our expectations.
   (7) She claims that she is related _____ the Queen.
   (8) The church wedding ceremony as performed in the West has now come _____ fashion in China.

4. Error Correction: Each of the following sentences has at least one grammatical error. Identify the errors and correct them.
   (1) Modernism was a complex and diverse international movement in all the creative arts, originated about the end of the 19th century.
   (2) It restates the same questions about existence and human nature founded in 19th-century works of art and literature.
   (3) Not any of the previous period in history has ever seen so many experiments in form and style.
   (4) The term "modernist" is usually reserved for more experimental and innovative modern works, those view experience in new ways and adopt new forms.
   (5) As the rapid development in economic and social fields, intellectual crisis appeared in art, literature and other cultural areas.
   (6) Many of the Modernist writers focused on it seemed irrational representation of their dissatisfaction and exposure of the weakness of human nature.
   (7) Symbolism at least partly based on Schopenhauer's pessimism and affected by Bergson's intuitionalism.
   (8) They insisted that artists ignored the reality around them and using intuitional power, expressed those idealistic beauties in abstract images.
   (9) The most frequent themes almost always was death and was most often depicted was dusk,

autumn, fallen leaves, tolls at the grave and burned-out candles.

(10) Imagism related to Bergson's intuitionalism and French symbolism.

(11) Imagism holds that the artist's mission is catch images in life by intuitional power.

(12) The characters in modernist fiction, basing on the representation of alienation, reflect the modern world's chaotic social order.

(13) The most notable Expressionists were Eugene O'Neill and Bertolt Brecht, all of whom demonstrated a sense of the profound crisis of contemporary capitalist society.

(14) These views became a new form of classicism which seemed so difficult and abstract to follow it and therefore did not last long as a movement.

(15) Great changes were occurred between the last three decades of the 19th century and the first three of the 20th century.

## Comprehensive Work

### 1. Share Ideas: Modernist Painting

Modernist paintings take many facets. Study the following paintings, and discuss with your partner to identify their artistic styles.

**Painting 1:** *The Death of the Gravedigger* **by Carlos Schwabe**

(1) What do you see in this painting?
_____

(2) How do you feel when you see it?
_____

(3) I think this painting is a representative of _____.
   a. futurism
   b. impressionism
   c. symbolism
   Reason: _____

**Painting 2:** *Mountains+Valleys+Streets Joffre,* **by Filippo Marinetti**

(1) What do you see in this painting?
_____

(2) How do you feel when you see it?
_____

(3) I think this painting is a representative of _____.
   a. futurism
   b. impressionism
   c. symbolism
   Reason: _____

**Painting 3: *The Scream* by Edvard Munch**

(1) What do you see in this painting?

   _____

(2) How do you feel when you see it?

   _____

(3) I think this painting is a representative of _____.
   a. futurism
   b. impressionism
   c. symbolism
   Reason:_____

## 2. Writing

Choose one of the paintings above. Write a composition, describing the painting and offering your interpretation of and comments on the painting.

## 3. Research Work

Form groups of three or four. Each group of students chooses a modern art movement as the subject of a mini art history research (examples of modern art movements include cubism, futurism, expressionism, imagism, surrealism, and symbolism). Using all available resources, research on the following about your chosen topic:

● definition of the movement
● time period
● media often employed
● common themes
● artists considered "masters" of this movement with examples of their works
● connection between this art movement and society as a whole at this point in history

Upon completion of research, each group designs a poster to display in the classroom that presents the answers to the research questions.

**Read More**

### Text B  Modernism after World War II (I)

In Britain and America, Modernism as a literary movement is generally considered to be relevant up to the early 1930s, and "Modernist" is rarely used to describe authors prominent after 1945. This is somewhat true for all areas of culture, with the exception of the visual and performing arts.

The post-war period left the capitals of Europe in upheaval with an urgency to economically and physically rebuild and to politically regroup. In Paris (the former center of European culture and the former capital of the art world) the climate for art was a disaster. Important collectors, dealers, and modernist artists, writers, and poets had fled Europe for America (especially New York). The Surrealists, and modern artists from every cultural center of Europe had fled the onslaught of the Nazis for safe haven in the United States. Many of those that didn't flee perished. A few artists, notably Pablo Picasso, Henri Matisse, and Pierre Bonnard, remained in France and survived.

The 1940s in New York City heralded the triumph of American Abstract Expressionism, a modernist movement that combined lessons learned from Henri Matisse, Pablo Picasso, Surrealism, Joan Miró, Cubism, Fauvism, and early Modernism via great teachers in America like Hans Hofmann and John D. Graham. American artists benefited from the presence of Piet Mondrian, Fernand Léger, Max Ernst and the André Breton group, Pierre Matisse's gallery, and Peggy Guggenheim's gallery *The Art of This Century*, as well as other factors.

## Pollock and Abstract Influences

During the late 1940s Jackson Pollock's radical approach to painting revolutionized the potential for all Contemporary art that followed him. To some extent Pollock realized that the journey toward making a work of art was as important as the work of art itself. Like Pablo Picasso's innovative reinventions of painting and sculpture near the turn of the century via Cubism and constructed sculpture, Pollock redefined the way art gets made. His move away from easel painting and conventionality was a liberating signal to the artists of his era and to all that came after. Artists realized that Jackson Pollock's process—the placing of unstretched raw canvas on the floor where it could be attacked from all four sides using artist materials and industrial materials; linear skeins of paint dripped and thrown; drawing, staining, brushing; imagery and non-imagery—essentially blasted art-making beyond any prior boundary. Abstract Expressionism in general expanded and developed the definitions and possibilities that artists had available for the creation of new works of art.

The other Abstract expressionists followed Pollock's breakthrough with new breakthroughs of their own. In a sense the innovations of Jackson Pollock, Willem de Kooning, Franz Kline, Mark Rothko, Philip Guston, Hans Hofmann, Clyfford Still, Barnett Newman, Ad Reinhardt, Robert Motherwell, Peter Voulkos and others opened the floodgates to the diversity and scope of all the art that followed them. Rereadings into abstract art, done by art historians such as Linda Nochlin, Griselda Pollock and Catherine de Zegher critically shows, however, that pioneer women artists who have produced major innovations in modern art had been ignored by the official accounts of its history.

**In the 1960s after Abstract Expressionism**

In abstract painting during the 1950s and 1960s several new directions like Hard-edge painting and other forms of Geometric abstraction, as a reaction against the Subjectivism of Abstract Expressionism began to appear in artist studios and in radical avant-garde circles. Clement Greenberg became the voice of Post-painterly abstraction by creating an influential exhibition of new paintings that toured important art museums throughout the United States in 1964. Color field painting, Hard-edge painting and Lyrical Abstraction emerged as radical new directions.

By the late 1960s, however, Postminimalism, Process Art and Arte Povera also emerged as revolutionary concepts and movements that encompassed both painting and sculpture, via Lyrical Abstraction and the Postminimalist movement, and in early Conceptual Art. Process Art as inspired by Pollock enabled artists to experiment with and make use of a diverse encyclopedia of style, content, material, placement, sense of time, and plastic and real space. Nancy Graves, Ronald Davis, Howard Hodgkin, Larry Poons, Jannis Kounellis, Brice Marden, Bruce Nauman, Richard Tuttle, Alan Saret, Walter Darby Bannard, Lynda Benglis, Dan Christensen, Larry Zox, Ronnie Landfield, Eva Hesse, Keith Sonnier, Richard Serra, Sam Gilliam, Mario Merz, Peter Reginato were some of the younger artists who emerged during the era of late modernism that spawned the heyday of the art of the late 1960s.

**Pop Art**

In 1962 the Sidney Janis Gallery mounted The *New Realists*, the first major Pop Art group exhibition, in an uptown art gallery in New York City. Sidney Janis mounted the exhibition in a 57th Street storefront near his gallery at 15 E. 57th Street. The show sent shockwaves through the New York School and reverberated worldwide. Earlier in England in 1958 the term "Pop Art" was used by Lawrence Alloway to describe paintings that celebrated Consumerism of the post World War II era. This movement rejected Abstract Expressionism and its focus on the hermeneutic and psychological interior, in favor of art which depicted, and often celebrated material consumer culture, advertising, and iconography of the mass production age. The early works of David Hockney and the works of Richard Hamilton and Eduardo Paolozzi were considered seminal examples in the movement. While in the downtown scene in New York's East Village 10th Street galleries artists were formulating an American version of Pop

Art. Claes Oldenburg had his storefront, and the Green Gallery on 57th Street began to show Tom Wesselmann and James Rosenquist. Later Leo Castelli exhibited other American artists, including Andy Warhol and Roy Lichtenstein for most of their careers. There is a connection between the radical works of Marcel Duchamp and Man Ray, the rebellious Dadaists with a sense of humor, and Pop Artists like Claes Oldenburg, Andy Warhol, and Roy Lichtenstein, whose paintings reproduce the look of Ben-Day dots, a technique used in commercial reproduction.

### Questions for Reflection
(1) What schools of art were popular during the post-war period?
(2) Who is Pollock? What is Abstract Expressionism?
(3) What is "Pop Art"? Name a few artists of "Pop Art".

## Text C  Modernism after World War II (II)

### Minimalism

By the early 1960s, Minimalism emerged as an abstract movement in art (with roots in geometric abstraction via Malevich, the Bauhaus and Mondrian) which rejected the idea of relational, and subjective painting, the complexity of Abstract expressionist surfaces, and the emotional zeitgeist and polemics present in the arena of Action painting. Minimalism argued that extreme simplicity could capture all of the sublime representation needed in art. Associated with painters such as Frank Stella, Minimalism in painting, as opposed to other areas, is a modernist movement. Depending on the context, Minimalism might be construed as a precursor to the postmodern movement. Seen from the perspective of writers who sometimes classify it as a postmodern movement, early Minimalism began and succeeded as a modernist movement to yield advanced works, but which partially abandoned this project when a few artists changed direction in favor of the anti-form movement. In the late 1960s, the term Postminimalism was coined by Robert Pincus-Witten to describe minimalist derived art which had content and contextual overtones which Minimalism rejected, and was applied to the work of Eva Hesse, Keith Sonnier, Richard Serra and new work by former minimalists Robert Smithson, Robert Morris, and Sol Lewitt, and Barry Le Va, and others. Minimalists like Donald Judd, Dan Flavin, Carl Andre, Agnes Martin, John McCracken and others continued to produce their late modernist paintings and sculpture for the remainder of their careers.

In the 1960s the work of the avant-garde Minimalist composers La Monte Young, Philip Glass, Steve Reich, and Terry Riley also became prominent in the New York art world.

Since this time, many artists have embraced minimal or postminimal styles, and the label "postmodern", has been attached to them.

## Neo-Dada

In the early 20th century Marcel Duchamp exhibited a urinal as a sculpture. His professed point was to have people look at the urinal as if it were a work of art because he said it was a work of art. He referred to his work as "Readymades". *Fountain* was a urinal signed with the pseudonym R. Mutt that shocked the art world in 1917. This and Duchamp's other works are generally labeled as Dada. Duchamp can be seen as a precursor to conceptual art, other famous examples being John Cage's *4' 33"*, which is four minutes and thirty-three seconds of silence, and Rauschenberg's *Erased De Kooning Drawing*. 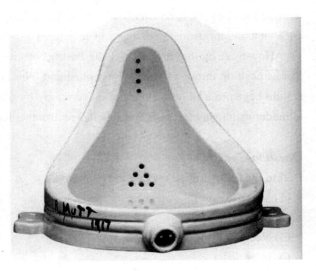 Many conceptual works take the position that art is created by the viewer viewing an object or act as art, not from the intrinsic qualities of the work itself. Thus, because *Fountain* was exhibited, it was a sculpture.

Marcel Duchamp famously gave up "art" in favor of chess. Avant-garde composer David Tudor created a piece, *Reunion* (1968), written jointly with Lowell Cross that features a chess game, where each move triggers a lighting effect or projection. At the premiere, the game was played between Duchamp and John Cage.

Another trend in art that can be associated with the term Neo-Dada is the use of a number of different media together. Intermedia, a term coined by Dick Higgins and meant to convey new artforms along the lines of Fluxus, Concrete Poetry, Found Objects, Performance Art, and Computer Art. Higgins was the publisher of the Something Else Press, a Concrete poet, married to artist Alison Knowles and an admirer of Marcel Duchamp.

## Late Period

Artists from many disciplines continue to work in modernist styles into the 21st century. The continuation of Abstract Expressionism, Color Field Painting, Lyrical Abstraction, Geometric Abstraction, Minimalism, Abstract Illusionism, Process Art, Pop Art, Postminimalism, and other late 20th century modernist movements in both painting and sculpture continue through the first decade of the 21st century.

At the turn of the 21st century, well-established artists such as Sir Anthony Caro, Lucian Freud, Cy Twombly, Robert Rauschenberg, Jasper Johns, Agnes Martin, Al Held, Ellsworth Kelly, Helen Frankenthaler, Frank Stella, Kenneth Noland, Jules Olitski, Claes Oldenburg, Jim Dine, James Rosenquist, Alex Katz, Philip Pearlstein, and younger artists like Brice Marden, Chuck Close, Sam Gilliam, Isaac Witkin, Sean Scully, Joseph Nechvatal, Elizabeth Murray, Larry Poons, Richard Serra, Walter Darby Bannard, Larry Zox, Ronnie Landfield, Ronald Davis, Dan Christensen, Joel Shapiro, Tom Otterness, Joan Snyder, Ross Bleckner, Archie Rand, Susan Crile, and dozens of others continued to produce vital and influential paintings and sculptures.

However, by the early 1980s, the Postmodern movement in art and architecture began to establish its position through various Conceptual and Intermedia formats. Postmodernism in music and literature began to take hold even earlier, some say by the 1950s. While Postmodernism implies an end to modernism many theorists and scholars realize that late Modernism continues into the 21st century.

## Questions for Reflection
**Define the following terms in your own words.**
(1) Minimalism
(2) Postminimalism
(3) Neo-Dadaism
(4) Intermedia

## Website to Visit
http://witcombe.sbc.edu/modernism/ (accessed Apr. 28, 2020)
On this website, you may find an illustrated study on Modernism in five chapters, including the roots of Modernism, Modernism and Politics, Modernism and Postmodernism, etc.

## Movie to Watch

### Surviving Picasso (1996)
In 1943, a young painter, Françoise Gilot (1921— ) meets Pablo Picasso (1881—1973), already the most celebrated artist in the world. For the next ten years, she is his mistress, bears him two children, is his muse, and paints within his element. She also learns slowly about the other women who have been or still are in his life: Dora Maar, Marie-Thérèse (whose daughter is Picasso's), and Olga Koklowa, each of whom seems deeply scarred by their life with Picasso. Gilot's response is to bring each into her relationship with Picasso. How does one survive Picasso? She keeps painting, and she keeps her good humor and her independence. When the time comes, she has the strength to leave.

# Bibliography

[1] Beatty, John L. & Oliver A. Johnson. (2004) *Heritage of Western Civilization* (*9th Edition*). Prentice Hall.

[2] Beck, Roger B. (2007) *World History: Patterns of Interaction* (*Student Edition*). McDougal Littell.

[3] Bonnett, Alastair. (2004) *The Idea of the West: Culture, Politics, and History*. Red Globe Press.

[4] Coffin, Judith G. & Robert C. Stacey. (2017) *Western Civilizations: Their History & Their Culture* (*19th Edition*). W. W. Norton & Company, Inc.

[5] Duiker, William J. & Jackson J. Spielvogel. (2018) *World History* (*9th Edition*). Cengage Learning.

[6] King, Margaret L. (2005) *Western Civilization: A Social and Cultural History* (*3rd Edition*). Prentice Hall.

[7] Kishlansky, Mark, Patrick Geary & Patricia O'Brien. (2006) *A Brief History of Western Civilization: The Unfinished Legacy* (*5th Edition*). Longman.

[8] Macrohistory. http://www.fsmitha.com/. Accessed Feb. 13, 2020.

[9] Platt, Dewitt & Roy Mathews. (2003) *The Western Humanities, Vol 2: The Renaissance to the Present* (*5th Edition*). McGraw-Hill Humanities.

[10] School History. http://www.schoolhistory.co.uk/sitemap.html. Accessed Feb. 13, 2020.

[11] World History: Hyperhistory. http://www.hyperhistory.com/online_n2/History_n2/a.html. Accessed Feb. 13, 2020.

[12] 丹尼斯·舍曼等编著. (2007) 世界文明史(第四版). 北京:中国人民大学出版社.

[13] 邓红风主编. (2005) 西方文明史. 青岛:中国海洋大学出版社.

[14] 董晓燕. (2001) 西方文明史纲. 杭州:浙江大学出版社.

[15] 杰里·本特利、赫伯特·齐格勒、希瑟·斯特里兹. (2008) 简明新全球史. 北京:北京大学出版社.

[16] 井卫华、王红欣主编. (2004) 西方文明史概述. 北京:中国电力出版社.

[17] 罗伯特·E. 勒纳. (1994) 西方文明史. 北京:中国青年出版社

[18] 王斯德主编. (2001) 世界通史:现代文明的发展与选择. 上海:华东师范大学出版社.

[19] 王佐良. (2002) 欧洲文化入门. 北京:外语教学与研究出版社.

[20] 叶胜年. (2005) 西方文化导论. 上海:上海外语教育出版社.

# 欧洲文化入门（第2版）

尊敬的老师：

您好！

本书练习题配有参考答案，请联系责任编辑索取。同时，为了方便您更好地使用本教材，获得最佳教学效果，我们特向使用该书作为教材的教师赠送本教材配套电子资料。如有需要，请完整填写"教师联系表"并加盖所在单位系（院）公章，免费向出版社索取。

北京大学出版社

## 教 师 联 系 表

| 教材名称 | | | 欧洲文化入门（第2版） | | | |
|---|---|---|---|---|---|---|
| 姓名： | | 性别： | | 职务： | | 职称： |
| E-mail： | | | 联系电话： | | 邮政编码： | |
| 供职学校： | | | 所在院系： | | | （章） |
| 学校地址： | | | | | | |
| 教学科目与年级： | | | 班级人数： | | | |
| 通信地址： | | | | | | |

填写完毕后，请将此表邮寄给我们，我们将为您免费寄送本教材配套资料，谢谢！

北京市海淀区成府路205号
北京大学出版社外语编辑部　吴宇森
邮政编码：100871
电子邮箱：wuyusen@pup.cn

外语编辑部电话：010-62759634
邮　购　部　电　话：010-62534449
市场营销部电话：010-62750672